Palgrave Studies in Economic History

Series editor
Kent Deng
London School of Economics
London, UK

Palgrave Studies in Economic History is designed to illuminate and enrich our understanding of economies and economic phenomena of the past. The series covers a vast range of topics including financial history, labour history, development economics, commercialisation, urbanisation, industrialisation, modernisation, globalisation, and changes in world economic orders.

More information about this series at
http://www.palgrave.com/gp/series/14632

Ellen Hillbom • Jutta Bolt

Botswana – A Modern Economic History

An African Diamond in the Rough

palgrave
macmillan

Ellen Hillbom
University of Lund
Lund, Sweden

Jutta Bolt
Lund University
Lund, Sweden

University of Groningen
Groningen, The Netherlands

Palgrave Studies in Economic History
ISBN 978-3-030-10323-1 ISBN 978-3-319-73144-5 (eBook)
https://doi.org/10.1007/978-3-319-73144-5

Cover illustration: Xinhua / Alamy Stock Photo

Printed on acid-free paper

This Palgrave Macmillan imprint is published by Springer Nature
The registered company is Springer International Publishing AG
The registered company address is: Gewerbestrasse 11, 6330 Cham, Switzerland

Preface/Acknowledgements

Why write the economic history of Botswana? Behind every rational academic answer to the question of why a certain case or country has been picked for in-depth studies, there is often a more personal story. This is our personal story about how this book project came to be.

In the autumn of 1994 Ellen was a bachelor student at the Department of Anthropology at Lund University looking for a topic for her thesis. She was asked by a childhood friend if she wanted to join in on a fieldwork trip to Botswana and as any eager student with a sense of adventure she said yes. She was in luck because her thesis supervisor, Professor Kajsa Ekholm Friedman, had some money left over in a research project and paid for the air fare and off she went. These chance circumstances would determine her ongoing interest in the African region. Previously she did not have any specific plans to spend her life within academia, but the experience of trying to figure out the rationality behind small-scale cattle holders' market integration woke her curiosity. Figuring out the schedules for the minibuses in Gaborone, bunking with friends and research assistants in local clinics in small villages in Kgatleng District, being burned by the hot African sun, and visiting cattle kraals on the vast grazing range by jeep and by foot all added to the experience.

Later on Ellen moved to the Department of Economic History at Lund University and combined the study of Botswana with that of other African countries. Over the years there have been numerous research projects, several funded by the Swedish International Development Agency and the Swedish Research Council. The outcome has been numerous publications in journals and books on a range of topics such as long-term changes in property rights to agricultural resources, smallholder farming and agricultural growth, natural resource dependency, economic diversification and structural transformation, development of state structures, and long-term inequality trends.

Meanwhile, Jutta studied Economics at the University of Groningen. After an internship at the Ministry of Finance to write her master thesis on the real economic effects of debt reductions in various African countries, she decided that she was not yet prepared to leave academia and continued as a PhD student in Groningen. Initially she worked mostly on long-term development in a comparative perspective. As a proper economist, she was trying to understand the general mechanisms and draw general lessons about development issues. Increasingly, however, she felt that the average lessons, although useful perhaps in unfolding patterns, concealed a lot of underlying diversity. What does an average tell us about individual stories? By incorporating both comparative and case study perspectives in her work, Jutta became an exponent of using long-term correlations between certain factors at various points in time to be a point of departure for asking interesting questions and investigating those questions in in-depth case studies.

Eventually Ellen and Jutta met at the Economic History World Congress in Stellenbosch in 2012 and saw the potential for future collaborations. At the time Ellen was involved in a project on colonial extraction headed by Professor Christer Gunnarsson. Within the framework of that project Ellen and Jutta started to work on constructing social tables and calculating Gini coefficients for Botswana for the colonial era. The combination of Ellen's background in anthropology and almost 20 years of research on Botswana and Jutta's training as an economist proved to be dynamic.

Since we started our collaboration we have published together on the development of the formal sector during the colonial era as well as on long-term inequality trends. Currently we are working on a large project on long-term inequality, economic growth, and sectorial change in various African economies in which we use social tables to measure inequality and capture sectorial transformation. In our work, Botswana has served as a pilot for initiating theoretical thinking about inequality and developing methods to measure it, but studies on Ghana, Tanzania, Zambia, Zimbabwe, Malawi, Uganda, and Mauritius are also being conducted. The research is currently funded by the Jan Wallander and Tom Hedelius Foundation and the Marcus and Marianne Wallenberg Foundation. In the project we are inspired by collaborations with several colleagues—Prince Aboagye, Michiel de Haas, Erik Green, Morten Jerven, and Sascha Klocke.

This book is an output of our current inequality project, but it is also a collection of over two decades of reading, visits to archives in London and Gaborone, interviewing cattle holders and village leaders, waiting for government officials, presenting at conferences, publishing, and thinking about the development path of Botswana. Over the years many more colleagues and friends have contributed to the process, and although all of them cannot be named here, the colleagues at the Department of Economic History in Lund as well as Ewout Frankema, Branko Milanovic, and Jeffrey Williamson deserve to be mentioned. We would also specifically like to extend our gratitude to Prince Aboagye, Tobias Axelsson, Erik Green, and Sascha Klocke for taking time to read and comment on the book manuscript itself. Their critical eyes were a significant help, and all the remaining flaws are our responsibility.

Further, we have also enjoyed the practical support of our joint department and, in the last stages, our research assistant, Mesfin Araya. We would also like to thank the team at Palgrave Macmillan—Kent Deng, Laura Pacey, and James Safford—for their feedback.

Finally, as all academics know, we are all at a loss without the love and support from our families. Our husbands and children have patiently seen us spend summer holidays, weekends, evenings, and ridiculously early mornings working on the manuscript. Niklas, Saga, Joel, Herbert, Luuk, and Emilie—we owe you for your understanding. Unfortunately, we cannot promise that it will not happen again.

Lund, Sweden — Ellen Hillbom

Lund University and University of Groningen — Jutta Bolt

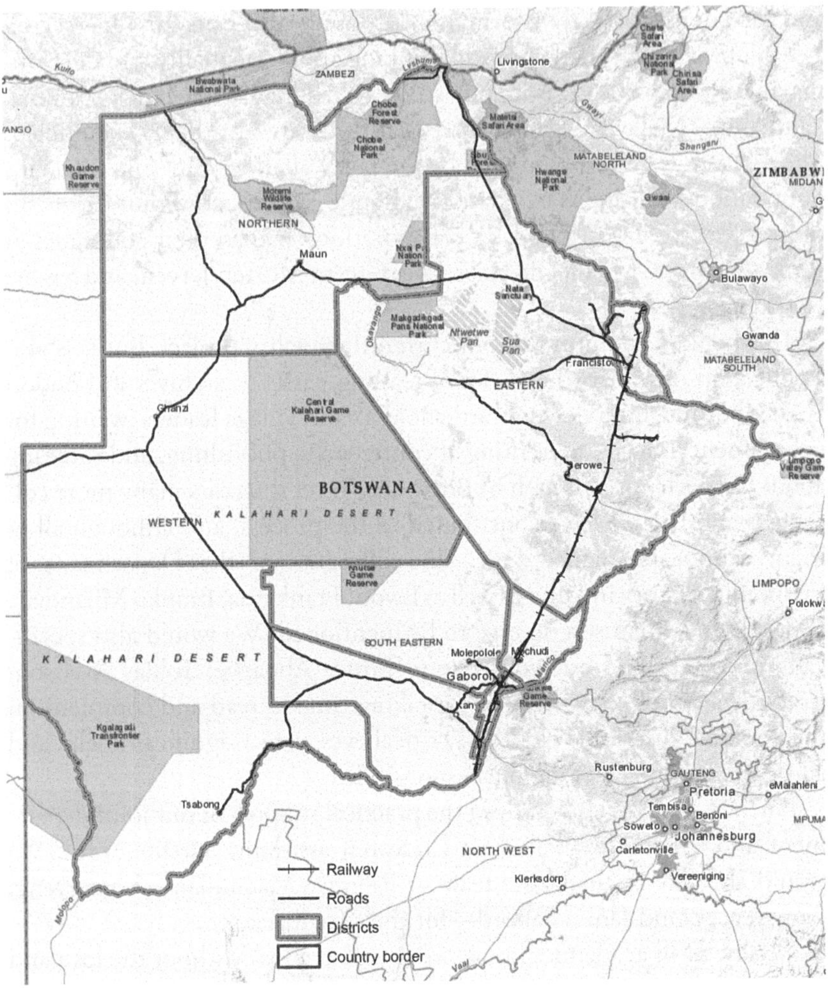
Livingstone
ZAMBEZI
ZIMBABWE
Bulawayo
Gwanda
MATABELELAND NORTH
MATABELELAND SOUTH
Hwange National Park
Chobe Forest Reserve
Chobe National Park
Moremi Wildlife Reserve
NORTHERN
Maun
Nata Sanctuary
Makgadikgadi Pans National Park
Ntwetwe Pan
Sua Pan
Francistown
EASTERN
Ghanzi
Central Kalahari Game Reserve
BOTSWANA
KALAHARI DESERT
WESTERN
LIMPOPO
SOUTH EASTERN
Molepolole
Gaborone
KALAHARI DESERT
Kgalagadi Transfrontier Park
Tsabong
Rustenburg
GAUTENG
Pretoria
Tembisa
Benoni
Soweto
Johannesburg
Carletonville
Vereeniging
Klerksdorp
NORTH WEST
eMalahleni
Railway
Roads
Districts
Country border

Contents

List of Figures

List of Maps

List of Tables

Part I

Part 1

1

An African Diamond in the Rough

1.1 Introduction

Botswana is, in terms of population, a small African country, and overall it has played a modest role in the economic and political history of the region. At the same time, its exceptional diamond-led economic growth record since independence has generated significant attention from both scholars and the policy community. The reason for this lies not only in a will to understand how a country that used to be among the poorest in the world, situated in a region often characterized by underdevelopment and conflict, has managed to achieve consistent long-run economic growth. It is also spurred by an interest in unravelling and explaining an uncharacteristic case of a natural resource-rich developing country that has managed to pair natural resource dependency with economic progress, substantial social development, and peaceful political maturity. The common experience, globally as well as in Africa, is that natural resource wealth has been negatively correlated with economic growth (Auty, 2001; Sachs & Warner, 1995). In many developing countries, the abundance of valuable natural resources has even been transformed into a curse characterized by economic crisis, corruption, and political instability including

E. Hillbom, J. Bolt, *Botswana – A Modern Economic History*, Palgrave Studies in Economic History, https://doi.org/10.1007/978-3-319-73144-5_1

violence. In contrast to this overall discouraging experience, Botswana constitutes a positive and unique example from which we can extract lessons in terms of how to ensure that natural resource wealth becomes a driver of economic growth and not a pitfall for development.

Existing explanations frequently found in the literature for Botswana's successful management of diamond incomes and subsequent growth miracle can crudely be divided into four main lines of argument. First, it is stated that limited European settlement during the colonial era and the fact that most resources remained in the hands of the indigenous population meant that the country suffered little from the adverse consequences of colonial influence. This argument ties to the second claim that precolonial political institutions characterized by accountability and broad-based negotiations persisted throughout the colonial period up until today. Third, the persistence of good precolonial institutions is said to explain a development-enabling quality found in contemporary political institutions, and this has catered for a prudent management of natural resource incomes and sound economic policies. Finally, in the midst of the institutional explanation, the country is said to be fortunate in that it has had wise leaders from independence onwards who have promoted political stability and national development instead of appropriating the state, turning it into a source for personal enrichment at the expense of national poverty and unrest. (For this literature, see, e.g. Acemoglu et al., 2003; Acemoglu & Robinson, 2010; Beaulier & Subrick, 2006; Harvey & Lewis, 1990; Iimi, 2006; Leith, 2005; Masire, 2006; Mpabanga, 1997; Owusu & Ismail Samatar, 1997; Robinson & Parsons, 2006; Samatar, 1999.)

We agree that an investigation into long-term institutional development is key for understanding Botswana's development trajectory and that the first generation of independence leaders played a decisive role in instigating the country's specific growth experience. At the same time we claim that the above cited explanations constitute an oversimplification of both the dynamics inherent in Botswana's economic history generally, and of the remaining challenges for the diamond-led growth miracle specifically. To start with, colonial influence was limited only during the first half of the colonial period, and we will show that from the 1930s onwards with the establishment and growth of the cattle export sector colonial policies actually had a profound effect on socioeconomic development. In addition, structures that were developed during the colonial era have persisted until today and continue to be part of the challenges for the future. Specifically, this refers to the continuous mono-product natural resource-dependent economy and the high levels of inequality. The long term effect of precolonial legacies also needs to be carefully considered. While several precolonial structures indeed have survived, they have been transformed over time and have been not only enabling but also hindering development progress depending on which groups in society we are considering. The precolonial legacy is much more complex than a straightforward causality between specific precolonial institutions and contemporary development-enhancing government policies. Further, while Botswana had leaders during the first decades of independence who ensured that diamond wealth benefitted the large majority of the population, the more recent political elite is increasingly criticized for corruption and elite capturing. Finally, it can be debated whether political continuity and stability, that is, the Botswana Democratic Party consistently ruling the country since independence, has come at the price of lacking change in socioeconomic structures towards inclusive economic development.

In this book we aim to give recognition to these and many more aspects of the complexities entrenched in both Botswana's long-term economic history and its contemporary growth miracle. Such an elaborate and critical examination is necessary if we are to draw accurate conclusions from our case that can constitute lessons relevant for other natural resource-rich developing countries. Our study offers evidence on which we base our arguments that in the midst of progress, the country remains with two overarching challenges. First, its economy is stuck in a natural resource trap and has yet to figure out how to move away from natural resource-based growth to a more diversified economy where additional high-productive sectors are playing a role in generating employment and stimulating growth. Second, the persistent high levels of inequality, in terms of income as well as division of resources and opportunities, give cause for concern. Botswana has a dual society where exceptional growth, substantial wealth, high rates of urbanization, social development, and socioeconomic modernization are found next to high unemployment rates, lingering poverty, and neglected rural areas. Further, we show that neither natural resource-dependent growth nor lack of diversification and high levels of inequality are unique to the current diamond economy. They are part of Botswana's long-term development trajectory and can be traced back to the equally relevant, though far less spectacular, cattle-led growth period during the colonial era. The relevance of this first growth period does not lie in the magnitude of growth or size of incomes and investments. Instead, it is the development of an economy and a society characterized by natural resource dependency with reliance on export revenues from a single resource as well as lack of inclusion and equitable access to opportunities for the broader population that makes the period important to analyse. These characteristics have remained and are still found in the current diamond economy.

While much of Botswana's fame relates to the last four decades of spectacular economic growth, our comprehensive study into the country's economic history stretches over more than one and a half century. Our period of investigation starts when the Tswana groups of contemporary Botswana settled in their present areas in roughly 1850, and we cover all significant events until the present. This approach providing a consistent analysis of processes of change is commonly referred to as the decompressing of history. Throughout the analysis we alternate between emphasizing institutions and geography/factor endowments as the prime drivers of said change. We discuss the precolonial Tswana agro-pastoral system of production as the basis for both building state capacity during the precolonial period and the development of the commercial cattle sector during the colonial period. Further, we analyse the two growth periods central to Botswana's economic history, the first driven by cattle and the latter by diamonds. Finally, we examine challenges that remain for the future, not from the viewpoint of growth and political stability, but from that of structural transformation and inclusive economic development. Throughout we pay ample attention to the characteristics of state structures as we understand them to be imperative for shaping the country's pathway of development.

This introductory chapter continues with a concise history of Botswana's growth experience, including elaborations on the main challenges the country is facing. We then present and expand on our three cross-cutting analytical approaches—the decompression of history, the interaction between institutions and geography/factor endowments, and the role of the state. In the next section we lay out the structure of the book. The final section sums up and bridges over to Chap. 2.

1.2 Botswana's Challenges in the Midst of Success

Botswana's diamond economy from the 1970s onwards is a well-known case of natural resource-led growth, and it is from the success during this era that scholars and policymakers commonly draw their lessons. With this book we contribute two important additions to the existing mainstream literature. First, we claim that there is a need of increased awareness that the diamond economy is the second period of natural resource-dependent growth in the history of the country, the first being the colonial cattle-led growth period which started in the 1930s. With its modest outcomes, the cattle-led growth period has been dwarfed in comparison to the latter diamond economy and therefore has attracted little attention. We will show that it, nevertheless, constitutes a key period as it is where we find the roots of contemporary socioeconomic structures shaping the diamond economy. Second, we argue that there should be a much more critical reflection on the characteristics of the diamond economy including a recognition of the challenges inherent in the lack of economic diversification for sustainable future growth and high levels of inequality (Bolt & Hillbom, 2015, 2016; Hillbom, 2008, 2014; Hillbom & Bolt, 2015). The result presented in this book is a modification of the current understanding of the background, development, and characteristics of Botswana's success story, and below we provide a brief summary of events leading up to contemporary challenges.

In the early colonial period the administration gained its incomes from taxation of the poor inhabitants of the territory, a strategy that provided only modest incomes. As aspirations to raise additional government funding developed in 1930, the colonial government turned its attention to the Tswana agro-pastoral system of production that contained substantial cattle wealth. As long as commercial domestic and export markets were basically non-existent, this wealth could, however, not serve as a basis for monetary incomes, neither for the state nor for the individual cattle holders. There was a subsequent realization on the part of the colonial authorities that the establishment of an export sector for cattle would open up new opportunities for taxation generating state revenues which in turn could be used for enacting development policies. While there was a regional cattle market in Southern Africa which the colonial administration could tap into, the identification of the territory's comparative advantage was not a response to an existing demand, but rather a strategy for securing revenues by supplying exports generated by an available agricultural product (Parsons and Crowder, 1988).

In the subsequent colonial cattle economy there was for the first time consistent economic growth, albeit rates were modest, and the cattle sector was characterized by low levels of technology and productivity. Per capita income in 1950 was a low 1,343 dollars per year (PPP-converted 2011 US dollars, Maddison Project database, Bolt et al., 2018). Because the large-scale cattle holders and the indigenous political elite were more or less made up of the same individuals, the colonial and the indigenous authorities had a shared interest in investing in the cattle sector. The outcome was increasing incomes for both the administration and the Tswana large-scale cattle holders. Meanwhile, the territory as a whole remained poor and underdeveloped, and the lives of the majority of the population continued to be tainted with poverty and malnutrition (Schapera & Comaroff, 1991).

In 1967 the discovery of diamond deposits was announced, and once exports took off in the mid-1970s, four decades of exceptional economic growth followed. During the 1980s, the economy of Botswana grew by 13 per cent annually, and in total over the first four decades after independence, the country registered the highest long-term growth rates in the world, including the Asian Tigers. Today, Botswana is classified as an upper middle income country with an estimated GDP per capita of 15,513 in 2016 (2011 PPP constant dollars[1]) (Leith, 2005, p. 4; Mpabanga, 1997, p. 369; World Bank, 2017). Although growth rates have levelled off in recent years, there does not appear to be any immediate end to economic expansion with a continued average annual GDP increase of roughly 5 per cent during the period 2010–2016 (World Bank, 2017).

The most exceptional element in the growth experience has not, however, been the abundance of a highly valuable natural resource enabling significant growth. Such commodity-driven growth spurts are not uncommon, albeit diamonds are unusually valuable and extraction has been high and consistent. Instead, it is the quality of the political institutional structure and the government's long-term good management of diamond incomes that makes Botswana stand out as a unique case. The country's outstanding performance in these respects is what has led numerous scholars to characterize it as a growth miracle and economic success story (Acemoglu et al., 2003; Samatar, 1999). While not questioning the growth miracle as such, it is the success story that we find to be simplistic and which we set out to discuss.

It is undisputable that sizeable state revenues have enabled the government to invest significantly into social development benefitting all citizens—education, health care, infrastructure, clean water, and so on. It has also helped people living in poverty fight acute hardship by offering temporary employment in various government programmes. In addition, independence was peaceful, and contrary to many other newly founded African countries where the state was hijacked by corrupt dictators, the government established a well-functioning multiparty democracy and showed an ability to govern the economy prudently. As a result the country's regulatory quality has been high and Botswana is considered not only the least corrupt country in Africa, but to be on par with various Western European countries in terms of state capacity. (For literature see, e.g. Acemoglu et al., 2003; Beaulier & Subrick, 2006; Hill, 1991; Leith, 2005; Lekoko & van der Merwe, 2006; Nthomang, 2004; Robinson & Parsons, 2006.) Adding up economic, social, and political progress, it is not surprising that contemporary Botswana is regarded as a sign of hope for prosperity in an otherwise poor and conflict-ridden region. The high levels of ambition of the government have even caused some scholars to define Botswana as one of very few African developmental states (Maundeni, 2001; Mbabazi & Taylor, 2005; Meisenhelder, 1997; Mkandawire, 2001).

What we stress, however, is that in the midst of this success story there is, nevertheless, cause for concern for the future, and many of the socio-economic challenges we see today have remained the same over both growth periods. Growth has consistently been correlated with exploitation of natural resources while sectorial change with cohesive technological progress and increased labour productivity has been absent. During the colonial era, the economy was based on the low-productive and low-value cattle sector. As a result, government revenues were limited, which gave modest room for investments in new technology and development of alternative sectors. During this period, incomes for the majority of the population remained modest, which reduced the scope also for demand-driven diversification. Meanwhile, the subsequent second growth period has been based on the extraction of high-value diamonds. Currently Botswana is the leading diamond-producing country in the world in terms of value, and the second largest in terms of volume, producing 25 per cent of global rough diamond market shares (Kimberley Process Rough Diamond Statistics, 2017). With diamonds making up 89 per cent of export incomes in June 2016 (Botswana International Merchandise Trade Statistics, 2017), the natural resource dependency has continued.

During the independence era the mining sector's share of GDP has risen from 5 per cent in 1966, peaked at above 50 per cent in 1986, and then declined in relative terms to roughly one-quarter of GDP after 2010. Meanwhile, agriculture has plummeted from roughly 40 per cent of GDP to 2–3 per cent of GDP and manufacturing has been stagnant at roughly 5 per cent of GDP during the same time period (Timmer et al., 2015; World Bank, 2017). The other sector, apart from mining, that has expanded its share of GDP is services which at present account for about 65 per cent (World Bank, 2017). At a first glance these changes might be taken for a transformation and modernization of the economy. Yet, industry more or less can be equated with diamond mining while the service sector is primarily made up of low-productive services such as the public sector, hotels, and restaurants. This means that the change does not correspond to the diversification, broad technological change, and increased overall labour productivity commonly associated with structural transformation. If successful management of diamond incomes made Botswana unique, the country's current situation of being stuck in a natural resource trap is a challenge that it shares with numerous natural resource-rich developing countries (Collier, 2008, chapter 2).

Further, in both growth periods driven by natural resources, economic progress has been accompanied by high levels of inequality, an association that is also common amongst developing countries. After the establishment of the cattle export sector in the 1930s, new opportunities opened up to transform latent cattle wealth into incomes. Access to agricultural resources became increasingly polarized at the same time as cattle prices increased and cattle incomes were only within reach for a smaller group of large-scale cattle holders. Meanwhile, the state apparatus grew, financed by rising export revenues, and wages to government officials improved. The forging ahead of large-scale cattle holders and government employees led to increasing income inequality in the 1940s and income inequality continued rising to the mid-1970s with Ginis reaching a little over 0.6. Subsequently income inequality only marginally increased during the height of diamond-led growth in the 1980–1990s, after which it has stagnated or potentially even slightly declined in recent years (Bolt & Hillbom, 2016; Hillbom & Bolt, 2015).

The high levels of income inequality since independence have gone hand in hand with unequal opportunities in the form of high unemployment, prevalence of poverty, neglect of the rural areas, and the discrimination of minority groups, particularly the Basarwa population (Good, 2008; Lekoko & van der Merwe, 2006; Nthomang, 2004; Phaladze & Tlou, 2006; World Bank, 2017). While the Botswana state is commonly applauded for its social development efforts associated with the success story, there are also critics pointing out that elite capturing and institutional inequality have hindered development (Good, 2008; Gulbrandsen, 1996; Makgala, 2006).

With our comprehensive and critical investigation of Botswana's economic history, we aim to show how both characterizations—Botswana as a growth miracle investing in social development, on the one hand, and poverty in the midst of plenty, inequality, and elite capturing, on the other hand—are accurate in their own right and exist side by side. In recognizing the complexity of the Botswana development experience and the duality of contemporary socioeconomic structures we offer a more informed foundation on which both Botswana and other natural resource-rich developing countries can base lessons for their future development.

1.3 Cross-cutting Analytical Approaches

Our study is held together by three cross-cutting analytical approaches—the decompressing of history, the interaction between institutions and geography or factor endowments, and the role of the state. While they are more or less strongly emphasized in the different chapters, they consistently remain the key ingredients for our efforts to provide a comprehensive understanding of Botswana's economic history.

1.3.1 Decompressing of History

In a growing and increasingly influential literature in historical economics, statistical analysis is used to identify correlations between historical events and contemporary development outcomes. This strand of literature has contributed greatly to the debate by raising broader research questions, stimulating the collection of previously unused historical data, and encouraging the development of quantitative methods (see, e.g. Acemoglu et al., 2001, 2002; Fenske, 2010; Nunn, 2008). It has, however, also been criticized for 'compressing history' and not informing us about the actual mechanisms driving processes of consistent continuity and change in between the different points in time (Austin, 2008; Hopkins, 2009). As a reaction there has been a call for the 'decompressing of history', which for all intents and purposes is not a new methodological invention, but rather represents a revival of old traditions within social and economic history. In our view the decompressing of history is imperative as a methodological approach as it compels us to move beyond the identification of correlations between two points in time and instead provide a continuous analysis wherein the relevance of all events are taken into consideration. As a consequence, it focuses the analysis on explaining the mechanisms of processes of change as well as identifying the drivers of said change instead of addressing only the end points.

In the case of Botswana, the compressing of history has concretely resulted in arguments to the effect that current economic progress is primarily explained by the good quality of precolonial political institutions. Further, that these institutions, due to limited colonial influence, have remained intact throughout the colonial period and now form the backbone of the independent state's democratic system and economic strategies (Acemoglu et al., 2003; Acemoglu & Robinson, 2010; Beaulier & Subrick, 2006; Masire, 2006; Robinson & Parsons, 2006). These claims have in turn resulted in an insufficient analysis of colonial economic legacies. In contrast, we instead pay consistent attention to all major events during a longer time period, 1850 to the present. The most important outcome of our approach is that it leads us to emphasize the latter part of the colonial era as a key time period wherein we identify the development of socioeconomic structures explaining the characteristics of the latter post-independence resource-driven growth and inequality trends (Bolt & Hillbom, 2015, 2016).

An important tool for us when decompressing history and opening up for a more dynamic and comprehensive analysis based on a continuous search for underlying mechanisms driving change is our identification of critical junctures which represent breaking points in Botswana's economic history. The more common division of time periods when studying African countries is to adhere to the political breaks between the precolonial, colonial, and postcolonial periods. We instead apply an alternative periodization where the precolonial economy stretches until the establishment of intrusive colonial policies in the 1930s and the structures of the colonial cattle economy in turn stay on until the next structural break, which is the maturity of the diamond economy in the mid-1970s. In addition, the time periods of Chaps. 4, 5, and 6 are delimited by their thematic scopes and not by political events.

1.3.2 Institutions, Geography, and Factor Endowments

Over the last decade and a half there has been an increasing polarization in the theoretical debate on identifying historical explanations for factors driving long-term trajectories of economic growth and development. On the one hand, we have scholars emphasizing the superior explanatory power of institutions, primarily political institutions. Others in contrast are pushing for the primacy of geographical explanations and factor endowments. The literature on Botswana's impressive post-independence growth trajectory is a poignant example of this polarization. Some researchers claim that the growth miracle is based on the presence of good political institutions with their roots in precolonial structures (Acemoglu et al., 2003; Acemoglu & Robinson, 2010, 2012; Beaulier & Subrick, 2006: Iimi, 2006; Robinson & Parsons, 2006).

Meanwhile, others have shown that the growth trajectory is clearly correlated with the successful extraction of diamonds in the post-independence era (Jerven, 2010; Sachs, 2012; van der Ploeg, 2011).

Rather than getting caught up in the dichotomized institutions versus geography/factor endowments debate, we position ourselves in a scholarly tradition where the interaction between institutions, as the rules of the game, and geography and factor endowments, as the preconditions for playing the game, is understood as multicausal (Austin, 2008; Herbst, 2000; North, 1990). For each case under study the complex puzzle to solve is how they interact and under what conditions one aspect can dominate temporarily and be the prime driving force of change in a specific historical setting. Our point of departure is that geographic preconditions and factor endowments affect the setup of economic and political institutions and that these institutions in turn feed back into how geography and factor endowments are moulded, exploited, and managed. Both aspects are consistently considered relevant in our study although one may be emphasized over the other depending on which processes we focus on.

Concretely, this approach determines how we in the book explain a variety of issues, the most important ones being the location of the Tswana groups within the territory that is contemporary Botswana; how the Tswana residential and land use patterns enabled the development of centralized political institutions; the agro-pastoral system of production based on abundant land and the subsequent identification of cattle as the main export product; how the need for deep mining to access diamond deposits enabled the state to monopolize extraction and prevent a natural resource curse; and the state's prudent management of diamond incomes but also lack of incentives for diversification away from diamonds.

1.3.3 The Role of the State

With the poor outcome for many African economies after independence, and especially after the lost decades in the 1980–1990s, the failure of the African state has repeatedly been presented as a primary explanation for a consistent economic crisis (see, e.g. Bates, 2005, 2008; van de Walle,

2001). In contrast, Botswana has been seen as an exception where recognition of good governance is instead essential for understanding the economy's success. The country has been hailed for its good political institutions, and the combination of economic success and social development has led some scholars to discuss Botswana in terms of an African *developmental state* thereby implying kinship with the East Asian Tigers (Maundeni, 2001; Mbabazi & Taylor, 2005; Mkandawire, 2001).

As economic historians our take is, however, that the original East Asian developmental state model requires the launching of very specific government policies and is applicable only to a small number of countries. The continued natural resource dependency, failure to build a strong private sector, the lack of industrialization strategies, and the ongoing close relationship between the government bureaucracy and the cattle-keeping elite in our view disqualifies Botswana from this category (Hillbom, 2012). While we agree with the emphasis on the need to unravel the fundamental characteristics of existing state structures to explain development trajectories at the macro level, we disagree with the typologization of Botswana as a developmental state. Instead, we identify the *gate-keeping state* concept as proposed by Frederick Cooper (2002) as the most appropriate when typologizing the state in Botswana. The classification of a gate-keeping state is primarily based on how challenges to secure sufficient government revenues to pay for socioeconomic development shape government policies. In situations where states face limited government revenues, the gate-keeping state theory suggests that this causes states to limit their activities and often focus on trying to increase revenues by designing export strategies and taxing trade.

These characteristics were particularly clear during the establishment of the colonial state. During the colonial period every African administration had to strive towards self-sufficiency and the rational way forward was to extract valuable natural resources and/or provide agricultural products for exports in combination with keeping administrative costs down. These incentives resulted in administrations that spent their resources on controlling the territory's border regions and European settlements while having limited interaction with the inland and the indigenous population, taxing the flow of goods in and out of the colony, and primarily investing in export-enhancing activities. Colonial Botswana was no exception to this general rule, and for the analysis of the impact of the gate-keeping state structures, we trace sources for government revenues, that is, taxation and customs duties, and investigate the effects of government policies determining expenditures, that is, targeted investments. To us the greatest advantage is that the gate-keeping state concept provides economically based rationales for trajectories of state development instead of focusing on political events or individuals' actions. It also contributes to our decompressing of history as we show how, with the absence of structural breaks, state characteristics transcend from the colonial into the independence era. While the contemporary state now has significant government revenues and can afford to be development oriented, the old challenges of persistent natural resource dependency and non-inclusive development found in the gate-keeping state have for all intents and purposes survived until the present.

1.4 The Structure of the Book

The book is divided into four parts. Part I includes this introduction and a background chapter accounting for the Tswana agro-pastoral society during the precolonial and early colonial eras. It starts in roughly 1850 with the post *Difaqane*[2] situation in Southern Africa and the settlement of a number of Tswana groups in the area that is current-day Botswana. It discusses the Tswana agro-pastoral system of production including its organization of access to agricultural resources as well as the unique residential pattern and the central role the system of production played in the development of political institutions. The second half of the chapter is dedicated to the tug between the British South Africa Company, South Africa, Britain, and the indigenous Tswana over what in 1885 became Bechuanaland Protectorate and the establishment of British colonial rule. We argue that the first decades of colonial rule until the 1930s brought limited change in economic structures and therefore we include them in our discussion of precolonial structures.

Part II consists of Chap. 3 dealing with colonial shocks in the form of the establishment of the colonial cattle economy in the 1930s and stretches until the switch over to the diamond economy in the mid-1970s. Here we discuss how the colonial administration which was strapped for revenues identified cattle as the comparative advantage of Bechuanaland Protectorate and developed the cattle export sector as the main source of government revenues. While the development process involved modest absolute sums, the impact was significant as it did not include any other sectors than cattle, and because diversification of the economy was not encouraged. In addition, we analyse colonial state building, understanding institutional characteristics to be the result of development ambitions in the midst of financial limitations. Again, we base the time period on economic structures and not political events such as independence in 1966.

Part III consists of three thematic chapters. The first, Chap. 4, is dedicated to an in-depth analysis of the drivers of the two growth periods. Our theoretical framework refers to the debate where, on the one hand, initial conditions in the form of location, space, climate, and natural resource endowments (e.g. Bloom et al., 1998; Landes, 1998) and, on the other hand, economic and political institutions managing resources (e.g. Acemoglu & Robinson, 2012; North, 2005) are seen as fundamental for analysing growth. For the modest cattle-led growth period we to a large extent lack national accounts and therefore we capture growth primarily through changes in occupational structures and wage and income levels. For balance we inquire about labour and wages also for the diamond-led growth period, but here we have better national accounts and they constitute the primary base for our analysis. Finally, while agriculture was the sole dominating sector during the first growth period, the diamond economy is much more complex compelling us to provide an in-depth sectoral analysis of changes in agriculture, industry, and services including movement of labour.

Chapter 5 addresses the challenges of moving beyond natural resource-based growth and instigating technological progress, improved labour productivity, and economic diversification, in combination leading to structural transformation and inclusive sustainable economic development (Kuznets, 1955, 1973; Lewis, 1954, 1955). The focus is on the diamond economy from the mid-1970s onwards and the 'natural resource trap'. During this period large export incomes and high annual growth rates could in theory have opened a window of opportunity for investing to develop alternative sectors. Yet, despite good institutional quality, sound financial policies, and the avoidance of a natural resource curse, there was a crowding out of industrialization efforts. Botswana has yet to find ways to diversify the economy away from natural resource dependency. Economic growth, social development, and political stability have proven to be enough for the country to be labelled a growth miracle, but not to break with the reproduction of old economic and political structures. We spend the last section discussing prevailing economic and political institutions grounded in colonial state structures, which we term the development-oriented gate-keeping state. We show how they have created a dual society lacking in terms of inclusion in the midst of economic plenty and social development.

The theme of Chap. 6 picks up on the discussion on why economies characterized by land abundance and mineral wealth tend to be less equal in both income and resource distribution (Bourguignon & Morrisson, 1990). Taking a point of departure in the drivers of the Kuznets curve (Kuznets, 1955) we elaborate on the relationship between long-term inequality trends and sectorial development during both growth periods. In this regard Botswana's colonial era is understudied and to capture income inequality we present social tables and Ginis for the cattle economy. Our data allow us to identify the timing of the increase in inequality as well as the factors driving the dynamics over time. Also, for the diamond economy we map income inequality as we evaluate official Ginis through a regional comparison and in relation to (the lack of) domestic sectorial change. The Ginis are further deconstructed and scrutinized as we trace changes in the composition of the labour force and incomes for various percentiles. Understanding income inequality is, however, not enough for our analysis, and we close the chapter with a discussion on underlying institutional inequality including the unequal distribution of resources and opportunities.

Part IV consists of the concluding Chap. 7 wherein we give a short recapitulation of the study and sum up the main messages to take away from the book. We identify what general lessons can be learned from Botswana's economic history that are of relevance for understanding historical as well as contemporary experiences of economic growth paired with the absence of structural transformation in natural resource-abundant developing countries. Finally, we highlight our methodological contribution and indicate future directions in research.

1.5 Summing Up and Moving On …

In a regional perspective Botswana has stood out as the most rapidly growing economy during Africa's independence era. During the course of four decades the country has risen from being one of the poorest in the world to an upper middle income country; it has been termed a growth miracle and a success story. The combination of prudent management of diamond incomes, social development, and political stability makes Botswana an illustrative example for other developing countries to learn from.

In this chapter we have introduced Botswana's diamond-led growth miracle, but we have also raised concerns regarding two main challenges for the future—the lack of diversification including the development of alternative productive sectors and the high levels of inequality. We have further presented how we in this book go about offering a comprehensive understanding of Botswana's economic history from the mid-nineteenth century to the present by applying three cross-cutting analytical approaches—the decompressing of history, the interaction between institutions and geography/factor endowments, and the role of the state. Finally, we have presented the structure of the book.

In the following chapter we give a background to the settlement of the area that is now Botswana and discuss the economic, social, and political structures of the precolonial Tswana agro-pastoral system of production. In Eurocentric history writing, Africa's 'precolonial' era is commonly equated to the whole period before the establishment of foreign, that is, European, rule, independent of how long that period might have been. We do, however, delimit the period and start with the settlement of the Tswana groups inhabiting current-day Botswana in the mid-1800s. Understanding the precolonial socioeconomic structures and the centralized state building is essential for our later analysis of the colonial and independence eras. As our chapters are delimited by structural breaks in the systems of production and not political events, we include the early colonial period in this chapter claiming that it was not until the 1930s that colonial influence became substantial enough to constitute such a structural break.

Notes

1. Throughout this book we have made use of income estimates expressed in 2011 PPP-converted US dollars. These estimates correct for price difference between countries. This enables a comparison across countries and over time, without the estimates being distorted by changes in relative prices.
2. *Difaqane*, a period of unrest in Southern Africa during the first half of the nineteenth century (see Chap. 2).

References

Acemoglu, D., Johnson, S., & Robinson, J. (2001). The colonial origins of comparative development: An empirical investigation. *The American Economic Review, 91*(5), 1369–1401.

Acemoglu, D., Johnson, S., & Robinson, J. A. (2002). Reversal of fortune: Geography and institutions in the making of the modern world income distribution. *The Quarterly Journal of Economics, 117*(4), 1231–1294.

Acemoglu, D., Johnson, S., & Robinson, J. A. (2003). An African success story: Botswana. In D. Rodrik (Ed.), *In search of prosperity: Analytic narratives on economic growth* (pp. 80–119). Princeton and Oxford: Princeton University Press.

Acemoglu, D., & Robinson, J. A. (2010). Why is Africa poor? *Economic History of Developing Regions, 25*(1), 21–50.

Acemoglu, D., & Robinson, J. A. (2012). *Why nations fail: The origins of power, prosperity, and poverty*. New York: Crown Publishing Group.

Austin, G. (2008). The 'reversal of fortune 'thesis and the compression of history: Perspectives from African and comparative economic history. *Journal of International Development, 20*(8), 996–1027.

Auty, R. M. (2001). The political economy of resource-driven growth. *European Economic Review, 45*(4), 839–846.

Bates, R. H. (2005). *Markets and states in tropical Africa: The political basis of agricultural policies*. Berkeley: University of California Press.

Bates, R. H. (2008). *When things fell apart: State failure in late-century Africa*. Cambridge: Cambridge University Press.

Beaulier, S. A., & Subrick, J. R. (2006). The political foundations of development: The case of Botswana. *Constitutional Political Economy, 17*(2), 103–115.

Bloom, D. E., Sachs, J. D., Collier, P., & Udry, C. (1998). Geography, demography, and economic growth in Africa. *Brookings Papers on Economic Activity, 1998*(2), 207–295.

Bolt, J., & Hillbom, E. (2015). Potential for diversification? The role of the formal sector in Bechuanaland Protectorate's economy, 1900–65. *Economic History of Developing Regions, 30*(2), 95–124.

Bolt, J., & Hillbom, E. (2016). Long-term trends in economic inequality: Lessons from colonial Botswana, 1921–1974. *Economic History Review, 69*(4), 1255–1284.

Bolt, J., Inklaar, R., de Jong, H., & van Zanden, J. L. (2018). Rebasing 'Maddison': new income comparisons and the shape of long-run economic development, GGDC Research Memorandum 174, Maddison Project Database, version 2018.

Bourguignon, F., & Morrisson, C. (1990). Income distribution, development and foreign trade: A cross-sectional analysis. *European Economic Review, 34*(6), 1113–1132.

Collier, P. (2008). *The bottom billion: Why the poorest countries are failing and what can be done about it.* New York: Oxford University Press.

Cooper, F. (2002). *Africa since 1940: The past of the present.* Cambridge and New York: Cambridge University Press.

Fenske, J. (2010). The causal history of Africa: A response to Hopkins. *Economic History of Developing Regions, 25*(2), 177–212.

Good, K. (2008). *Diamonds, dispossession & democracy in Botswana.* Oxford: James Currey.

Gulbrandsen, Ø. (1996). *Poverty in the midst of Plenty: Socio-economic marginalization, ecological deterioration and political stability in a Tswana society* (No. 45). Bergen: Norse Publications.

Harvey, C., & Lewis, S. R., Jr. (1990). *Policy choice and development performance in Botswana.* London: Macmillan in Association with the OECD Development Centre.

Herbst, J. (2000). *States and power in Africa: Comparative lessons in authority and control.* Princeton: Princeton University Press.

Hill, C. B. (1991). Managing commodity booms in Botswana. *World Development, 19*(9), 1185–1196.

Hillbom, E. (2008). Diamonds or development? A structural assessment of Botswana's forty years of success. *The Journal of Modern African Studies, 46*(2), 191–214.

Hillbom, E. (2012). Botswana: A development oriented gate keeping state. *African Affairs, 111*(442), 67–89.

Hillbom, E. (2014). Cattle, Diamonds and Institutions: Main drivers of Botswana's economic development, 1850 to present. *Journal of International Development, 26*(2), 155–176.

Hillbom, E., & Bolt, J. (2015). *Changing income inequality and structural transformation: The case of Botswana 1921–2010* (No. 2015/028). WIDER Working Paper. UNU-WIDER, Helsinki.

Hopkins, A. (2009). The new economic history of Africa. *Journal of African History, 50*, 155–177.

Iimi, A. (2006). Did Botswana escape from the resource curse? IMF Working Paper 06/138, International Monetary Fund, Washington, DC.

Jerven, M. (2010). Accounting for the African growth miracle: The official evidence–Botswana 1965–1995. *Journal of Southern African Studies, 36*(1), 73–94.

Kuznets, S. (1955). Economic growth and income inequality. *The American Economic Review, 45*(1), 1–28.

Kuznets, S. (1973). Modern economic growth: Findings and reflections. *The American Economic Review, 63*(3), 247–258.

Landes, D. S. (1998). *The wealth and poverty of nations: Why some countries are so rich and some so poor.* New York: WW Noton.

Leith, J. C. (2005). *Why Botswana prospered.* Montreal and Kingston: McGill-Queen's University Press.

Lekoko, R. N., & Van Der Merwe, M. (2006). Beyond the rhetoric of empowerment: Speak the language, live the experience of the rural poor. *International Review of Education, 52*(3–4), 323–332.

Lewis, A. (1955). *The theory on economic growth.* London: Allen & Unwin.

Lewis, W. A. (1954). Economic development with unlimited supplies of labour. *The Manchester School, 22*(2), 139–191.

Makgala, C. J. (2006). *Elite conflict in Botswana: A history.* Pretoria: African Institute of South Africa.

Masire, K., & Lewis, S. R. (2006). *Very brave or very foolish? Memoires of an African democrat.* Gaborone: Macmillan Botswana Publishing Co (Pty) Ltd.

Maundeni, Z. (2001). State culture and development in Botswana and Zimbabwe. *Journal of Modern African Studies, 40*(1), 105–132.

Mbabazi, P., & Taylor, I. (2005). *The potentiality of 'developmental states' in Africa.* Botswana and Uganda Compared, Dakar: CODESRIA.

Mkandawire, T. (2001). Thinking about developmental states in Africa. *Cambridge Journal of Economics, 25*(3), 289–314.

Mpabanga, D. (1997). Constraints to industrial development. In J. S. Salkin, D. Mpabanga, D. Cowan, J. Selwe, & M. Wright (Eds.), *Aspects of the Botswana economy* (pp. 369–387). Gaborone: Lentswe La Lesedi.

North, D. C. (1990). *Institutions, institutional change and economic performance.* Cambridge: Cambridge University Press.

North, D. C. (2005). *Understanding the process of economic change.* Princeton: Princeton University Press.

Nthomang, K. (2004). Relentless colonialism: The case of the Remote Area Development Programme (RADP) and the Basarwa in Botswana. *The Journal of Modern African Studies, 42*(3), 415–435.

Nunn, N. (2008). The long-term effects of Africa's slave trades. *The Quarterly Journal of Economics, 123*(1), 139–176.

Meisenhelder, T. (1997). The developmental state in Mauritius. *The Journal of Modern African Studies, 35*(2), 279–297.

Owusu, F., & Ismail Samatar, A. (1997). Industrial strategy and the African State: The Botswana experience. *Canadian Journal of African Studies, 31*(2), 268–299.

Parsons, N., & Crowder, M. (1988). *Monarch of all I survey: Bechuanaland Diaries 1929–37.* Gaborone: The Botswana Society.

Phaladze, N., & Tlou, S. (2006). Gender and HIV/AIDS in Botswana: A focus on inequalities and discrimination. *Gender & Development, 14*(1), 23–35.

Robinson, J. A., & Parsons, Q. N. (2006). State formation and governance in Botswana. *Journal of African Economies, 15*(AERC Suppl 1), 100–140.

Sachs, J., & Warner, A. (1995). Natural resource abundance and economic growth. NBER Working Paper 5398.

Sachs, J. D. (2012). Government, geography, and growth: The true drivers of economic development. *Foreign Affairs*, September/October.

Samatar, A. I. (1999). *An African miracle: State and class leadership and colonial legacy in Botswana development.* Portsmouth, NH: Heinemann.

Schapera, I., & Comaroff, J. L. (1991). *The Tswana* (Revised ed.). London: Kegan Paul International.

Timmer, M. P., de Vries, G. J., & de Vries, K. (2015). Patterns of structural change in developing countries. In J. Weiss & M. Tribe (Eds.), *Routledge handbook of industry and development* (pp. 65–83). London: Routledge.

Van de Walle, N. (2001). *African economies and the politics of permanent crisis, 1979–1999.* New York: Cambridge University Press.

Van der Ploeg, F. (2011). Natural resources: Curse or blessing? *Journal of Economic Literature, 49*(2), 366–420.

Online Sources

Botswana International Merchandise Trade Statistics. (2017). Retrieved 2017, from https://knoema.com/BWIMTS2016/botswana-international-merchandise-trade-statistics-monthly-update

World Bank. (2017). *World development indicators*. Washington, DC. Retrieved August, 2017, from http://databank.worldbank.org/data/reports.aspx?source=world-development-indicators

2

Precolonial Economy and Society, c. 1850–1930

2.1 Introduction

In the time before our investigation, Basarwa populations living in nomadic hunting–gathering communities inhabited the area that constitutes contemporary Botswana. In the mid-nineteenth century, the domino effect of a period of political unrest in Southern Africa, known as the *Difaqane*, caused the resettlement of a number of Tswana groups. Upon arrival, the geographic conditions such as the combination of access to agricultural resources, that is, land and water, and the disease environment, determined where the Tswana groups eventually settled. The area in its entirety was land abundant and population density was extremely low. However, not all of the area was suitable for the Tswana agro-pastoral system of production or healthy for human and livestock populations.

On arrival at their respective locations, the Tswana groups established their unique local settlement pattern characterized by numerous centralized residential areas, or villages, surrounded by arable lands and further away the communal grazing range dotted with individual cattle posts (Silitshena & McLeod, 1998). A common theme in explaining contemporary economic progress in Botswana is the claim that the tradition of

E. Hillbom, J. Bolt, *Botswana – A Modern Economic History*, Palgrave Studies in Economic History, https://doi.org/10.1007/978-3-319-73144-5_2

centralized state capacity has constituted a basis for the development of good precolonial political institutions (Acemoglu et al., 2003; Masire, 2006; Robinson & Parsons, 2006). We will show how the roots of this institutional development can be traced back to the geography of the Tswana settlement patterns. Climatic conditions, especially the bareness of the land, restricted the opportunities for crop farming in the area. Instead, the Tswana agro-pastoral system of production focused on cattle keeping wherein the ownership of livestock translated into wealth, social status, and access to labour. In this hierarchical society, the largest cattle holders were also the political elite. With markets and monetary incomes being very scarce, the elite invested their cattle wealth in building patron–client relationships and securing political loyalty (Schapera, 1994; Schapera & Comaroff, 1991).

While there is an undisputable political break between the precolonial independent Tswana society and the establishment of the Bechuanaland Protectorate in 1885, the event did not constitute an economic structural break. In line with our cross-cutting analytical approach of decompressing history, we therefore opt for a periodization where we consider the early colonial era to be a continuation of the precolonial cattle economy. New elements that became important in the economy included the expansion of labour migration to primarily South Africa and the colonial administration's efforts to establish a new system for taxation. Both represent changes implemented by the colonial government, but they had limited effects on the structure of the economy at large. Consequently, for this early colonial period we concur with the assertion that colonial influence in Bechuanaland was limited (Acemoglu et al., 2003; Beaulier & Subrick, 2006; Robinson & Parsons, 2006).

In this chapter we first elaborate on the Tswana settlement pattern and its effect on precolonial state building and then we move on to discuss the agro-pastoral system of production. Subsequently, we present how the arrival of the Europeans, the increasing wage employment opportunities in the region, the establishment of colonial rule, and the initial introduction of taxation structured both society and the economy during the early colonial period. We conclude with a summing up and indicate central issues in Chap. 3.

2.2 The Tswana Agro-pastoral Society

Due to limited archaeological, written, and oral evidence, much of the Tswana peoples' history prior to the nineteenth century remains unknown. As in many other parts of Africa, archaeological finds are modest, both because the old settlements left scarce material remains and because systematic archaeological excavations to piece together the history of the region have just begun. Meanwhile, written evidence only goes back to the beginning of the nineteenth century and is heavily dominated by European travellers, missionaries, colonial administrators, and academics, giving limited and biased accounts of African history. Local oral tradition and eyewitness accounts potentially offer valuable alternatives and complementing information. Unfortunately, these are sources that more quickly become distorted or disappear with the passing of time. The uncovering of early Stone Age skeletons and tools, however, tells us that the area that is now Eastern Botswana was inhabited for some 500,000 years and the contemporary Basarwa population is made up of the descendants of these early inhabitants. Around AD 200 Bantu-speaking people arrived in the area, first the Kgalagadi, and from AD 400 we have archaeological evidence suggesting the presence of Tswana groups (Ramsay et al., 1996, pp. 3–13; Schapera & Comaroff, 1991, p. 8).

The Tswana arrived in Southern Africa as part of the larger Bantu migration mentioned above and today 1.6 million Tswana live in Botswana while another 4 million reside in South Africa and roughly 100,000 in Zimbabwe and Namibia. Botswana's current total population is 2.35 million, and the second largest group next to the Tswana are the Kalanga, representing some 11 per cent of the total population. The Basarwa constitute a small minority making up around 3 per cent of the country's inhabitants. The remaining population groups originate from consistent migration inflow since the late nineteenth century of Europeans, Asians, and other Africans attracted by trade, colonization, and eventually new opportunities in the growing diamond economy.

2.2.1 Settlement and State Building

Over the centuries, the Tswana of Southern Africa broke up into a number of politically organized subgroups. Each unit was headed by a male leader who held a hereditary position that gave legislative, administrative, and judicial power and was characterized by outstanding privilege and authority. In return, the leader was responsible for catering for the needs of the members of his unit—he was viewed as the ultimate paternal caretaker. The Tswana term for their political unit was *morafe*, in plural *merafe*, and its leader was called *kgosi*, in plural *dikgosi*. In the language of the British colonial administration, *morafe* became equated to the term 'tribe' and *kgosi* to 'chief' (Schapera, 1994, pp. 1–7; Wylie, 1990, chapter 1).

The present-day location and societal structure of the larger *merafe* in Botswana, such as the Kwena, Ngwaketse, Ngwato, and Twana, were not settled until the 1840s. This was after the *Difaqane*, or *Mfecane*, a name that translates into 'the crushing', signifying a period in Southern African history during the first half of the nineteenth century when population growth and increased competition over resources both between various African groups, and between Africans and Europeans, led to disruption, migration, and war. Explanations for what instigated the *Difaqane* vary, but it appears to have been a combination of several intertwined processes. From 1810 onwards, the Northern Nguni people in Natal split into several fractions fighting one another in a series of wars that had repercussions as far north as present-day Tanzania. The peak was the military expansion of the Zulu Nation under their king Shaka in the 1820s and 1830s. During these decades there was also increasing competition over the Portuguese trade with ivory and slaves at the ports of southern Mozambique, including a disruptive increase in slave raiding from the mid-1820s. Finally, in an effort to escape British control, the Afrikaner population in Cape Colony moved northward in the 1830s and 1840s in waves of migration referred to as the Great Treks. When resettling, the Afrikaners claimed new land from indigenous populations which led to armed conflicts (Eldredge, 1992; Parsons, 1993, pp. 68–79; Ramsay et al., 1996, pp. 62–63). In combination, these events created a domino effect of displacement and unrest.

The Tswana groups that came to live within the borders of present-day Botswana were not directly involved in Shaka's wars, the slave raids, or Afrikaner migration. They were, however, indirectly affected as the subsequent migration of the Bakololo (1825–1845) and the Amandebele (1837–1840) in turn displaced them from what were their homelands prior to the *Difaqane* (Ramsay et al., 1996, p. 65). When resettling they adjusted to various geographical delimitations. In the west lay the Kalahari Desert, an environmental region that today is commonly termed the *sandveld.* It is covered by deep Kalahari sand and is by its natural conditions too dry for crop farming and cattle rearing. Until the later drilling of modern boreholes from the 1920s onwards, this area was populated almost solely by hunting and gathering Basarwa groups. In the north there was water, the Okavango and Chobe Rivers, but also malaria and tsetse flies. In search for a combination of access to water and a healthy climate, the Tswana primarily settled in the eastern region, also known as the *hardveld*, consisting of rocky hill ranges and shallow sand offering the potential for some crop farming and substantial animal husbandry (Schapera & Comaroff, 1991, pp. 13–14) (see Map 2.1).

Due to the mentioned geographical limitations land was abundant and population density stayed low. According to the earliest population census that we can obtain, the total population was estimated to a little below 121,000 Africans and 1,000 Europeans in 1904 (Annual Report of the Bechuanaland Protectorate, 1903/1904). Recently revised population estimates indicate that these early censuses probably constituted significant underestimations and that the actual population was probably closer to around 176,000 (Frankema & Jerven, 2014). Given the dryness of the area, the Tswana could inhabit, at the most, half the surface that is present-day Botswana. This meant a low population density of around 0.6 individuals per square kilometre. In addition, based on the fact that we cannot find any early colonial reports indicating concern for overgrazing, it is most likely that at the time of colonial conquest in the late nineteenth century, the size of the cattle population stayed well below the carrying capacity of the grazing range.

According to Herbst (2000), Africa's historically weak state structures can be explained by the general low population density on the continent. He argues that societies characterized by land abundance and labour scarcity

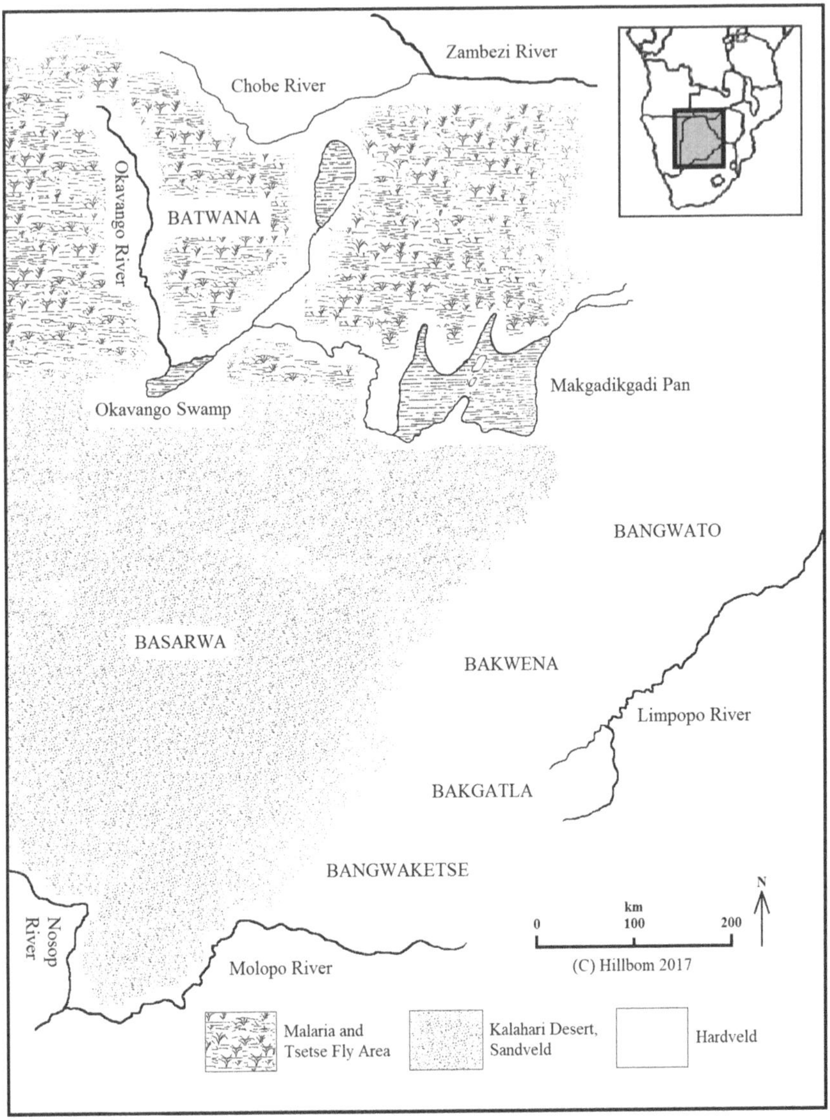

Map 2.1 Settlement by larger Tswana merafe, c. 1860

will develop extensive agricultural systems of production and scattered settlement patterns. This creates a challenge to any political power seeking control and unity, and opens up for decentralized systems of authority rather than centralized state structures. This explanation for how initial factor endowments influence the development of political institutions is relevant for many parts of Africa. The Tswana states, however, constitute an exception as state structures were centralized despite prevalent low population density. Various scholars have subsequently referred to a heritage of advanced state capacity as a key factor for explaining Botswana's contemporary good institutional quality and economic progress (Acemoglu et al., 2003; Masire, 2006; Robinson & Parsons, 2006). They do not, however, immerse themselves into the puzzle of explaining the precise mechanisms enabling the development of centralized systems of authority in a low population density society.

To analyse the unique history of state development among the Tswana we first need to understand how the organization of geographic space influences institutional development. Specifically, we have to understand Tswana's traditional local settlement patterns. While the *hardveld* was less dry than the *sandveld*, the whole area, while suited for subsistence agriculture, lacked the potential for successful surplus crop farming. Consequently, the Tswana relied heavily on cattle, but contrary to most African pastoralist populations they were sedentary agro-pastoralists, combining cattle herding and subsistence crop farming. Each *morafe* was divided into several larger and smaller village settlements. The village where the *kgosi* resided made up the 'capital' and could be quite sizeable. Schapera (1994, p. 8), for example, reports that Serowe, the headquarters of the Ngwato, had an estimated population of 25,000 around the mid-1930s. The smaller village units were led by headmen acting on behalf of the *kgosi*.

Every household belonged to a village unit, and it was mandatory to have a residential plot for the main hut in a village settlement. Surrounding each village was an area with arable fields where each household grew their crops. This was primarily the task of the female household members and when the workload was high, they would stay in a secondary hut near the fields. Beyond the arable lands lay the communal grazing range where households with cattle set up cattle posts consisting of a *kraal* and possibly a water point in the form of a hand-dug well. The male household members were responsible for herding and managing the cattle and took turns staying at the cattle post. Each household thus held land in two or even three different locations and depending on season and productive activities household members moved between their different dwellings (Mgadla, 1998; Schapera, 1994; Silitshena & McLeod, 1998). Importantly though, they regularly returned to the residential plot in the village and thereby they could be reached by the Tswana authorities, the headmen, and the *kgosi*, and be incorporated into hierarchal and centralized political structures which contributed to the building of state capacity.

In each *morafe* the *kgosi* controlled the group's joint wealth, natural resources, and production. He held both land and cattle in trust for his people and decided how resources would be allocated and used. Further, he could command his subjects' labour, a scarce and valuable resource in this low population density society. To balance his significant power, the *kgosi* was expected to consult a group of councillors and elders before making any major political decisions, and to be generous towards his subjects. For everyday matters, the *kgosi* delegated his powers to the village headmen. In each village there were subunits, so-called wards, and the number of wards depended on the size of the village. Members of a ward were generally related to one another and were under the leadership of a hereditary headman. This headman in turn answered to the village headman. In relation to the ward, the ward headman held a similar position as the *kgosi* did in relation to the *morafe*. The wards in turn consisted of a number of families, each family sharing a household and being under the authority of a male head, a *pater familias*. In sum, Tswana society was organized according to a strict hierarchal and patriarchal pyramid structure (Mgadla, 1998; Schapera, 1994, chapter 1; Schapera & Comaroff, 1991, pp. 13–14, 39–41, 45–48).

Within this structure the *kgotla*, indicating both a centrally located physical place and the actual meetings held there, constituted an arena where people could air their grievances towards other members of the *morafe*, including their own leaders. There existed a *kgotla* for each ward and village and they were presided over by the headmen of the wards and villages. In addition, the *kgosi* had a *kgotla* located in the *morafe*'s capital that was the centre for his administration where he conducted trials and interacted with his subjects and visitors (Schapera, 1994). The *kgotla* is often presented as a phenomenon unique to the Tswana. The opportunity given to ordinary people to discuss the decrees of the authorities in public and the requirement for leaders to spread information is commonly identified as an imperative precolonial political institution creating a tradition of political openness to debate and negotiations (Acemoglu et al., 2003; Masire, 2006). Undoubtedly, the *kgotla* was an important tool for keeping the *kgosi* and his advisors accountable to the public as well as a way of guaranteeing some level of freedom of speech to his subjects. Yet, it is important to remember that it was not open to all members of society as it could only be attended by men recognized as members of the *morafe*, and far from all matters of the state were discussed (Mgadla, 1998). Later, the colonial period brought a shift in the role of the *kgotla* as British rule strengthened the *dikgosi* in relation to the *morafe*, making them less dependent on the *kgotla* meetings for confirming their legitimacy. This turned the *kgotla* more into an arena for announcements and less for debates (Mamdani, 1996, pp. 46–47).

Opinions vary regarding the levels of tolerance, equity, and accountability present within the Tswana socioeconomic and political structures. The *merafe* were not stagnant groups. Instead, members were generally willing to include various migrants on relatively equal terms (Robinson & Parsons, 2006; Schapera, 1994, chapter 1). There were, however, exceptions to this attitude of openness and generosity. Going back for centuries to early encounters between various Tswana groups and the Basarwa and Kgalagadi people, the latter were compelled into a system of bonded labour, or serfdom, referred to as *bolata*. Although individuals, *malata*, were not generally sold by their masters, they could not move away without permission and could be inherited. They were rarely paid more than food and housing in return for their labour (Ramsay et al., 1996, p. 19). Based on numbers for the colonial era, it is reasonable to estimate that *malata* in late precolonial times made up at the most around 6 per cent of the population in Bechuanaland. In addition to this account discrimination based on ethnic belonging, it should be emphasized that the patriarchal Tswana society was also characterized by gender discrimination. In the *morafe* women neither held leading positions nor were invited to participate in the *kgotla*, and in the household the wife was subject to the authority of her husband (Mgadla, 1998; Schapera, 1994; Schapera & Comaroff, 1991; Wylie, 1990).

Cutting across the political hierarchical structure, all adults belonged to age regiments, each headed by a member of the royal family and having specific duties to perform. The age regiments provided a pool of labour that could be used for communal tasks such as setting up regiments of soldiers, looking for missing people, rounding up stray cattle, going on hunting expeditions, and keeping the village clean. Or they could be working directly for the personal gains of the *kgosi*, for example, clearing fields or building houses (Schapera & Comaroff, 1991, pp. 22–23). The low population density that characterized the Tswana societies is often indicative of labour scarcities. However, as the key activity for male labour in the cattle economy, herding, was not labour intensive, labour in these societies does not appear to have been scarce after all. As a result, there appears to have been no need to develop elaborate and extensive authoritarian institutions for labour control.

2.2.2 The Traditional Cattle Economy

The climatic preconditions on the *hardveld* where the Tswana *merafe* were primarily located were dry but mostly compatible with the Tswana's agro-pastoral system of production constituting limited crop farming with a focus on livestock herding. Iliffe (1995) characterizes Africa as historically being land abundant, an initial condition that gave rise to extensive farming systems. This characterization fits well with the areas inhabited by the Tswana. Arable land was readily available for any (primarily male) *morafe* member and cattle were kept on vast communal grazing ranges.

In this agricultural-based society, crop farming was a low-technology subsistence activity that was necessary for every household, but fields were commonly only the size of a few acres. Farming was dependent on limited and erratic rainfall, and due to reoccurring droughts, fields were left uncultivated as often as every three or four years. The principal staple crop was sorghum, but as was the general trend for Southern Africa, maize production was steadily increasing in the mid-nineteenth century.

Also millet, groundnuts, and beans were cultivated in smaller quantities. Any modest surplus production was primarily sold on the local markets (Schapera & Comaroff, 1991, pp. 15–16). While agriculture provided the Tswana with staple foods, it was animal husbandry generally, and cattle keeping specifically, that constituted the proper source of wealth and social status.

The cattle economy sprung out of a long tradition of livestock management. Archaeological finds show that domesticated animals were kept in the area for 2,200 years (Ramsay et al., 1996, p. 10). While land for grazing was abundant, access to water resources was consistently the primary limiting factor for cattle rearing (Emongor, 2006). Several severe droughts were recorded in the region and each time the national herd was significantly reduced. Until the 1920s and the adaption of modern technology for the drilling of deep boreholes, animals and herders were relying on open natural waters and hand-dug shallow wells in the *hardveld*. The modern boreholes provided seasonally reliable water sources and they eventually also opened up new grazing areas in the dryer *sandveld* (Hillbom, 2010).

In the literature we find several scholars discussing the interrelationship between relative prices of factor endowments and the development of key socioeconomic structures such as property rights systems (e.g. Engerman & Sokoloff, 2002 for Latin America). In the Tswana cattle economy, the abundance of land, limited access to water, modest labour requirements, and the high value of cattle are all factors that have put their mark on the principles guiding the regulations of ownership, user rights, and access to agricultural resources and livestock.

Natural resources such as land and water were, as an overriding principle, seen as belonging to the *morafe* in their entirety and kept in trust by the *kgosi*, but in practice there were significant differences as to who controlled and who was allowed to access these resources. Land allocations in the form of private user rights to specific land sites, such as residential plots, arable fields, and cattle posts, were granted by the *kgosi* together with the village and ward headmen primarily to male heads of household. Failure to actively use the land sites as well as repeated violations of the conditions under which the user rights had been given led to a reversal of the allocation. While crop farming was conditioned by securing individual user rights to farm land, cattle was herded on the communal grazing range which any *morafe* member could freely access (Hillbom, 2010; Mgadla, 1998; Schapera, 1994, chapter 11; Schapera & Comaroff, 1991, pp. 14–15).

Natural waters were also treated as a public good to which no individual could claim private property rights and the non-exclusion principles were particularly prominent due to the life-supporting qualities of water resources (Carlsson, 2003; Peters, 1994). By combining the allocated private user rights to communally owned natural resources with the input of privately controlled family labour resources, the head of the household could secure private ownership over man-made structures such as houses or water points, as well as over agricultural production (Mgadla, 1998; Schapera, 1994, chapter 11). Generally in African customary property regimes, investments of labour and financial inputs in construction and maintenance together have been an important strategy for claiming resources and obtaining private property rights. This is unlike European property rights institutions, where the granting of private ownership is expected to come first in order to encourage investments (Sjaastad & Bromley, 1997).

Meanwhile, cattle were held in common by the *morafe* and managed by the *kgosi* or held as private property belonging to various members of society. The spread of the number of animals owned was large, from only a few to several thousands. Whoever controlled enough cattle could use them to build patron–client relationships through *mafisa*, a system of lending out animals to cattle-less subjects and relatives on a long-term basis. The system held advantages for both parties; while the recipient gained access to milk and draft power as well as ownership of potential future offspring, the lender could both spread risks and claim labour and political loyalty in return (Schapera, 1994, chapter 12). In a society where the primary scarce factor of production was labour, the *mafisa* system meant that an individual's ability to control or own cattle and exchange the use of animals for the control of labour resources became the basis for economic wealth, but also of social status and ability to mobilize political support. Acemoglu et al. (2003) have claimed that the private ownership of cattle in the precolonial era constituted the foundation of development-enhancing institutions of the postcolonial productive Botswana state. In contrast, we argue that the extensive communal property rights regimes and principles of granting user and access rights to dependents challenge such a heavy emphasis on private property right structures. What the system of *mafisa* instead reveals is that it was through the sharing of property, rather than exclusion based on the private property rights structures, that elites best managed their herds while in the meantime putting their capital (cattle) to good use by investing it in the building of socioeconomic networks, controlling labour, and securing political power. In the meantime, the system ensured that the cattle-less were prevented from falling below subsistence. This led to the creation of a benevolent elite, who benefited most from the system, but at the same time were required to show responsibility for the poor members of society. The rise of this new elite impacted principles guiding economic and political institutions. After independence these principles developed in the Tswana society spilled over to independent Botswana state structures.

Customary property rights in Africa have generally been shown to be flexible and negotiable, allowing for both security of access and amassment. The inherent negotiability is understood by some as ultimately protecting and promoting the interests of the economically and socially weak in society (Berry, 2002; Odgaard, 2003). Others emphasize that negotiations take place between individuals of varying social, economic, and political status and thereby provide an opportunity for the powerful and wealthy to amass resources (Peters, 2004). For Botswana, several researchers have argued that the precolonial redistributive system created institutions that facilitated later amassment of agricultural resources and cattle by economic and political elites (Good, 1994; Gulbrandsen, 1996; Hillbom, 2010; Peters, 1994; Wylie, 1990). It appears to have, if not promoted, at least enabled unequal distribution and polarization.

2.3 Early Colonial Era

Limited colonial influence has been identified by some scholars as a key explanatory factor for the success of independent Botswana (e.g. Acemoglu et al., 2003; Robinson & Parsons, 2006). We instead claim that it is only the impact of the first half of the colonial period that has been limited. We identify an economic structural break dividing the colonial period into two subperiods separated by their different degrees of colonial ambition, one before and one after the establishment of the colonial cattle export sector (Bolt & Hillbom, 2016; Hillbom, 2014). The early colonial period 1885–1930 was principally characterized by the continuation of existing precolonial economic structures and therefore we deal with it in this chapter. Conversely, we argue that policies implemented during the second half of the colonial period had long-term consequences and constituted colonial shocks. They are discussed in depth in Chap. 3.

2.3.1 Arrival of Europeans and the Establishment of Colonial Rule

In 1816 members of the London Missionary Society (LMS) became the first Europeans to venture into the area that is now southern Botswana. Although other churches followed in the 1820s, the LMS stayed dominant. At first conversions went slow, but the pace picked up after the *Difaqane* and by 1910 all the Tswana *dikgosi* had adopted Christianity and introduced it to their respective *morafe*. The LMS' most famous minister was David Livingstone who settled among the Bakwena in 1845. After a short and unsuccessful stay—it is said that he only converted one or two individuals—Livingstone moved on and eventually found his calling in explorations. Christianity had a profound impact on Tswana society and culture, its potentially single most important effect coming from strategies to provide education. The missionary schools provided higher education for the children of the traditional Tswana elite, including the new generation of ministers who took over after independence (Ramsay et al., 1996, pp. 178–191).

Following the missionaries, European traders started to penetrate the inland, arriving in the 1830s to buy goods such as ivory, skins, and ostrich feathers and eggs. Until 1870, trade with outsiders was monopolized by the *dikgosi* and their relatives ensuring privileged access to significant wealth for them. In addition to providing a more comfortable lifestyle to the traditional elite, trade introduced the *merafe* to new foods and tools, some of which outcompeted existing local production (Ramsay et al., 1996, pp. 193–196). A more voluminous inflow of Europeans came with the opening of gold mines in what was to become the Tati District (see Map 2.2) in 1868/1869, setting off Southern Africa's first European gold

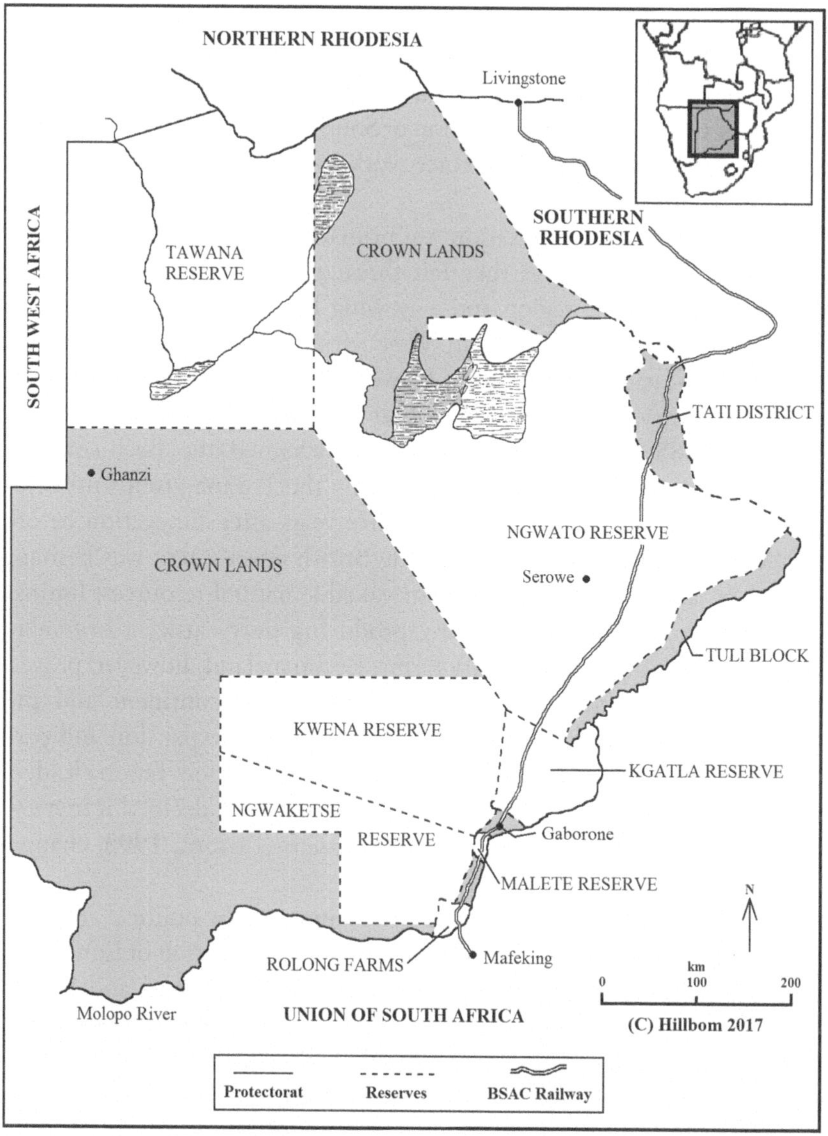

Map 2.2 The Bechuanaland Protectorate, c. 1915

rush. The ores where, however, soon depleted (Ramsay et al., 1996, pp. 142–143). With diamond mines opening in Kimberly in the late 1860s and gold being discovered in Witwatersrand in the 1880s, two areas later incorporated in the Union of South Africa, the Tswana primarily came to constitute a labour force working in mines located in neighbouring territories.

Subsequent British annexation was primarily driven by political rather than economic motives as they felt threatened when Germany, a new colonial player in the region and a growing European political and economic power, occupied German West Africa, contemporary Namibia. Due to increasing competition between the European powers over African territory, Britain thought it best to control as much land as possible. In 1885 the British unilaterally proclaimed the Bechuanaland Protectorate covering the area inhabited by the Tswana groups north of Molopo River (see Map 2.2). It took five years after annexation before full colonial control was exercised. The British government was hesitant to take on an area with few apparent valuable natural resources, limited labour resources, and an economy producing only cattle, a low-value agricultural product in monetary terms. Bechuanaland, however, proved useful as a road into the interior of the African continent and the Protectorate became a stepping stone for northward expansion and part of the ambition to build the 'Cape-Cairo Line'. While few Tswana leaders welcomed the idea of being under colonial rule, most deemed it inevitable due to the military power of the Europeans (Parsons, 1993, chapter 10; Ramsay et al., 1996, pp. 145–159).

Colonial expansion in Africa was driven not only by political and economic interests in Europe, but also by a growing population of Europeans already living in Africa and seeking to control more land and labour (Cain & Hopkins, 1993, chapter 11; Ramsay et al., 1996, p. 148). One of the major players on the scene, Cecil Rhodes with his British South Africa Company (BSAC), as well as the Afrikaner of the Transvaal and the British in the Cape Colony were all interested in expanding northward. The British government was planning for the administration of Bechuanaland to be taken over by a regional actor loyal to Britain's political ambitions and it held far-reaching negotiations with Rhodes. To the Tswana, however, the prospect of falling under the administration of the

BSAC was not appealing and they decided to turn directly to the British government to plead their case. The three most influential *dikgosi*, Khama of the Ngwato, Sebele of the Kwena, and Bathoen of the Ngwaketse, together travelled to London in 1895 to seek the support of the British public and an audience with Queen Victoria. With the help of LMS they managed to appeal to the Christian moralist middle class and the Secretary of State for the Colonies, Joseph Chamberlain. Partly due to their diplomatic trip and partly due to Rhodes' own political mistake of supporting a raid into the Afrikaner republic of Transvaal, it was decided that Bechuanaland Protectorate would stay as an entity within the British Empire (Parsons, 1993, chapter 11, 1998; Ramsay et al., 1996, pp. 171–176).

A significant part of Bechuanaland Protectorate became Crown Land or was held under company rule. The Tati District was primarily controlled by the Tati Company and inhabited by both indigenous and European farmers. The large section to the west and south-west was part of the Kalahari Desert and was occupied by small numbers of the Basarwa as well as some Afrikaner cattle farmers around Ghanzi. The BSAC and European settlers possessed land in the Tuli Block in the east and the BSAC also controlled land along the length of the railway line it constructed from the Cape, via Mafeking to Livingstone (Ramsay et al., 1996, pp. 203–204, 218–231). When added up, sizeable pieces of land were under foreign control, but they only corresponded to 3 per cent of total farmland and during the colonial era Europeans never made up more than 1 per cent of the territory's population (Colclough & McCarthy, 1980; Lewis, 2006, p. 7).

The administrative capital was located first in Vryburg, but from 1895 to 1964 it reallocated to Mafeking, both towns located in South Africa. The fact that the European administrators of Bechuanaland were primarily living in South Africa meant that they took modest part in the Protectorate's economy and society. In addition, situated across the border, the British administration exercised limited control over the Tswana *dikgosi* who were left with extensive judicial and administrative powers, including collecting colonial taxes. With the support of the colonial administration, the *dikgosi* felt a decreasing need to seek council from their headmen and popular assemblies, the *kgotla*. Slacking accountability gave them leverage which they used to build up their personal political power and cattle wealth (Parsons, 1993, p. 183; Ramsay et al., 1996). The combination of limited European settlement, continuous indigenous control of land, and strengthening of the prevailing Tswana political systems meant that Bechuanaland throughout the colonial era remained a so-called peasant economy (Mosley, 1983).

2.3.2 Labour Migration and Taxation

Whilst the colonial power saw limited opportunities for the development of agricultural or mineral production within Bechuanaland in the early colonial era, the Protectorate was still, like all colonies, expected to pay its own way within the British Empire. To this end, two primary strategies were designed that would influence the economic structures of the Tswana states from the onset of colonial rule—encouragement of labour migration and establishment of a taxation system to ensure government revenues.

As the whole of the Southern African region was sparsely populated, the colonial powers generally sought various ways of controlling labour resources. The Tswana's interest in wage labour started in the mid-nineteenth century with a growing demand for guns, used for hunting and warfare, but initial labour migration was modest. The regional expansion of the mining sector from the 1860s onwards, first in Kimberly and later in Witwatersrand, however, meant that labour demand increased substantially. As a result, the British colonial administration looked for new ways to encourage further labour movements. The Bechuanaland Protectorate was given the role of a regional labour reserve, but unlike colonies like South Rhodesia and South Africa, no actual Native Reserves were created. Instead, economic incentives such as the introduction of taxes and the payment of relatively generous salaries in neighbouring South Africa were used to encourage temporary wage labour migration. For example, mining wages varied between 20 and 64 shillings per month between 1888 and 1930, whereas the average wage for unskilled labour in Bechuanaland was around 23 shillings between 1900 and 1930 (Bolt & Hillbom, 2015; Parsons, 1993, pp. 143–151,

173–174). While mining was the most important sector for southward male labour migration, people also took up employment as farm hands and women primarily worked as domestic help.

It is difficult to determine the exact magnitude of labour migration because the majority of it took place without being officially recorded. In the colonial documents for 1938, a little over 8000 labour passes, the equivalent of 1.7 per cent of the population, are registered. Anthropological sources, however, tell a very different story. Schapera & Comaroff (1991, p. 24) suggest that 28 per cent of all adult males were absent in 1943, and Schapera (1994) reports that in many areas in the south as much as half of the productive population could have been absent in the 1920 and 1930s. Some scholars suggest that migration became of such magnitude that it significantly negatively affected domestic agricultural production in Bechuanaland. Decreasing populations and increasing difficulties in controlling labour affected the relationship between tribal authorities and their subjects as it threatened to undermine the authoritarian rule of the centralized Tswana states. While this could have led to more authoritarian institutions for controlling labour, it seems that the *dikgosi* instead chose to persuade people to stay by proposing a more benevolent and inclusive rule in combination with traditional hierarchal structures (Parsons, 1993; Ramsay et al., 1996; Schapera, 1994; Schapera & Comaroff, 1991).

Next to generous salaries paid in South Africa, the introduction of a colonial tax system was a primary driver of labour migration. Initially a hut tax was introduced in 1899, but it was substituted by a poll tax in 1909 and in 1949 the poll tax was replaced by a graded tax system (in Chap. 3 we elaborate further on the tax system over the whole colonial era). The hut tax was first set at 10 shillings, but the amount was raised to £1 poll tax in 1909 and poll taxes gradually increased to 25 shillings per annum in 1930. If we relate tax levels before 1930 to incomes earned by mineworkers, which as previously mentioned fluctuated between 20 and 64 shillings before 1930, it seems that a month's income was enough to pay the yearly hut tax (Bolt & Hillbom, 2015; Makgala, 2004). Compared to non-African regions in the British Empire tax levels in Bechuanaland were kept low throughout the colonial era, but they were substantially higher than in the other Southern Africa colonial territories. It took an unskilled urban worker in Bechuanaland 23 working days on average to earn enough to pay the tax in 1925. In comparison, the average of number of working days required for Southern Rhodesia, Northern Rhodesia, and Nyasaland in the same year was 12.8 days (Frankema, 2010: Appendix 2, Table 2; Gardner, 2012).

In the years after the introduction of the tax, the administration used the *dikgosi* for the collection of colonial taxes and gave them a 10 per cent commission as an incentive to perform conscientiously. In the 1920s the *dikgosi* were no longer paid on commission and in the 1930s the government took over the colonial tax collection for a few years (Makgala, 2006; Ramsay et al., 1996, p. 205; Schapera & Comaroff, 1991, p. 25).

One explanation for the relatively high taxes in Bechuanaland compared to neighbouring countries could be that the colonial government had limited alternative sources of revenue until the 1930s when it started to receive both colonial aid and export duties from cattle exports. As each colony in the British Empire was expected to be self-supporting, the only option for the colonial government in the absence of exports was to tax the population (Gardner, 2012). Another explanation could be that the colonial administration saw an opportunity to benefit from increasing labour migration and the relatively high wages earned by mineworkers abroad. Indeed, remittances sent home by migrant workers were one of the most important income sources for paying taxes (Morapedi, 1999). Finally, introducing high taxes could have been a way for the colonial government to benefit from the Tswana's cattle wealth. Even though the population in the Protectorate was poor in terms of nutritional intake and average cash incomes, the large majority of the population held some wealth in form of livestock, either cattle or small stock. Schapera and Comaroff (1991) document that large- and medium-scale cattle holders sometimes sold cattle to pay for taxes and that the sale of one animal could pay the annual tax several times over. However, given the vulnerability of cattle herds to drought and diseases, the average cattle owner was reluctant to sell animals if it was not absolutely necessary (Bolt & Hillbom, 2016).

The high tax levels meant that for the colonial administration tax revenues *per capita* were relatively high in an African perspective, 99 and 131 pence per year in 1911 and 1925, respectively (Frankema, 2010: Appendix 2). However, due to the overall small population, scarce domestic wage-earning opportunities, and non-existent export sector, the accumulated tax base during the early colonial era generated limited *total* revenues for the Bechuanaland administration. Consequently, it failed to secure sufficient incomes to pay for any development strategies beyond basic policing and administration of the territory.

In addition to paying to the colonial administration the Tswana were also taxed by their own leaders. Already in the precolonial era subjects paid tribute in kind—spoils from hunting expeditions, livestock, grain, and so on—to their *kgosi*. The levels where set in relation to the productive outcome, a sort of negotiable graded tax system (Schapera & Comaroff, 1991, pp. 20–21). In 1919 this was transformed into a monetary system with fixed tariffs under the heading of a 'native tax'. The native tax was initially set at three shillings per annum, but raised to five shillings per annum in 1925. In comparison to other African countries, this was not very high. In Kenya, for example, the native tax was initially a little over six shillings per annum and was raised to 11 shillings in 1915, and in Southern Rhodesia the poll tax was set at 20 shillings per annum (Gardner, 2012, pp. 97, 110). The tax in Bechuanaland was to be paid to the local Tribal Funds and used by the tribal authorities. Subsequently, chiefs were paid from the fund and the balance was to be spent on economic and social development in the reserves, for example, building schools, providing water for domestic use in the villages, and drilling boreholes for watering animals on the grazing range (Schapera & Comaroff, 1991, pp. 25–26). The Tswana authorities, however, shared the challenges of the colonial administration that incomes were too modest to allow for any ambitious development projects.

2.4 Summing Up and Moving On ...

In this chapter we described the main features characterizing the precolonial settlement patters and agro-pastoral system of production of the Tswana living in current-day Botswana. Understanding the factors shaping their socioeconomic and political structures during this era is vital for a further understanding of subsequent processes of continuity and change in both the colonial and independence eras. In the precolonial society we find the formation of basic principles later determining access to agricultural resources, cattle production, wealth inequality, and development of political institutions.

Limited direct colonial control over valuable agricultural land and indigenous labour, modest European settlement, the physical absence of British officials, and the delegation of administrative powers to the *dikgosi*—these are all factors that have led various scholars to claim that colonial influence was limited in Bechuanaland throughout the colonial era. This in turn would explain the survival of good precolonial institutions laying the ground for Botswana's current state capacity and also explain the good management of diamond revenues. We agree with the story of limited colonial influence for the early colonial period up until 1930s. However, in Chap. 3 we will show that for the later part of the colonial period colonial strategies actually came to have a profound impact on the economic, social, and political pathway of development in both colonial Bechuanaland and independent Botswana—an impact that has often been underestimated in the literature.

References

Acemoglu, D., Johnson, S., & Robinson, J. A. (2003). An African success story: Botswana. In D. Rodrik (Ed.), *In search of prosperity: Analytic narratives on economic growth* (pp. 80–119). Princeton and Oxford: Princeton University Press.

Beaulier, S. A., & Subrick, J. R. (2006). The political foundations of development: The case of Botswana. *Constitutional Political Economy, 17*(2), 103–115.

Berry, S. (2002). Debating the land question in Africa. *Comparative Studies in Society and History, 44*(4), 638–668.

Bolt, J., & Hillbom, E. (2015). Potential for diversification? The role of the formal sector in Bechuanaland Protectorate's economy, 1900–65. *Economic History of Developing Regions, 30*(2), 95–124.

Bolt, J., & Hillbom, E. (2016). Long-term trends in economic inequality: Lessons from colonial Botswana, 1921–1974. *Economic History Review, 69*(4), 1255–1284.

Cain, P. J., & Hopkins, A. G. (1993). *British imperialism, innovation and expansion, 1688–1914*. London and New York: Longman.

Carlsson, E. 2003. *To have and to hold: Continuity and change in property rights institutions governing water resources among the Meru of Tanzania and the BaKgtala in Botswana; 1925–2000*. Lund Studies in Economic History, 28. Stockholm: Almqvist & Wiksell International.

Colclough, C., & McCarthy, S. (1980). *The political economy of Botswana: A study of growth and distribution*. Oxford: Oxford University Press.

Eldredge, E. A. (1992). Sources of conflict in southern Africa, c. 1800–30: The 'Mfecane' reconsidered. *The Journal of African History, 33*(1), 1–35.

Emongor, V. E. (2006). Use of secondary effluent in food production in Botswana. *Journal of Applied Science, 6*(2), 318–324.

Engerman, S. L., & Sokoloff, K. L. (2002). Factor endowments, inequality, and paths of development among new world economics. *Economia, 3*(1), 41–108.

Frankema, E. (2010). Raising revenue in the British empire, 1870–1940: How 'extractive' were colonial taxes? *Journal of Global History, 5*(3), 447–477.

Frankema, E., & Jerven, M. (2014). Writing history backwards or sideways: Towards a consensus on African population, 1850–2010. *The Economic History Review, 67*(4), 907–931.

Gardner, L. (2012). *Taxing colonial Africa: The political economy of British imperialism*. Oxford: Oxford University Press.

Good, K. (1994). Corruption and mismanagement in Botswana: A best-case example? *The Journal of Modern African Studies, 32*(3), 499–521.

Gulbrandsen, Ø. (1996). *Poverty in the midst of Plenty: Socio-economic marginalization, ecological deterioration and political stability in a Tswana society* (No. 45). Bergen: Norse Publications.

Herbst, J. (2000). *States and power in Africa: Comparative lessons in authority and control*. Princeton: Princeton University Press.

Hillbom, E. (2010). Agricultural development and the distribution of water resources in Kgatleng District, Botswana. *Development Southern Africa, 27*(3), 413–427.

Hillbom, E. (2014). Cattle, Diamonds and Institutions: Main drivers of Botswana's economic development, 1850 to present. *Journal of International Development, 26*(2), 155–176.

Iliffe, J. (1995). *Africans. The history of a continent*. Cambridge: Cambridge university press.

Lewis, S. (2006). Explaining Botswana's success. In L. Harrison & P. Berger (Eds.), *Developing cultures*. New York: Case Studies.

Makgala, C. J. (2004). Taxation in the tribal areas of the Bechuanaland Protectorate, 1899–1957. *The Journal of African History, 45*(2), 279–303.

Makgala, C. J. (2006). *Elite conflict in Botswana: A history*. Pretoria: African Institute of South Africa.

Mamdani, M. (1996). *Citizen and subject: Contemporary Africa and the legacy of late colonialism*. Princeton, NJ: Princeton University Press.

Masire, K. (2006). *Very brave or very foolish? Memoires of an African democrat.* Gaborone: Macmillan Botswana Publishing Co (Pty) Ltd.

Mgadla, P. T. (1998). The Kgosi in a traditional Tswana setting. In *Botswana: Politics and Society*. Gaborone: Macmillan Botswana.

Morapedi, W. G. (1999). Migrant labour and the Peasantry in the Bechuanaland Protectorate, 1930–1965. *Journal of Southern African Studies, 25*(2), 197–214.

Mosley, P. (1983). *The settler economies: Kenya and Southern Rhodesia 1900–1963.* Cambridge: Cambridge University Press.

Odgaard, R. (2003). Scrambling for land in Tanzania: Processes of formalization and legitimization of land rights. In T. Benjaminsen & C. Lund (Eds.), *Securing land rights in Africa*. London: Frank Cass.

Parsons, N. (1993). *A new history of Southern Africa* (2nd ed.). London: Macmillan Education Ltd.

Parsons, N. (1998). *King Khama, emperor Joe, and the great white queen: Victorian Britain through African eyes.* Chicago: University of Chicago Press.

Peters, P. E. (1994). *Dividing the commons: Politics, policy, and culture in Botswana*. Charlottesville: University Press of Virginia.

Peters, P. E. (2004). Inequality and social conflict over land in Africa. *Journal of Agrarian Change, 4*(3), 269–314.

Ramsay, J., Mgadla, P. T., & Morton, B. (1996). *Building a nation: A history of Botswana from 1800 to 1910*. Gaborone: Longman Botswana.

Robinson, J. A., & Parsons, Q. N. (2006). State formation and governance in Botswana. *Journal of African Economies, 15*(AERC Suppl 1), 100–140.

Schapera, I. (1994). *A handbook of Tswana law and custom.* Münster: LIT Verlag.

Schapera, I., & Comaroff, J. L. (1991). *The Tswana* (Revised ed.). London: Kegan Paul International.

Silitshena, R. M. K., & McLeod, G. (1998). *Botswana: A physical, social, and economic geography* (2nd ed.). Gaborone: Longman Botswana Ltd.

Sjaastad, E., & Bromley, D. W. (1997). Indigenous land rights in Sub-Saharan Africa: Appropriation, security and investment demand. *World Development, 25*(4), 549–562.

Wylie, D. (1990). *A little god: The twilight of patriarchy in a Southern African chiefdom*. Hanover: Wesleyan University Press.

Archive Material

Annual Report of the Bechuanaland Protectorate. Issues 1903/1904, London School of Economics Library.

Part II

Part 2

3

Colonial Policies and the Cattle Economy, c. 1930–1975

3.1 Introduction

In the broad literature on colonial legacies, a larger population of European settlers is often linked to higher long-term economic growth. The mechanisms underlying this 'settler effect' are thought to work via greater access and diffusion of European technologies, human capital development via the transfer of skills and knowledge including the introduction of European education, and the creation of European 'developmental' or 'inclusive' institutions (Acemoglu, Johnson, & Robinson, 2001, 2002; Easterly & Levine, 2016; Putterman & Weil, 2010). Due to the average low degree of European intrusion, the relevance of this literature for the African experience has been debated. Colonialism in Africa only lasted for a relatively short period roughly from the mid-1880s to the mid-1960s, and the large majority of territories experienced relative low levels of settlement and expropriation (Frankema et al., 2016; Mosley, 1983).

In contrast to the colonial settlement explanation, the economic progress of independent Botswana has instead been linked to limited European presence, modest colonial influence, and the persistence of

E. Hillbom, J. Bolt, *Botswana – A Modern Economic History*, Palgrave Studies in Economic History, https://doi.org/10.1007/978-3-319-73144-5_3

precolonial institutions (Acemoglu et al., 2003; Acemoglu & Robinson, 2010; Robinson & Parsons, 2006). It is true that Bechuanaland throughout the colonial period remained a typical peasant colony, only attracting a small number of European settlers while the overwhelming majority of land and other productive resources remained in African hands. We argue, however, that this did not mean that the colonial period did not significantly affect long-term development. In this chapter we show that policies implemented during the second half of the colonial period, most importantly the establishment of a commercial cattle economy in the 1930s, constituted a colonial shock marking a clear socioeconomic structural break with the precolonial period. The economic structures of the colonial cattle economy dominated until the next structural break, the takeover of the diamond economy in the mid-1970s, and its legacies have continued to profoundly impact independent Botswana's development path.

The key to understanding the long-term impact of the later colonial era is to analyse colonial policies and their transformation of existing socioeconomic structures. The intrinsic logic of those colonial policies can be made clear only by understanding the incentives inherent in the colonial state. First of all, the European colonial powers demanded that all colonies financed their own development strategies (Cooper, 2002; Gardner, 2012). Meanwhile, in the case of Britain, direct investments to the African territories were generally restricted, and the transfer of European technology, knowledge, and institutions remained limited (Bowden et al., 2008; Mosley, 1983). Further, most of the colonial administrations had too little domestic revenues to pay for any development-oriented investments. In combination, these financial constraints resulted in the development of a minimalistic state, a gate-keeping state, characterized by government policies focused on instigating export-led growth that could be taxed with relative little effort while increasing total government revenues significantly (Cooper, 2002).

Bechuanaland was no exception to this general characterization. To prove this point, we explore both the sources and levels of the government's domestic revenues, as well as the investment choices made by the colonial government. Considering the modest amounts involved in colonial incomes one could, based on these indicators alone, mistakenly conclude that there was little change and thus limited colonial impact. However, we argue that it is not the absolute amounts but the relative importance of the various revenue-raising activities and direction of investments that is of primary interest. Mapping revenues and investments is therefore a means to unravel the long-term impact of the colonial administration's development strategy. While the establishment and development of the cattle export sector never became a very lucrative activity, it profoundly affected the economy. It was the only colonial activity that resulted in some, albeit modest, economic growth. When looking at the outcomes in terms of changes in economic and political structures the colonial legacy was significant as it created preconditions for coming development challenges in terms of incentives and opportunities for sectorial change and the distribution of resources and welfare. This will be further discussed in our thematic Chaps. 4, 5, and 6.

We start this chapter with outlining the development of the African colonial state and focus especially on the gate-keeping state concept introduced by Cooper (2002). The gate-keeping state describs a state structure that due to its inability to raise sufficient revenues is restricted in its socioeconomic development ambitions. This results in a small government, focusing on maintaining its basic administration and control. In the next section we apply this framework of state development to Bechuanaland. First, we analyse in depth the fiscal capacity of the colonial government, what strategies the administration pursued to raise revenues, and how much revenues it managed to raise. Second, we discuss the choices the colonial government made in terms of investments and transfers, and how these in turn re-enforced existing economic structures. The third section deals with the establishment of the cattle export sector and how this initiative came to dominate the economy. We move on to present the time of the political change leading up to independence as well as the new independent government's initial policies. Finally, we sum up and and indicate the central issues discussed in Chap. 4.

3.2 Colonial State Development in Africa

During the 'scramble for Africa', signifying the time period roughly between the Berlin Conference in 1884–1885 and World War I, the European colonial powers were primarily interested in conquering the African continent, establishing political power, and setting up a tax collection system to raise revenue in order to pay for colonial activities (Pakenham, 1992). It was not until the 1920s and 1930s that the various European powers began viewing their African colonies not just as territories open for exploitation and extraction, but as member states in their empires. With this shift in perception began a search for strategies both to expand the formal taxation systems to generate incomes from surplus production within the colonies and to identify investments to develop the colonial economies further. The aim was to increase government revenues in order to enable colonial administrations to launch more ambitious development strategies. In addition, natural resources, minerals, and agricultural products in Africa were expected to add to the national wealth of the European countries (Cooper, 2002).

Due to limited state capacity and little financial means the colonial administrations opted out of taking on the demanding and expensive task of building tax capacity by developing a state apparatus for direct tax collection and broadening the tax base. Instead colonial governments focused on developing the colonies' primary sectors, extracting valuable natural resources, producing cash crops for exports, and taxing trade. This was a strategically rational choice in view of the existing circumstance, as controlling borders and taxing the export sector was the easier, cheaper, and more effective way of raising revenues compared to developing the state bureaucracy needed for the collection of direct taxes. The outcome was the creation of administrations that focused their efforts on developing export sectors rather than domestic markets, and spent their resources on controlling the borders and the flow of goods in and out of the colony while having limited interaction with the inland. These principles governing colonial state policies and shaping the economic structures from the 1930s onwards provide the basis for Cooper's (2002) 'gate-keeping state' concept. Even though initial conditions and production factors, that is, natural resources, land and labour, and consequently specific colonial strategies varied between the African territories, there were far-reaching similarities between African colonies, resulting in the development of similar gate-keeping states across the region.

The creation of the gate-keeping states and their specific development strategies has strongly influenced development paths in the region. The narrow tax base and limited transfers from the European colonial powers caused local colonial governments to encourage and facilitate the production of a limited number of valuable primary exports goods which could then be taxed at the borders. This commonly resulted in the development of mono-mineral and mono-crop economies which were vulnerable to fluctuations in commodity prices on the global market. While these mono-sector economies did raise government revenues as intended, incomes were in most instances not enough to remove the financial constraints that the colonial governments experienced. Consequently, the gate-keeping states continued throughout the colonial era to be restrictive when it came to investing in or encouraging the development of alternative productive sectors of the economy (Cooper, 2002; Hillbom, 2012).

Based on the absence of valuable minerals, dry climatic conditions, and existing agro-pastoral system of production, the colonial administration in Bechuanaland eventually identified ranching as the comparative advantage of the territory. Sir Charles Rey, arriving as the new Resident Commissioner in 1930, was in the spirit of the new colonial ambitions expected to develop the Protectorate's economy. He saw a great potential in the large herds held by the Tswana and the vast open grazing ranges (Parsons & Crowder, 1988). From the start, however, there were inherent limitations to the strategy of choosing cattle as the main export commodity as it constituted neither a very valuable nor a unique resource. While there existed cattle markets in Southern Africa that Bechuanaland exports could tap into, cattle was held in large quantities in neighbouring territories such as South Africa, Southern Rhodesia, and Northern Rhodesia. The administrations of these territories were already aiming for strategies to provide beef to their own populations, primarily in the urban areas. This lack of regional demand did not, however, discourage Bechuanaland's administration from deciding to stimulate exports that added to existing supply.

In the absence of an abattoir, beef was primarily exported in the form of the herding of live animals across the border to the neighbouring territories. This made it a bulk good that was not conditioned by infrastructure development such as railways, but still had high transaction costs in the form of inefficient transportation. The new export sector was further challenged by the fact that Bechuanaland was landlocked. The most easily reachable sizeable export market was the Union of South Africa, and as pointed out above this country already had a significant beef production of its own (Parsons & Crowder, 1988). The global market was out of reach as there was significant international competition at the time in the form of much more efficient producer countries. For example, the cattle sectors in Argentina and Uruguay had much higher productivity being linked, as they were, to technological and structural changes via investments in transportation and information infrastructure, slaughter houses, and a leather industry. Products from these Latin American countries were dominant in the global market (Salvucci, 2006). Rey must have understood that the unsupplied demand for beef regionally as well as globally was modest, but options for finding an alternative revenue-making export product in Bechuanaland were limited. Consequently, the colonial administration continued its support of the cattle export sector drilling boreholes, providing veterinary services, and so on. While securing only modest incomes, the cattle sector became the backbone of the colonial economy.

For peasant colonies in Africa the primary sector focus endured throughout the colonial era, and sometimes beyond. Industrialization, which could have been one diversification strategy, was generally not an option for the African colonial administrations as such efforts were beyond their financial and governmental capabilities. Industrial developments only took place in a few settler colonies, for example, Congo, South Rhodesia (Zimbabwe) and South West Africa (Namibia), and South Africa. The latter, which became independent in 1910, was the only African country to have a proper industrialization strategy by the mid-twentieth century (Freund, 1984; Schneider, 2000).

In Bechuanaland, modest government revenues and difficulties in identifying specific opportunities translated into a lack of colonial interest in developing the manufacturing sector. At the time of independence, the manufacturing sector contributed only 5 per cent to total GDP (Leith, 2005, p. 100). In terms of the share of the population employed in manufacturing the numbers are even less significant. The census of 1946 indicates that around 7,500 persons, or around 2 per cent of the population, were working outside agriculture and services. Out of those, around 4,500 individuals were employed in domestic mining activities and around 3,000 were active as (skilled) labourers in handicrafts. In 1964, the domestic mining sector only employed around 700 people, reducing the total number of workers in industrial, manufacturing, or handicraft-related activities in the domestic economy to around 5,000. This meant that they made up less than 1 per cent of the total population around the time of independence (Annual Report, 1963/1964; Population Census Bechuanaland, 1964).

Depending on the resource, the colonial gate-keeping states' focus on developing natural resource-based exports sometimes resulted in urbanization and increasing urban wage labour opportunities. For example, in Northern Rhodesia (Zambia) the construction of the copper mines led to the creation of a relatively large urban population in the decades before World War II. This in turn created a domestic demand for surplus food production, stimulating the development of an agricultural sector geared towards providing the urban areas with maize and, to some extent, beef (Hillbom & Jenkin, 2018). In Bechuanaland there existed no colonial regulations or forced movement of labour. With only marginal mining and manufacturing sectors and thus modest opportunities for urban wage employment, urbanization was limited throughout the colonial era. In 1960 no more than 3 per cent of the population lived in urban areas (World Bank, 2017). Further, the overall development of real wages, was poor throughout the colonial period (Bolt & Hillbom, 2015). This meant that most wage earners had no surplus income to stimulate demand driven production, either in agriculture or in manufacturing.

Meanwhile, the inhabitants of the rural areas who were engaged in informal self-employment in the agricultural sector and constituted some 80 per cent of the total population were generally even more cash poor. The majority of them held only a few animals which they would sell only when they were being pressurized to pay taxes, or, alternatively, they owned no animals at all. The only rural group who could afford any substantial above-subsistence consumption were the large-scale cattle holders making up at the most 5 per cent of the population during the colonial era. They only started gaining substantial cash incomes after the takeoff of the cattle export sector (Bolt & Hillbom, 2015, 2016). All in all, the basis for a demand-driven diversification of the domestic market was narrow.

In all of colonial Africa, the great majority of the population continued to live in rural areas that were mostly unknown and unregulated by the colonial administration. This laid the foundation for a dual economy which had, on the one hand, a formal sector consisting of a limited wage labour class and, on the other hand, a large residual informal sector (Cooper, 2002; Freund, 1984; Mamdani, 1996). The separation between the formal and the informal often corresponded to a divide between the spheres of the Europeans and the indigenous populations. While the separation came to its extreme in South Africa's apartheid system (1948–1994) (Evans, 1997; Posel, 1991), its principles were established earlier and were more generally spread throughout the gate-keeping states of the region. In this system, African societies were expected to cater for the needs of their own members without much support from the central administration. This meant that the overall colonial development project became detached from the masses in the rural areas as well as the urban informal economy. These dual socioeconomic structures have lived on and have become one of the most severe structural challenges for contemporary African states (Cooper, 2002; Freund, 1984; Mamdani, 1996; Muthien & Houston, 2002).

At a first glance Bechuanaland with its scant European settlement, limited urbanization, and pre-existing domestic cattle economy appears to separate itself from the typical colonial dual economy story. The economy and society remained fairly homogeneous in the colonial era in the sense that it remained mostly rural and was based on the same agro-pastoral system of production as during precolonial times. Nevertheless, with its highly unequal distribution of cattle wealth and the amalgamation of economic and political elites, it contained the roots of the dual structures that would later become more pronounced. The commercialization of the cattle sector and new opportunities to turn cattle wealth into incomes, in combination with an expanding public sector, resulted in sharply increasing inequality already during the colonial era. The mechanisms behind this development will be discussed in depth in Chap. 6. The creation of a dual economy did not really, however, establish itself until after independence with the development of the diamond economy leading to fast urbanization and rapid, though partial, modernization and this is a theme discussed in Chap. 5.

In addition to the divide between the formal and informal sectors, the gate-keeping state also created a public–private divide within the formal sector, a divide that has persisted and has had significant implications also for independent Africa. The main sources of incomes for the gate-keeping state were obtained from state-owned national resources and taxation of trade. Increasing government revenues often resulted in rising wages for government officials. Meanwhile, since there was little encouragement of rural and urban private entrepreneurship during the colonial era, the private sector remained underdeveloped. For the political elite it became important to control the state as this also entailed profiting from its riches. Contemporary gate-keeping states continue to be hotbeds for power struggles due to lacking alternative economic opportunities. When controlling the state continues to be the only way to obtain wealth, political leaders tend to take desperate measures to stay in power, or alternatively try to grab it (Berry, 1993; Cooper, 2002; Leonard & Straus, 2003).

As we will discuss more in Chap. 4, Bechuanaland during the cattle-led growth period was a typical case of the forging ahead of the public sector. While wages paid to skilled labourers and government employees were on a par in the mid-1940s, this balance changed from 1950 onwards as wages in the public sector rapidly increased to 4.5 times the level of the private sector wages for skilled labour. The public sector not only expanded in terms of increasing wages, but a growing number of people found employment in the public sector during this period. This expansion was paid for by increased revenues from the cattle export sector together with rising grants and loans from Britain (Bolt & Hillbom, 2015; Makgala, 2006).

3.3 Fiscal Capacity

Although colonial development strategies in Bechuanaland were modest and implemented relatively late during the colonial period, they still brought about a significant change in institutional and economic structures. The most fundamental change brought about by the colonial administration was driven by the search to increase revenues. Due to the lack of a broad tax base, the administration concentrated its efforts on developing a commercial cattle export sector and securing increasing export incomes. To structure our investigation into the colonial strategies in Bechuanaland with respect to raising revenues and investments made in the economy, we have subdivided this section into two. First we discuss the constraints the colonial government faced and the choices they made with regard to raising government revenues and investment opportunities.

3.3.1 Revenues

During the first half of the colonial period, the government budget had been very modest. Total revenues amounted to around £100,000 annually and most of this was derived from direct taxation of a population that was generally poor. Due to modest direct incomes, and lack of alternative income sources, the administration was severely constrained in regard to the sums it could spend on expanding the colonial state or encouraging economic activities. Figure 3.1 shows the very low levels of domestic revenues in 1930, when this chapter's period of investigation starts. As the colonial administration was expected to cover its own costs and there was not yet a developed export sector providing additional incomes, total recurrent expenditures were kept down. The colonial government continued to experience budget restrictions for a decade and a half, and we can see that it is not until the second half of the 1940s that both total domestic revenues and total recurrent expenditures started to rise. From the mid-1950s domestic revenues continue to increase slowly while recurrent expenditures initially increase more rapidly. Some of that can be accounted for by increases in spending on veterinary and agricultural services, and the rest is most likely the costs for the relocation of the capital from South

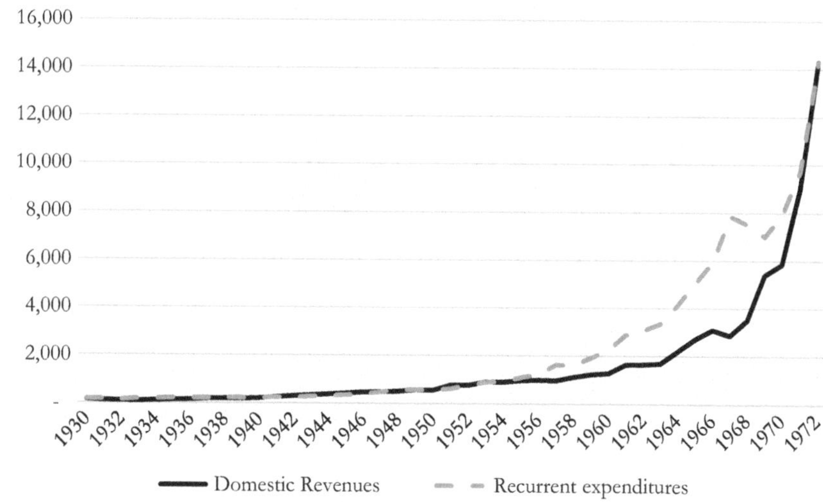

Fig. 3.1 Total domestic revenues versus total recurrent expenditures, 1930–1973 (£,000). Source: Hermans (1974: Table 1)

Africa to Gaborone; see also Sect. 3.3.2 (Colclough & McCarthy, 1980; Hermans, 1974).

In the years after independence the first revenues from diamond mining began flowing in and government incomes increased rapidly. As a result, the government was quickly able to restore a balanced budget, though at a much higher level than before. Due to the much higher value of diamond exports compared to cattle exports, our characterization of the gate-keeping state's strategies as shaped by a struggle with budgetary restrictions becomes distorted when we include diamond revenues. It is, however, unavoidable that there was a period of transition before the diamond-led growth period had matured and a structural break can be identified.

From the start of the colonial period until the mid-1940s, the collection of direct taxation from households and individuals formed the fiscal backbone of the state. In Fig. 3.2 we can see the share of domestic revenues generated by native hut and poll taxes and personal income tax from 1925 until independence, when the native taxes were abolished. Income tax was initiated in 1922 and was in practice only paid by Europeans and companies. The total amount of direct taxes, however,

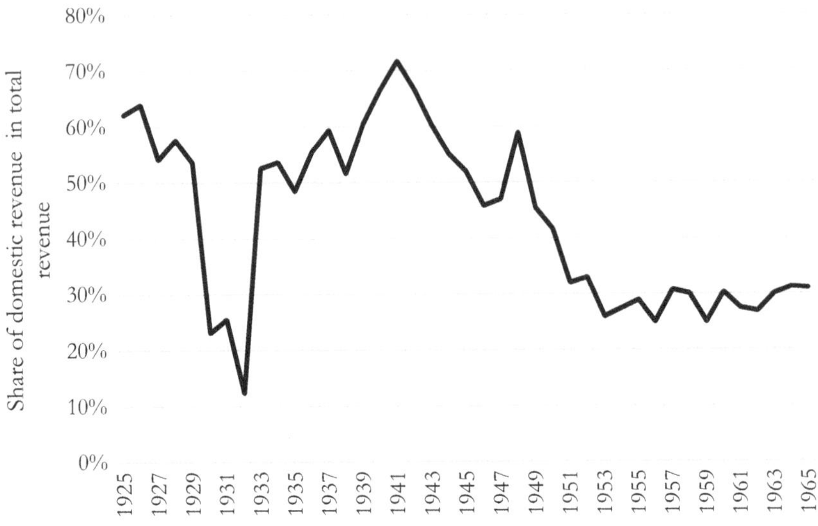

Fig. 3.2 Share of direct tax revenue, 1925–1966. Source: Hermans (1974: Table 1)

never exceeded 850,000 pounds per annum, remaining modest in absolute amounts. Additionally, these direct taxes were unpredictable as the population's ability to pay varied due to droughts and outbreaks of livestock diseases which affected incomes. The amount of direct taxes collected dropped drastically in the early 1930s as a result of the severe drought that hit the country, and again in the mid-1940s (see Fig. 3.2). Nevertheless, it averaged as much as 53 per cent of total domestic revenues in 1900–1930, peaking at 72 per cent in 1941 and then slowly declining to on average 30 per cent between 1950 and 1966. Between 1930 and independence, around 40 per cent of domestic revenues was generated by direct taxes.

Because the scope for taxing the cash-poor population of the Protectorate was evidently limited, the administration was eager to look for complementary revenues. In the 1930s it started developing two alternative strategies to raising revenues—requesting financial aid from Britain and stimulating the development of its only available natural resources at the time, the cattle sector, to raise revenues. These strategies would in time pay off in increasing total revenues, a development which is mirrored in Fig. 3.2 by the declining share of direct tax of total revenues.

The changing strategies of the Bechuanaland administration were not a local nor an isolated initiative, but part of changing general colonial policies. The 1930s saw a general launch of what Cooper (2002) has termed 'development colonialism', a growing ambition among the European powers generally to provide development support to their African colonies guided by the intention to instigate socioeconomic development. Preferably, development projects would still primarily be paid for by domestic revenues raised in the colonies, but in addition there was now increasing financial aid from the colonial powers. Changing colonial policies within the British Empire had a significant impact on Bechuanaland.

In search of ways to increase its revenues, Bechuanaland's colonial government turned to the British government for financial aid. In 1930 the territory started receiving proper colonial funding for the first time. In the beginning it was identified as *extraordinary revenue* and from the financial year 1934–1935 it was termed the *Colonial Development Fund*. From 1933 and a few years onwards, there was also substantial *parliamentary grant-in-aid*, which represented as much as 70 per cent of total revenue in 1933–1934. Although this was an extreme year, parliamentary grants-in-aid continued to be of significant importance until it was terminated with the outbreak of World War II. Figure 3.3 shows the parliamentary grant-in-aid and extraordinary revenue that the Protectorate received for its Colonial Development Fund. The relative importance of the external funding varied between the British colonies depending on their own ability to fund development projects. For a colony such as Bechuanaland where domestic revenue was modest, additional funding from the colonial power was of substantial importance. Both in the early 1930s and after the 1950s, the British grants sometimes nearly doubled the available budget. During the World War II years, however, colonial aid was halted and after independence in 1966 it was stopped.

As a supplement to direct taxation and aid, the colonial government carried out strategies for exploiting Bechuanaland's abundant natural

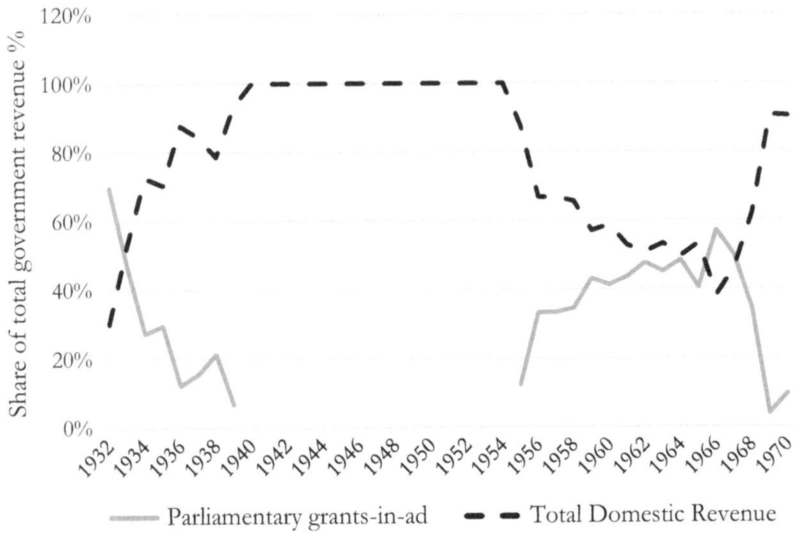

Fig. 3.3 Share of domestic revenue and colonial funding in total government revenue, 1931–1972. Source: Hermans (1974: Table 1)

resource, primarily the vast grazing range and substantial national cattle herd, by expanding opportunities to tax exports. Export duties were levied on live cattle and carcases during two time periods: 1916–1925 and 1942 onwards. In the first period these duties were directed towards the limited number of European large-scale cattle holders living in the Protectorate as they were not yet paying income tax. During the second period the scope was broadened and duties were levied on all exported cattle, most of them by then being provided by large-scale Tswana cattle holders. With the growth of the cattle export sector these revenues soon increased substantially. In addition to its own export earnings, Bechuanaland joined the Southern African Customs Union and from there the Protectorate received a share of the common pool of customs and excise duty collections (included in trade tax revenue in Fig. 3.4). This enabled the Protectorate to benefit to some degree from the economic development and increased exports and imports of the region as a whole (Hermans, 1974).

Incomes from trade taxes started to increase from the mid-1940s, albeit slowly. After the mid-1950s they surpassed direct tax revenue as the most important source of domestic income, and added more than 30 per

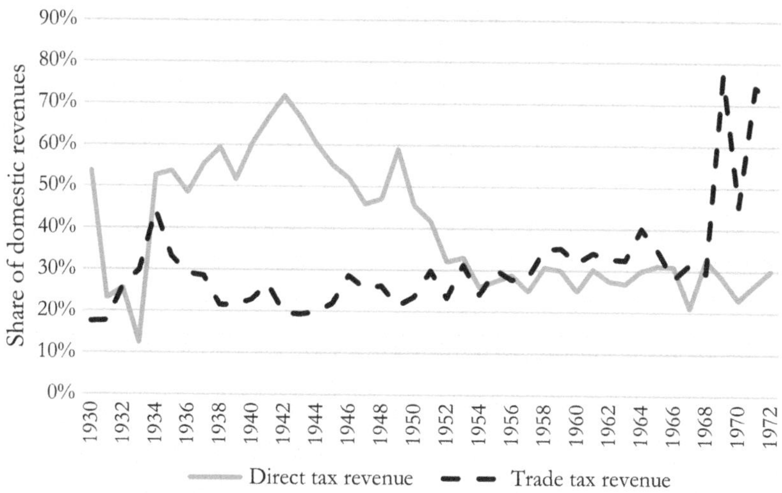

Fig. 3.4 Direct versus trade tax revenues, 1930–1972. Source: Hermans (1974: Table 1)

cent to the budget. Further, even though incomes from trade taxes did not increase enormously after the establishment of the cattle sector, the ability by the population to pay native taxes did, largely due to increased cattle sales. Total incomes originating in one way or the other from the livestock sector between 1930 and 1965 amounting to 60 per cent of the total annual government budget. While Bechuanaland developed a mono-product-based natural resource export dependency, the scope for sizeable increases of total government revenue due to increasing export incomes remained limited given the low value added of cattle. More important for our arguments for the outcome of colonial policies is that at the end of the day cattle completely dominated the export sector.

3.3.2 Expenditures

Taxing cattle exports were only one part of the colonial vision of how to turn Bechuanaland's natural resources into government revenues. In addition, the authorities made deliberate choices regarding how to spend income, and the hope was that investments would ensure continued, long-term incomes.

Table 3.1 Colonial administrative expenditure in Bechuanaland Protectorate, 1936–1966 (per cent)

	1936–1945	1946–1955	1956–1966
General administration	41.4	35.3	41.0
Police	11.5	10.8	6.6
Medical	9.4	9.9	5.9
Education	4.1	4.8	6.3
Veterinary & agriculture	12.8	12.6	10.0
Public works	9.5	12.9	4.9
Development expenditures	11.3	13.7	25.3
Total	100	100	100

Source: Colclough and McCarthy (1980: Table 1.1)

With the increase in colonial funding, slowly rising domestic revenues, and a growing taxable export sector, the administration increasingly gained some, albeit modest, financial means to invest in socioeconomic development. By analysing choices in regard to expenditures we can reveal much about colonial government strategies and hypothesize about future consequences based on the opportunities and incentive structures they created.

Table 3.1 shows the colonial administration's expenditures divided into various categories from the 1930s onwards. Around 40 per cent of total government expenditure was consistently spent on paying salaries for the administration itself throughout the period between the 1930s and independence. Additionally, another 5 to 10 percent of the budget was spend on the police force during this period. The relatively constant share of expenditures in relation to the increasing total incomes during the cattle-led growth period means that total sums spent on administration increased. It was especially increasing wages that accounted for the exanding expenditures, although also the number of government employees increased modestly (wages and wage differences will be further elaborated in Chaps. 4 and 6). In total there were some 20 or so administrators (not including the police force) assigned to govern an area the size of France. In total, however (still excluding the police), more than 150 people worked for the central government administration. The Protectorate actually had a high number of colonial administrators relative to the number of African subjects. In 1937 there were 13,193 Africans per administrator in Bechuanaland compared to the British Empire's average of 37,374 Africans per administrator (Richens, 2009: Table 1). These figures can be interpreted in two ways—either the colonial presence in Bechuanaland was significant or there was a limit to how small any administration could be in order to function. Either way, the size of staff in relation to the number of subjects indicates that colonial efforts to administrate Bechuanaland were not as negligible as is often indicated in the literature claiming the absence of colonial legacies (Acemoglu et al., 2003; Acemoglu & Robinson, 2010; Robinson & Parsons, 2006). As we will show in the following section when discussing the establishment of the cattle export sector, colonial efforts were definitely sizeable enough to significantly and permanently restructure the precolonial cattle economy.

Meanwhile, investments in social development as share of total spending on health, education, and public works initially increased right after World War II, only to decline again during the final decade of colonial rule. Despite the increase in the share spent on education, total investments in social development (health and education) in terms of absolute amounts spent, remained modest. The administration generally relied on the missionary societies and Native Authorities to cater for these types of services, for example, in the form of building primary schools. Investments in public works, such as infrastructure, were also limited and primarily aimed at supporting the administration with public buildings and other facilities (Hermans, 1974). Further, the grants and loans received from Britain, especially in the latter half of the period, were largely invested in telecommunications, power, water, and roads projects. These investments were the result of the decision to move the administrative headquarters of Bechuanaland from South Africa to Gaborone at the end of the colonial period. Most was spent on new office blocks, housing, and ancillary urban services for the new capital city (Colclough & McCarthy, 1980, p. 31). The move fully accounts for the increase in the 'Development Expenditure' spending. The poor outcome of modest colonial social development efforts can be illustrated with some examples—at independence Botswana had 12 kilometres of paved roads, 22 university graduates, and 100 students with a secondary school degree (Acemoglu et al., 2003). Importantly, this poor state of affairs was not primarily the result of extractive policies, but of the colonial administration's modest revenues due to dependency of a low-value natural resource with limited export opportunities. With almost half of those revenues being spent on paying for salaries in the expanding administration it left limited funds for investment in development projects.

Independent of the limitations of the cattle sector, it still constituted the most obvious opportunity to raise incomes and the colonial administration focused its restricted means on its expansion. Indeed, the cattle sector was the only economic sector that received substantial and consistent government investments, accumulating to on average a little over 10 per cent of the government budget. The Veterinary Department, established in 1905, was the first professional service department and veterinary and agricultural investments were part of recurrent expenditures (Hermans, 1974). Eventually, with the newfound interest in developing natural resources into revenue-earning exports and the grant-in-aid-financed programmes, additional investments were made into the cattle sector, for example, in the form of the erection of veterinary fences and the building of a first modern abattoir in Lobatse in 1954. The gate-keeping state strategy of focusing government investments on furthering one targeted economic activity, namely, the cattle sector, resulted in the creation of a mono-product economy based on cattle exports. In relation to its intents and purposes of encouraging the cattle sector for the sake of gaining export revenues the colonial administration has to be deemed successful in the sense that at the time of independence it represented 85 per cent of total export earnings (Colclough & McCarthy, 1980, p. 32; Harvey & Lewis, 1990, pp. 78–82; Makgala, 2006; Parsons & Crowder, 1988).

3.4 The Commercial Cattle Sector

In their work on Latin America, Engerman and Sokoloff (2002) have argued that the preconditions for accessing factor endowments turned out to be the strong determinant in increasing levels of inequality and this conclusion rings true also for Bechuanaland. In contrast to the Latin America case characterized by colonial extraction, unequal distribution of land, and the hacienda system dominated by settlers, in Bechuanaland it was not settlers but the Tswana elite who turned out to be winners due to their success in securing control over agricultural resources in the form of water points and grazing land.

In the previous section we showed how, over the decades from 1930s onwards, the administration, after having paid for its own salaries, the police force, and constructions, increasingly focused its investments to develop the cattle sector. In this section we move on to discuss the outcomes of government investments and policies. While there was consistent need for a continuous spending on basic agricultural and veterinary services, the most important targeted efforts lay in reducing vulnerability to natural disasters.

Even though the region was generally suited for cattle herding, it was again and again hit by severe regional droughts and outbreaks of foot-and-mouth disease. For example, during the 1930s, more than 60 per cent of the total cattle population perished due to a combination of droughts and an outbreak of foot-and-mouth disease. Such incidents directly affected government revenues and, as we learned in the previous section, during the 1930s the administration did not collect export duties, an outcome of the severe crisis in the cattle sector. It took two decades before the cattle population was back at its original level and eventually reached a new high of 1,352,000 in 1962 (see Fig. 3.5), only to be hit by a new devastating drought in the early 1960s taking another high toll on the national cattle herd.

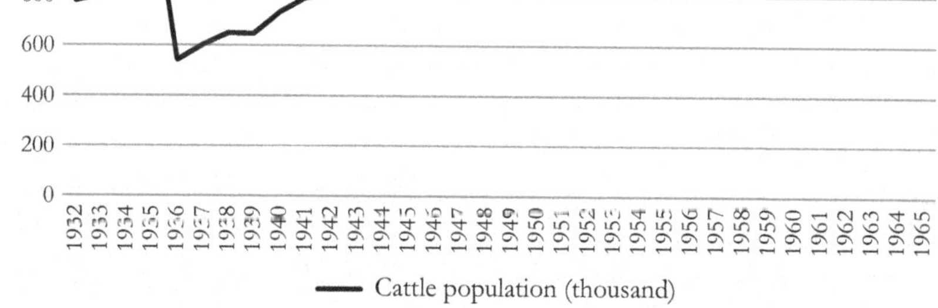

Fig. 3.5 Cattle population in Bechuanaland Protectorate, 1932–1965. Source: Roe (1980, p. 2: Table 1). Note: In the numbers presented by Roe that we use, there is a sharp increase in cattle population between 1933 and 1934. Roe does not explain this abnormality, and we lack any additional source to provide alternative numbers or elaborate on potential explanations for inconsistencies

The primary obstacle for expanding the national herd and to limit the effects of droughts was to secure permanent access to water on the grazing range. On the *hardveld* cattle could drink from seasonal and perennial natural waters such as ponds and streams and in addition there were man-made shallow wells. On the *sandveld*, however, the dry climate made the lack of water so severe that cattle could not survive in any substantial numbers. Meanwhile, in the areas in the north where water could be found in the Chobe and Okavango rivers the presence of tsetse flies made it impossible for both humans and animals to survive in any great numbers. In these circumstances determined by geography and climate the administration focused its efforts on finding solutions to the lack of water and to that effect it imported modern deep-drilling technologies for boreholes. With the modern boreholes water could be pumped up from the underground aqua spheres and the increased use of groundwater both reduced vulnerability and opened up additional grazing areas.

The necessity of drilling boreholes had already been recognized by the Tswana authorities. In a pioneering initiative in the 1920s the BaKgatla *kgosi* Isang initiated and carried out drilling within the BaKgatla Reserve. Although only seven out of sixteen boreholes drilled in the late 1920s became successful, this was the first large-scale water development scheme in the Protectorate (Peters, 1994, p. 58; Schapera, 1980, pp. 22–23). Then in the 1930s following the shift in colonial policies, the British administration started to collaborate with Tswana authorities, the BaKgatla as well as others, to develop additional permanent water points (Parsons & Crowder, 1988; Steenkamp, 1991). This was part of the colonial investment strategies to advance the cattle sector and raise government revenues. The Tswana leaders, on their part, wanted to modernize their respective reserves and, as they themselves were large-scale cattle holders, at the same time further increase their own personal incomes as well as those of their political allies by securing permanent water sources necessary for expanding their cattle herds further (BNA 230, 1933; Hillbom, 2010). In 1940 the British administration had sunk 27 boreholes in the BaKgatla reserve out of which 21 were successful (BNA s.376/3(B), 1961). World War II put a temporary halt to drilling, but in 1946–1959 another 88 boreholes were drilled, 44 of them successful (BNA s.376/2, 1958–1960). Additional efforts were carried out in the other Native Reserves.

The impact of the borehole schemes was threefold. First, while the numbers of boreholes might seem modest, they were an important part of a trend that has continued until the present day with new boreholes consistently being added over the decades. The new permanent water points became imperative for the cattle sector as they both opened up new grazing areas and reduced vulnerability to droughts. Second, while the absolute sums going into the schemes might have been modest due to the generally limited budgets of the colonial and Tswana administrations, they were of substantial size in relative terms as they absorbed most of the funds available for targeted efforts. No equivalent efforts were made to encourage alternative economic activities. The only other proper investments made were an abattoir and the construction of veterinary fences in the north to separate wildlife and the cattle populations, thereby preventing the spread of disease. Finally, the subsequent appropriation of the boreholes instigated a trend of increasing polarization in both the control over agricultural resources and distribution of animals within the cattle sector (Carlsson, 2003; Hillbom, 2010; Peters, 1994).

Once constructed, many boreholes were handed over to a person of high economic and political status, in which case the boreholes, and thus access to water, became private property. The majority of the boreholes were, however, handed over to so-called borehole syndicates. The syndicates were small, exclusive groups usually made up of cattle holders connected to the Tswana elite. As the boreholes were much more expensive in terms of maintenance and running costs than was the case with the previous hand-dug wells, it was necessary to share the costs between a number of property rights holders of certain means. By letting a small number of individuals, in the form of a syndicate, rather than the *morafe* as a whole, take care of all costs as well as reap all benefits of the borehole, it was hoped that the syndicate members would realize the long-term gains of proper maintenance and manage the water point well (BNA s.376/2, 1958–1960).

In general, animals on the grazing range could wander roughly 5 kilometres before they needed to drink. By situating the boreholes at a distance of at least 8 kilometres apart the herds belonging to the various boreholes were kept separate (although some animals strayed relying on natural waters). The indirect effect was that ownership over water points also gave control over the surrounding grazing range. The colonial and tribal distribution of boreholes to wealthy individuals and better-off syndicate members thereby contributed to a selective elite increasingly controlling the grazing range and an amassment of de jure and de facto property rights governing water and land, and an increasingly unequal distribution of agricultural resources (Carlsson, 2003; Peters, 1994). Hence, the wealthy and the high-status cattle holders showed their capacity to use their political influence, at first with the Tswana authorities and then the colonial administration, securing control over water points and thereby groundwater resources (Peters, 1994, pp. 59–62).

While the colonial administration's development strategies meant provisioning for an elitist commercial cattle industry, requests from the broad masses of subsistence farmers were given low priority (Hillbom, 2010). These smallholders owning few or no cattle were rather interested in the development of water sources on the arable lands and in the residential areas catering foremost for domestic use, for watering small stock, and (to a lesser degree) for agricultural use. Such requests were not, however, readily met by the colonial administration since they were not considered to be of economic interest in comparison to the furthering of the cattle sector. Consequently, these smallholders were left to secure water on their own and when they failed to do so they often could not keep their animals.

In the late 1950s and in the 1960s the rate of borehole drilling increased and drilling schemes were complemented by other efforts such as the continuous erection of veterinary fences and the building of the abattoir in Lobatse in 1954. While the era saw an augmented interest in economic development in the British colonies beyond a mere continuance of policies that had already been adopted, the Bechuanaland administration persisted in its concerns with water point management (Peters, 1994, pp. 77–78). Despite the creation of syndicates, the issue of governance was not solved in a satisfactory manner and several boreholes failed temporarily or permanently because of insufficient maintenance and poor management. In addition, efforts to reimburse the administration for its drilling and maintenance expenses and to shift costs from the public administration to the private beneficiaries failed (BNA s.381/8, 1963–1964).

A game changing outcome of the colonial administration's development of the commercial cattle sector was that government policies created new opportunities for the Tswana elite to transfer their existent cattle wealth into an incomes-earning venture. In conjunction with the existing Tswana property rights regimes, colonial government policies also provided the mechanisms through which the distribution of agricultural resources became increasingly unequal, resulting in a polarization of cattle ownership and growing income inequality. While the concentration of cattle wealth and incomes was furthered during colonial rule, it is important to point out that many of the mechanisms driving the process were based in the structures of the Tswana's hierarchical precolonial society and these underlying principles were already in place before the involvement of colonial policies. These long-term inequality trends, mechanisms, and outcomes will be discussed in depth in Chap. 6.

3.5 Dawn of Independence

Independence was a time of significant political change in the African region, but it did not automatically bring socioeconomic structural change. Instead, the principles guiding developmental colonialism and the structures of the gate-keeping state survived in many countries into the independence era. One explanation for the survival of the gate-keeping state structures was the continued lack of government funds to instigate sectorial change. Another explanation was that some future national leaders were already involved in the development process before they themselves came into power and they continued with existing policies. Especially in the British colonies, it was often the urban-based elites who entered into negotiations with the colonial administrations and led the political process towards independence. These elites shared many of the economic and political interests of the colonial administration while being detached from other sections of the societies they were going to rule. Meanwhile, grass-root movements organizing strikes and labour protests in the 1930s and 1940s were commonly focused on calls for development, which were not by necessity paired with claims for independence. Demanding economic and social justice often came before demanding political freedom and organizing the struggle in the form of political parties (Austen, 1987, chapter 9; Cooper, 2002).

Processes leading up to independence in Bechuanaland followed these trends. During the last decades of colonial rule development strategies were to a significant degree formulated in conjunction with the Tswana elites, including future post-independence presidents Sir Seretse Khama and Ketumile Masire, two of the Protectorate's largest cattle holders. In the 1950s these leaders were primarily looking to achieve social and economic development in the Protectorate and only later did they start engaging in strategies for independence (Masire, 2006). Good and Taylor (2008) write that as late as in 1961, only five years before independence, Khama identified himself primarily as a farmer and large-scale cattle holder and not a politician. With a politically passive population and leadership, it was, interestingly enough, the British who pushed for the independence movement, encouraging the Tswana political and economic cattle elite to form political parties and prepare for independence. The outcome of having politicians in powerful positions being the same before and after independence was that development policies generated within the colonial context stayed on to be reproduced in development efforts during the first decades of independence (Good & Taylor, 2008; Masire, 2006).

The first party to raise calls for independence in the early 1960s was the Bechuanaland People's Party (BPP), a radical party stimulated by the African National Congress (ANC) struggle in South Africa. BPP was not, however, seen by the British as the most suitable to take over the country. In the opinion of the British it would be better for stability if there could be a more European-friendly leadership. They had their successors in mind and encouraged Seretse Khama, who was also the hereditary *kgosi* of the BamaNgwato, the largest and most powerful of the Tswana *merafe*. In 1962 he finally agreed and left for good his position in the tribal authority structures and instead formed the Botswana Democratic Party (BDP). In 1965 a new constitution resulted in the first general elections ever held in the country. The BDP won, just as the party has won every election since then. The same year the seat of government moved from Mafeking to the newly established city, and future capital, of Gaborone.

The elections were followed by formal negotiations for independence. In June 1966 Botswana's leaders' proposal for independent democratic self-governance was accepted by Britain. The peaceful transfer of political power to majority rule made Botswana an exception in relation to its neighbours—South Africa, South West Africa (Namibia), Rhodesia (Zimbabwe), and Portuguese-controlled Angola and Mozambique—none of which could be regarded as democracies (Good & Taylor, 2008).

The new independent government continued with colonial development policies investing in the construction of water points, access to veterinary services, building of veterinary fences, and setting up the Botswana Meat Commission (BMC) (a monopoly buyer of cattle for exports) (Acemoglu et al., 2003, p. 101; Lawry, 1983, p. 14). As the early post-independence leaders were also to a significant degree prominent cattle holders profiting from the existing export sector, they had no profound interest in instigating structural change away from the colonial cattle economy. Non-radical development efforts and socioeconomic continuity between the colonial and early post-independence eras have often been quoted as a principal explanation for Botswana's subsequent success story of economic growth and political stability (e.g. Acemoglu et al., 2003; Acemoglu & Robinson, 2010; Beaulier & Subrick, 2006; Leith, 2005; Samatar, 1999). An alternative interpretation is that the new Tswana leaders simply took over the existing colonial gate-keeping state from the British and the continuity in state structures and political will resulted in the absence of initiatives to instigate structural change which could have held a potential for inclusive development (Hillbom, 2008, 2012).

With the continuation of the colonial cattle economy, institutions governing the allocation and management of key agricultural resources, that is, water and land, remained at the core of government policies and the state took over the formal responsibility from the Tswana authorities. At the time of independence the territory's population grew to around 550,000 people giving an estimated population density in the eastern *hardveld* areas of about 2.5 persons per square kilometre and the national cattle herd was at 1.1 million animals (Population Census, 1964; Roe, 1980, p. 2: Table 1). Nevertheless, the relative price of factors of production stayed largely the same—land was abundant and water remained the critical agricultural resource. All in all, this meant that incentives influencing economic and political institutions remained much the same.

In 1968 two new laws, the Water Act and the Tribal Land Act, were enacted. The first vested the responsibility for granting water rights in a government organization, the Water Apportionment Board. For the enforcement of the second piece of legislation, 12 Land Boards were created in 1970 with the responsibility of allocating land. With some modifications both pieces of legislation followed the allocation principles that had been prominent in customary law. Agricultural resources, land and water, were jointly owned, although now by the state instead of the *morafe*. Private user rights to land sites were allotted to individuals and smaller groups and on these sites they could erect constructions such as houses and water points which were then privately owned. The difference was that the responsibility for handing out the allocations was now vested in government bodies instead of the *dikgosi* although the old authorities continued to be influential through their participation in the new government structures, the Land Boards (Hillbom, 2010).

In 1975 the Tribal Grazing Land Policy (TGLP) brought about a more radical divide of land into three different categories: communal (staying under the authority of the Land Boards and working under the principles of customary tenure); commercial (giving groups and individuals exclusive rights in the form of leasehold tenure); and reserve (for future use and wildlife). Most of the more densely populated *hardveld* was designated as communal land while the more sparsely populated larger western *sandveld* areas became either commercial or reserve land. The expectation was that the larger cattle holders would move out of the communal areas and instead establish commercial farms on private land, thereby leaving room for the medium- and small-scale cattle holders (Gulbrandsen, 1996, pp. 10–18; Masalila, 1983, pp. 152–156; Parson, 1984). As it turned out, large cattle holders instead commonly held herds both on the communal grazing range and on their private farms, thereby profiting from both land types and the outcome was increasing inequality in opportunities to exploit agricultural resources (Hillbom, 2010).

Government efforts to reform property rights governing agricultural resources in Botswana in the early years after independence have followed a general trend in sub-Saharan Africa. It has been pointed out by scholars that, in many instances, elites in the post-independence era supported and maintained the customary institutional system established during colonial rule with the goal of enriching themselves. The unfortunate consequence of this has been increasing inequality and polarization within the rural sector as well as between the urban and the rural sectors (Carney & Farrington, 1998; Platteau, 1996; Ribot, 2000). In the case of Botswana this can be exemplified with the *dikgosi* and their overseers being appointed members to sit on the Land Boards with the argument that this would provide continuity with customary allocations and structures (Hillbom, 2010).

However, the years when beef was dominating the national economy were coming to an end one decade after independence. The modestly profitable colonial cattle economy was to be replaced by the much more spectacular diamond-led growth period. A few years before independence diamond deposits were discovered, but they were not announced until the year after independence. While the colonial era had seen efforts to develop a profitable mining sector with gold being mined in the Tati District, the contribution of the mining sector to national GDP prior to the exploitation of the diamond deposits had been trivial. Soon after the formal announcement of the discovery in 1967, diamond mining started and in 1973 the mining sector's contribution to GDP was already 11 per cent. The sector continued to grow rapidly and contributed close to 65 per cent of GDP in the mid-1980s and it is still the most productive sector in the economy (Gaolathe, 1997, p. 408: Table 2; World Bank, 2017). Meanwhile, agriculture, or more precisely the cattle sector, in terms of its contribution to GDP, plunged drastically from the mid-1960s to the mid-1980s and since then its share in GDP has stayed at low levels of roughly 2–3 per cent (World Bank, 2017). Based on the timing of the fall of the relative economic importance of agriculture and the dramatic surge of mining incomes, we identify the mid-1970s as constituting the structural breaking point between the colonial cattle economy and the post-independence diamond-led economy.

3.6 Summing Up and Moving On ...

In this chapter we have discussed the common view that Botswana has experienced only limited colonial influence. While we agree with this description for the early colonial era (see Chap. 2) we here argue that the later colonial period, starting roughly in 1930, instead has had a significant long-term impact on the economic structures of Bechuanaland and later independent Botswana. For this argument we have primarily emphasized colonial state structures, government policies in regard to raising revenues and investing in productive activities, and the development of the cattle export sector. We have argued that the colonial era saw the creation of so-called gate-keeping states, in Africa generally and in Bechuanaland specifically, characterized by financial constraints restricting its development strategies. The gate-keeping states' solution to having a limited tax base and modest colonial transfers while being expected to instigate economic and social development was to focus their energies on controlling and taxing trade and targeting investments towards the export sectors.

In Bechuanaland, the overall poverty of the Protectorate meant modest government revenues which were primarily spent on administrating the territory. However, with additional development funds from Britain starting to flow into the colonial budget in the 1930s the administration could afford to target the cattle sector with the aim of establishing an export sector to increase tax revenues. By the end of the colonial era and up until the maturing of the diamond economy in the mid-1970s, cattle dominated the economy. The colonial efforts were welcomed by the Tswana elite who in their capacity as being the large-scale cattle holder of the territory benefitted the most from government investments. The outcome was an increasing polarization in control over agricultural resources directly and eventually also cattle wealth and export incomes.

We see three overriding outcomes of the colonial efforts discussed in this chapter and these outcomes constitute the themes for the following chapters. First, in Chap. 4 we discuss the two consecutive growth periods that Botswana has experienced during our time of investigation, first driven by cattle and then by diamonds. The first growth period is modest but puts into place a resource dependency structure which still characterizes Botswana's economy. The second growth period is infinitely more successful than the first due to the higher value of diamonds compared to cattle and has national accounts on which we can base our discussion. Second, in the midst of spectacular diamond-led growth, the economic structures characterized by mono-product natural resource dependence established during the colonial era stayed very much the same after independence and this has resulted in a lack of diversification in the rest of the economy. The success of diamond-led growth meant a continuation of the mono-product-based natural resource export dependency locking the economy up in a persistent natural resource trap preventing it from instigating sectorial change. Importantly though, well-functioning political institutions saved the economy from being tainted by a natural resource curse. The continuation of gate-keeping state structures meant that although it could afford to launch significant social development it did not advocate inclusive economic development and the outcome has been the creation of a dual society. This is the theme for Chap. 5. Third, from the establishment of the cattle export sector there was increasing socio-economic inequality based on the elite's control over agricultural resources and polarized cattle ownership. Hence, Botswana entered the independence era as one of the most unequal countries in the world and high levels of inequality have persisted during the diamond economy. In Chap. 6 we calculate and analyse long-term trends in inequality.

References

Acemoglu, D., Johnson, S., & Robinson, J. (2001). The colonial origins of comparative development: An empirical investigation. *The American Economic Review, 91*(5), 1369–1401.

Acemoglu, D., Johnson, S., & Robinson, J. A. (2002). Reversal of fortune: Geography and institutions in the making of the modern world income distribution. *The Quarterly Journal of Economics, 117*(4), 1231–1294.

Acemoglu, D., Johnson, S., & Robinson, J. A. (2003). An African success story: Botswana. In D. Rodrik (Ed.), *In search of prosperity: Analytic narratives on economic growth* (pp. 80–119). Princeton and Oxford: Princeton University Press.

Acemoglu, D., & Robinson, J. A. (2010). Why is Africa poor? *Economic History of Developing Regions, 25*(1), 21–50.

Annual Report of the Bechuanaland Protectorate. Issue 1963/1964, London School of Economics Library.

Austen, R. A. (1987). *African economic history: Internal development and external dependency*. London: James Currey.

Beaulier, S. A., & Subrick, J. R. (2006). The political foundations of development: The case of Botswana. *Constitutional Political Economy, 17*(2), 103–115.

Berry, S. (1993). *No condition is permanent: The social dynamics of agrarian change in sub-Saharan Africa*. Madison, WI: University of Wisconsin Press.

Bolt, J., & Hillbom, E. (2015). Potential for diversification? The role of the formal sector in Bechuanaland Protectorate's economy, 1900–65. *Economic History of Developing Regions, 30*(2), 95–124.

Bolt, J., & Hillbom, E. (2016). Long-term Trends in Economic Inequality: Lessons from colonial Botswana, 1921–1974. *Economic History Review, 69*(4), 1255–1284.

Bowden, S., Chiripanhura, B., & Mosley, P. (2008). Measuring and explaining poverty in six African countries: A long-period approach. *Journal of International Development, 30*(8), 1049–1079.

Carlsson, E. (2003). *To Have and to Hold: Continuity and change in property rights institutions governing water resources among the Meru of Tanzania and the BaKgtala in Botswana; 1925–2000*. Lund Studies in Economic History, 28. Stockholm: Almqvist & Wiksell International.

Carney, D., & Farrington, J. (1998). *Natural resource management and institutional change*. London and New York: Routledge.

Colclough, C., & McCarthy, S. (1980). *The political economy of Botswana: A study of growth and distribution*. London: Oxford University Press.

Cooper, F. (2002). *Africa since 1940: The past of the present*. Cambridge: Cambridge University Press.

Easterly, W., & Levine, R. (2016). The European origins of economic development. *Journal of Economic Growth, 21*(3), 225–257.

Engerman, S. L., & Sokoloff, K. L. (2002). Factor endowments, inequality, and paths of development among new world economics. *Economia, 3*(1), 41–108.

Evans, I. (1997). *Bureaucracy and race: Native administration in South Africa*. Berkley: University of California Press.

Frankema, E., Green, E., & Hillbom, E. (2016). Endogenous processes of colonial settlement. The success and failure of European settler farming in Sub-

Saharan Africa. *Revista de Historia Economica-Journal of Iberian and Latin American Economic History, 34*(2), 237–265.
Freund, B. (1984). Labor and labor history in Africa: A review of the literature. *African Studies Review, 27*(2), 1–58.
Gaolathe, B. (1997). Development of Botswana's mineral sector. In J. S. Salkin, D. Mpabanga, D. Cowan, J. Selwe, & M. Wright (Eds.), *Aspects of the Botswana economy* (pp. 401–431). Gaborone: Lentswe La Lesedi.
Gardner, L. (2012). *Taxing colonial Africa: The political economy of British imperialism*. Oxford: Oxford University Press.
Good, K., & Taylor, I. (2008). Botswana: A minimalist democracy. *Democratization, 15*(4), 750–765.
Gulbrandsen, Ø. (1996). *Poverty in the midst of Plenty: Socio-economic marginalization, ecological deterioration and political stability in a Tswana society* (No. 45). Bergen: Norse Publications.
Harvey, C., & Lewis, S. R., Jr. (1990). *Policy choice and development performance in Botswana*. London: Macmillan in Association with the OECD Development Centre.
Hermans, Q. (1974). Towards budgetary independence a review of Botswana's financial history, 1900 to 1973. *Botswana Notes and Records, 6*, 89–116.
Hillbom, E. (2008). Diamonds or development? A structural assessment of Botswana's forty years of success. *The Journal of Modern African Studies, 46*(2), 191–214.
Hillbom, E. (2010). Agricultural development and the distribution of water resources in Kgatleng District, Botswana. *Development Southern Africa, 27*(3), 413–427.
Hillbom, E. (2012). Botswana: A development oriented gate keeping state. *African Affairs, 111*(442), 67–89.
Hillbom, E., & Jenkin, S. (2018). Maize for the mines: The shaping of Zambia's agricultural sector c. 1915–2015. In V. Pinilla & H. Willebald (Eds.), *Agricultural Development in the World Periphery: A global economic history approach*. London: Palgrave Macmillan.
Lawry, S. W. (1983). *Land tenure, land policy, and smallholder livestock development in Botswana* (No. 78). Madison: Land Tenure Center, University of Wisconsin.
Leith, J. C. (2005). *Why Botswana prospered*. Montreal and Kingston: McGill-Queen's University Press.
Leonard, D. K., & Straus, S. (2003). *Africa's stalled development: International causes and cures*. Boulder, CO: Lynne Rienner Publishers.
Makgala, C. J. (2006). *Elite conflict in Botswana: A history*. Pretoria: African Institute of South Africa.

Mamdani, M. (1996). *Citizen and subject: Contemporary Africa and the legacy of late colonialism*. Princeton, NJ: Princeton University Press.

Masalila, A. (1983). Botswana's national policy on tribal grazing land: Towards a strategy for rural development. In M. A. Oomen, F. K. Inganji, & L. D. Ngcongno (Eds.), *Botswana's economy since independence*. New Delhi: Tata McGraw-Hill Publishing Company.

Masire, K. (2006). *Very brave or very foolish? Memoires of an African democrat*. Gaborone: Macmillan Botswana Publishing Co (Pty) Ltd.

Mosley, P. (1983). *The settler economies: Kenya and Southern Rhodesia 1900–1963*. Cambridge: Cambridge University Press.

Muthien, Y., & Houston, G. (2002). *Transforming South African state and society: The challenge of constructing a developmental state* (pp. 53–99). The Africa State: Reconsiderations.

Pakenham, T. (1992). *The scamble for Africa: The White man's conquest of the dark continent*. London: Abacus.

Parson, J. (1984). *Botswana: Liberal democracy and labor reserve in Southern Africa*. Boulder, CO: Westview Press.

Parsons, N., & Crowder, M. (Eds.). (1988). *Monarch of all I survey: Bechuanaland diaries 1929–37*. Gaborone: The Botswana Society.

Peters, P. E. (1994). *Dividing the commons: Politics, policy, and culture in Botswana*. Charlottesville: University Press of Virginia.

Platteau, J. P. (1996). The evolutionary theory of land rights as applied to sub-Saharan Africa: A critical assessment. *Development and Change, 27*(1), 29–86.

Posel, D. (1991). *The making of apartheid, 1948–1961*. New York: Claredon Press.

Putterman, L., & Weil, D. N. (2010). Post-1500 population flows and the long-run determinants of economic growth and inequality. *The Quarterly Journal of Economics, 125*(4), 1627–1682.

Ribot, J. (2000). Decentralization, participation, and representation: Administrative apartheid in Sahelian forestry. In P. Peters (Ed.), *Development encounters: Sites of participation and knowledge*. Cambridge, MA: Harvard University Press for HIID.

Richens, P. (2009). The economic legacies of the "thin white line": Indirect rule and the comparative development of sub-Saharan Africa. *African Economic History, 37*, 33–102.

Robinson, J. A., & Parsons, Q. N. (2006). State formation and governance in Botswana. *Journal of African Economies, 15*(AERC Suppl 1), 100–140.

Roe, E. (1980). *Development of livestock, agriculture and water supplies in Eastern Botswana before independence: A short history and policy analysis*. Gaborone, Botswana: Ministry of Agriculture.

Salvucci, R. (2006). Export-led industrialization. *The Cambridge Economic History of Latin America, 2*, 249–292.
Samatar, A. I. (1999). *An African miracle: State and class leadership and colonial legacy in Botswana development*. Portsmouth, NH: Heinemann.
Schapera, I. (1980). *A history of the BaKgatla-bagaKgafêla*. Mochudi, Botswana: Phuthadikobo Museum.
Schneider, G. E. (2000). The development of the manufacturing sector in South Africa. *Journal of Economic Issues, 34*(2), 413–424.
Steenkamp, P. (1991). Cinderella of the empire?': Development policy in Bechuanaland in the 1930s. *Journal of Southern African Studies, 17*(2), 292–308.

Online Sources

World Bank. (2017). *World development indicators*. Washington, DC. Retrieved August, 2017, from http://databank.worldbank.org/data/reports.aspx?source=world-development-indicators

Archives

Bechuanaland Protectorate Government Census. (1946). London School of Economics Library.
Botswana National Archives (BNA) 230. (1933). *Financial and economic position of the bechuanaland protectorate*, report of the commission appointed by the Secretary of State for Dominion Affairs, London.
Botswana National Archives (BNA) s.376/2. (1958–1960). Water development. General correspondence, surveys, etc.
Botswana National Archives (BNA) s.376/3.
Botswana National Archives (BNA) s.376/3(B). (1961). Water development. General correspondence, surveys, etc.
Botswana National Archives (BNA) s.381/8. (1963–1964). Water development. Bore-hole maintenance.
CSO (Central Statistics Office). (1965). Ministry of Finance and Development Planning. *Population and Housing Census 1964*. Gaborone.

Part III

Part 3

4

Growth, Incomes, and Development, c. 1940–Present

4.1 Introduction

For some time the common perception was that the African region could be characterized by consistent economic stagnation and limited variation in growth experiences. This view was based on studies covering the post-colonial era up until the turn of the millennium that showed negative average economic development, chronic state failure, and the inability to profit from the region's potential (Collier & Gunning, 1999; Easterly & Levine, 1997). More recent research, however, has shown that African economies have not been stagnant throughout. Instead, the African growth experience is better described as recurrent periods of growth (Austin, 2008; Garner, 2006; Jerven, 2010; Prados de la Escosura, 2012).

A recent example of such a growth period was the global commodity boom of the first decade of the twenty-first century, which enabled several natural resource-rich African countries to experience exceptional growth rates. Between 2000 and 2010, six of the ten fastest-growing economies in the world were African. However, as soon as commodity prices started falling in 2015, the growth spurt came to a halt in most countries. Also when we look back in time, various African countries have experienced periods of substantial economic expansion during both

E. Hillbom, J. Bolt, *Botswana – A Modern Economic History*, Palgrave Studies in Economic History, https://doi.org/10.1007/978-3-319-73144-5_4

the colonial and postcolonial eras (Austin, 2008; Frankema & Van Waijenburg, 2012; Garner, 2006). As a rule though, these growth periods have not been transformed into sustained growth and structural transformation, and consequently they have stayed elusive to scholars and policymakers.

Like many other African countries, Botswana's economy is resource dependent, and it has experienced two periods of natural resource-led growth—cattle-led growth roughly during the period 1940 to 1975 and then diamond-led growth from 1975 until the present. Botswana's spectacular diamond-led growth has inspired researchers to describe the country as a growth miracle (Samatar, 1999) and a sign of hope for sub-Saharan Africa. Botswana has indeed come a long way from being the undeveloped and seldom heard of part of the world that it was at independence in 1966. In a long-term perspective, the first four decades of independence average growth rates were the highest ever recorded in the world and even surpassed the performance of the Pacific Asian Tigers (Leith, 2005, p. 4: Table 1.1). During the 1970s, GDP per capita increased annually with a spectacular 11 per cent, followed by an impressive 8 per cent on average during the 1980s (World Bank, 2017).[1] Today Botswana is classified as a middle-income country by the World Bank with a GDP per capita of US$15,513 in 2016 (PPP, constant 2011 dollars, World Bank, 2017). Although the exceptional growth numbers have become more modest in recent years, there are no signs of diamond-led growth coming to a halt in the near future. However, as no alternative productive sector(s) have been developed that can take over the role of securing government revenues and economic profits at a comparative level, the economy risks a collapse as soon as Botswana runs out of diamonds.

Compared to the diamond-led growth, the earlier cattle-led growth period was modest and it lasted for a shorter period of time. It ended not because it experienced a bust, but because it was replaced by the more spectacular second growth period. Hence, Botswana has experienced continuous growth from the 1940s until the present, and in this chapter, we analyse the drivers of growth as well as evaluate the growth processes themselves. Our analytical framework is based on the principle that there is a consistent multicausal interaction between geography and factor endowments, on the one hand, and institutions, on the other hand, determining economic growth. The importance of each of the factors varies, depending on the time period and processes under study. In the case of Botswana it is the primary sector, the extraction of natural resources, that has consistently constituted the basis for growth. At the same time, political institutions managing the highly valuable resources and subsequent incomes during the diamond-led growth also played a decisive role.

In our investigation we focus mostly on the supply side of growth although we also discuss, where relevant, demand side factors. The lack of national accounts for the cattle-led growth period makes the analysis challenging and compels us to capture the growth process by mapping and analysing occupational structures as well as levels of incomes and wages. For the diamond-led growth period we can rely to national accounts, but for the sake of balance we also include a discussion about incomes and wages. The in-depth critical examination of the growth experience is postponed to Chaps. 5 and 6, where we elaborate, first, on the limitations of the growth process in terms of lack of diversification developing alternative productive sectors and, second, on long-term trends of high levels of inequality.

The structure of the chapter is as follows. We start with presenting the main strands of literature guiding our understanding of potential drivers of economic growth. In the next section, we account for Botswana's long-term growth from a macro perspective. This is followed by a detailed discussion of the cattle-led growth period relying on both colonial data and anthropological studies to map wages for formal employment and assign incomes in the informal agricultural sector. In the subsequent section we turn to the diamond-led growth period, first breaking the economy into a sectorial growth analysis and then presenting changes in wages. Finally, we sum up and move ahead.

4.2 Drivers of Growth and Development

The study of economic growth distinguishes between, on the one hand, proximate and, on the other hand, fundamental or deeper determinants of growth. The proximate determinants are efforts to create new factors of production and to combine existing factors in more productive or efficient ways to create more output. Both these processes are influenced by the deeper determinants of economic growth and scholars generally agree on institutions and geography being the most important ones, while some are also adding culture to the equation (Weil, 2013).

The geography explanation for economic growth covers several aspects of location, general spatial characteristics of the area, and climate (Bloom et al., 1998; Landes, 1998, chapter 1). Land-locked countries, that is, countries located without access to navigable rivers or the sea, generally face higher transport costs which is disadvantageous when participating in international trade. Lowering transport cost often requires expensive infrastructural investments (Faye et al., 2004; Gallup et al., 1999; Sachs & Warner, 1995). In the same vein, the general spatial or geographic characteristics of a country such as rainforests, mountains, and deserts affects the physical movement of goods and people and may therefore influence economic growth. The severity of this impact depends on the extent to which such geographical factors are present, and should be put in relation to the goods that need to be transported and to the state of infrastructural developments. In the age of the third technological revolution, digitization, and the global marketing of services, location and other geographical characteristics might become increasingly less relevant for some economic activities (Milanovic, 2016).

The climate prevalent in countries in turn affects both the agricultural potential and the disease environment. Countries located in the tropics have more irregular rainfall patterns and temperatures are less conducive to agriculture compared to countries in more moderate climatic zones. Further, tropical soils are often more vulnerable to erosion. In addition, Africa, the cradle of mankind, is the region with the highest prevalence of tropical diseases such as sleeping sickness and malaria, and the effect this has on labour resources undermines the development and efficiency of systems of production (Frankema, 2015; Landes, 1998).

In all of the four above-mentioned respects—location, general spatial characteristics of the area, climate, and disease environment—Botswana has been challenged. The country is land locked, roughly two-thirds consists of the Kalahari Desert; rainfall is scarce, limiting the potential for crop farming and cattle keeping; and the north, which is home to the major rivers, is infested with malaria and tsetse flies.

The prevalence of natural resources is yet another geographic factor potentially providing opportunities for economic growth, and natural resources can crudely be divided into two broad categories. The first is agricultural lands, whose value is determined by general soil fertility and average rainfall. Botswana overall has not been blessed with fertile agricultural land, but the abundance of the land suitable for grazing was a decisive factor driving the economic expansion during the cattle-led growth period. The second kind of resources are so-called point source natural resources consisting of valuable resources such as oil or gas, but also diamonds, the abundance of which has been the basis for Botswana's second growth period. Throughout our period of investigation, the country has then profited from its factor endowments and managed to use them for achieving economic growth.

It is precisely their potential to generate economic growth that until the 1970s motivated most economists to perceive the availability of abundant natural resources as a positive asset for an economy (see, e.g. Habakkuk, 1962; Nurkse, 1953; Rostow, 1960). Many developing countries possessed great wealth in primary natural resources and this was thought of as almost a guarantee for future growth. The actual outcome, however, was very different than expected. The developing regions most affluently endowed with natural resources, Latin America and Africa, experienced disappointing economic growth rates. The economies in most Latin American countries stagnated for decades after 1950s and numerous countries in sub-Saharan Africa suffered from political and economic failure. When taking a global perspective, it turned out that on average, there has been a negative correlation between natural resource abundance and economic growth (Sachs & Warner, 1995; van der Ploeg, 2011).

Explanations given for the growth failures of many resource-abundant countries are numerous, but can be divided into four main categories:

overconsumption by the government, unsustainable extraction of resources, deindustrialization due to appreciating exchange rates, and political economy factors such as civil conflict, authoritarianism, and rent seeking. A broad literature has focused on the latter, pointing out that resource-dependent economies have higher prevalence of indolence, rent seeking, conflict between stakeholders, corruption, and predation, compared to countries which rely on other comparative advantages. Due to enormous profits to be made, leaders of natural resource-rich developing countries have often turned to corruption, selling off national natural assets to privately pocket the profits (Auty, 2001; Gylfason et al., 1999; Leite & Weidmann, 1999; Sachs & Warner, 1999; van der Ploeg, 2011). This has sometimes led to individuals and international companies becoming wealthy, while states and populations have stayed poor. In sharp contrast, the rapidly growing Asian economies based their comparative advantage on access to abundant low-wage labour instead of valuable natural resources and with this strategy they succeeded in achieving sustained growth (Auty, 2001; van der Ploeg, 2011).

Influenced by the generally disappointing growth experiences of resource-abundant regions, natural resources became increasingly considered a curse instead of a blessing (Leite & Weidmann, 1999). The question of how to avoid the resource curse directed the attention towards the importance of how economic resources are being managed. During the last decade, the role of institutions generally, and political institutions in particular, has increasingly been considered the most important factor driving economic growth. Institutions as the 'rules of the game' guide human interaction and reduce uncertainty by providing structure to everyday lives. Via the institutional framework, governments can shape the environment in which everyone in society goes about their activities. By enforcing the rule of law and, for example, protecting property rights people can engage in transactions and provide investments that are conducive to economic growth (North, 1990, 2005). During the diamond-led growth, Botswana has been an atypical natural resource-rich developing country in that it has had the institutional quality required to manage its incomes prudently.

Scholars such as Acemoglu, Johnson, and Robinson have claimed that political institutional quality is the most important factor explaining long-term economic progress. To them, good political institutions are the equivalent of institutions that effectively protect private property rights, thereby promoting economic activity conducive to growth. Conversely, extractive institutions, or institutions that enable authorities to expropriate property and profits from their populations, will result in slow or even negative growth and general underdevelopment (Acemoglu et al., 2001). Further, they argue that the historical roots of many of today's developing countries are found in their colonial past, and that these colonies experienced a 'reversal of fortune' in terms of economic development due to colonization (Acemoglu et al., 2001, 2002). Europeans tended to settle and introduce private property rights institutions in areas where the disease environment did not threaten them. These colonies were generally economically underdeveloped areas with low population density and moderate temperatures. Meanwhile, European settler mortality was much higher in the indigenously more densely populated tropical societies and in these areas colonial powers were instead motivated to establish extractive institutions to benefit from the available richness. These extractive institutions in turn have had a detrimental effect on economic development since colonization (Acemoglu et al., 2002). Within an African context where both settler and non-settler colonies existed, the institutional theory has, however, been unable to offer a satisfactory explanation to either the historical trajectories or current pathways of development (Albouy, 2012; Austin, 2008; Hopkins, 2009). Acemoglu, Johnson, and Robinson (2003) and Acemoglu and Robinson (2010) identified Botswana as an exception to their own theory, arguing that it is limited colonial influence and the survival of precolonial political institutions that explains the contemporary growth miracle.

Rather than going with either the geography or the institutions' explanations for our analysis of Botswana's growth periods we emphasize the *multicausal interaction* between economic institutions, political interest groups, geography, and factor endowments. This is in line with scholars such as North (1981, 1990) who states that changes in relative prices between factors of production have constituted one of the primary sources of long-term institutional change. Generally for Africa, Austin (2008) has taken this argument further by stating that, subject to the historical context, changes in factor endowments are potentially the primary explanatory factor driving change in the various economies in the region.

4.3 Macroeconomic Long-Term Growth

Chapters 2 and 3 have provided an extensive description of both the precolonial cattle economy and the development of the colonial cattle export sector. They show that while there was ample wealth stored in cattle in the precolonial era, this generated neither economic growth nor individual incomes as cattle was not marketed to any significant extent. With the establishment of the colonial cattle export sector in the 1930s, however, cattle wealth could be turned into a source of income both for the state and for large-scale cattle holders. This instigated the first period of economic expansion in Botswana's economic history, the era of cattle-led growth. In Chap. 3 we discussed how, in the 1930s, the development of the new export sector was negatively affected by droughts diminishing the national herd and that it was not until roughly 1940 that we can say that cattle exports definitely took off. This is consequently the time marking the starting point of Bechuanaland's first period growth.

Figure 4.1 shows Botswana's long-term increase in GDP per capita. Unfortunately, there are no national accounts covering the time prior from 1940 to 1950 and for the purpose of giving a complete overview of the period with cattle-led growth we are left with a somewhat incomplete curve. However, the graph shows that the time period leading up to independence consists of modest and stagnant annual growth rates and we have no reason to expect the missing decade prior to 1950 to be any different. In line with what we have stated previously, we can see that there is no bust related to cattle-led growth, but there is an accelerated second growth period covering the independence era.

From the second half of the 1960s Botswana's growth figures correlates perfectly with diamond sector development leading to the conclusion that the second growth period is diamond-led (Jerven, 2010). At the time of independence, the newly founded government vested all mineral rights under its authority. Possibly it already knew then that valuable diamond deposits existed and the South African company De Beers, one of the

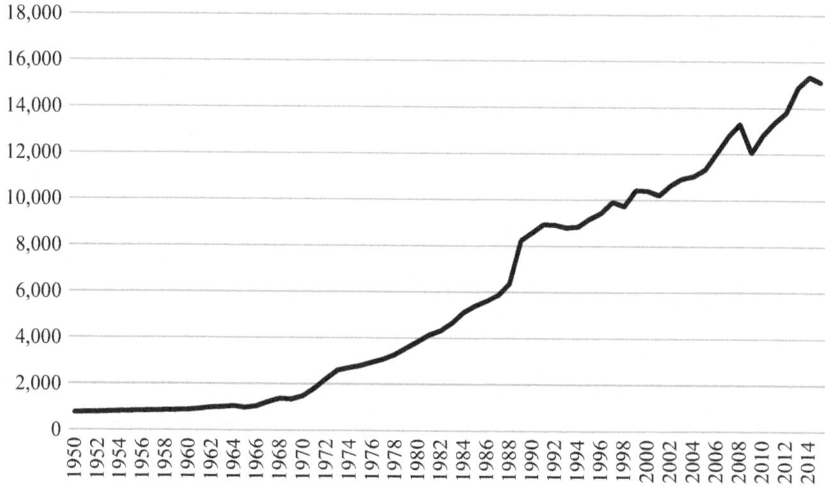

Fig. 4.1 Botswana's long-term increase in GDP per capita, 1950–2015. Sources: GDP per capita is in 2011 US dollars; The Maddison Project database, version 2018, Bolt et al. (2018)

world leaders in mining and specializing in diamonds, immediately showed interest in prospecting. In 1967 diamond discoveries were announced and the government saw opportunities to negotiate a substantial share of profits from mining extraction. In 1969 it went into a 50/50 joint venture with De Beers and together they formed Debswana Diamond Company Ltd. in 1978, thus ensuring the capture of sizeable mineral rents for the government (Gaolathe, 1997; Leith, 2005). While growth rates started accelerating with the first discoveries, we identify the mid-1970s as the time when the diamond-led economy has matured and taken over from the cattle economy.

Figure 4.1 clearly captures the exceptional diamond-led growth. During the four decades 1965–2005 the average real annual GDP growth was 9.5 per cent. This long-term trajectory included a staggering average 26 per cent increase in GDP per annum in the years 1971–1972 as well as the decade-long period 1980–1989 showing more than 11 per cent annual increase on average (Leith, 2005, p. 4; Samatar, 1999; World Bank, 2017). Right after the global recession of 2008–2009 growth turned negative, but it bounced back immediately to levels of around 4 per cent per year on average.

4.4 Incomes in the Colonial Cattle Economy

Due to scarce information about the economy and sketchy national accounts, an in-depth analysis into the colonial cattle economy's growth trajectory is challenging. In such situations, relative prices and wages becomes a crucial source of information about the structure of the economy (van Zanden, 2009). The importance of investigating occupations and wage levels for understanding the processes of economic growth and sectorial change has, for example, been shown by Allen (2009) in his seminal study of the British economy prior to, and during, the industrial revolution. Allen argues that Britain represents a special case in the sense that it combined high wages and cheap energy together creating both demand and opportunity for the development of new labour-saving technologies operated by growing numbers of skilled labourers. Thereby the changing characteristics of the formal labour market, for example, wage levels and skill premiums, were interlinked with processes of diversification and increasing productivity. While preindustrial Britain and Bechuanaland are very different empirical cases, Allen's methodological approach to map and analyse changes in occupational structures and wages at the micro level in order to capture economic change at the macro level is of universal applicability. We start with analysing the formal sector looking at wage employment relying on colonial records. Then we move on to map the much more elusive informal agricultural sector.

4.4.1 Wages and Premiums in the Formal Sector

During most of the colonial period only roughly 15 per cent of Bechuanaland's population was formally employed and thereby captured by the colonial statistics. The colonial records provide income information for three broad categories of domestic employment: *unskilled labourers* either in agriculture, as domestic help, or in the mines; *skilled labour*; and *government employees*. However, the earliest opportunities for wage employment were outside of the Protectorate. Already from the 1860s, young men had migrated to work in the mines of South Africa and throughout the colonial period more men worked abroad than in the

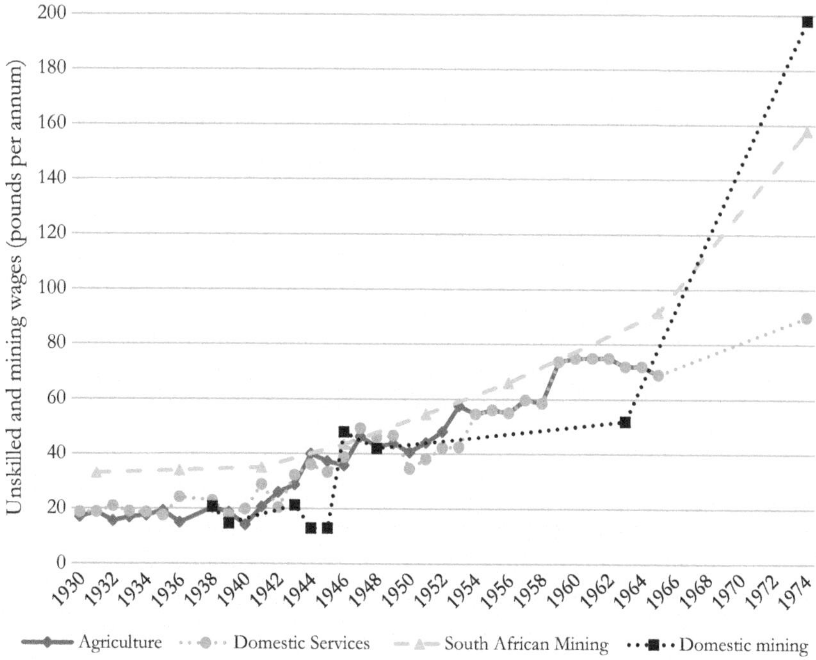

Fig. 4.2 Nominal wage developments for unskilled labour, 1930–1974 (pounds per annum). Source: Bolt and Hillbom (2015)

domestic mines (Parsons, 1993). Consequently, we complement our domestic wage categories with a fourth category—employment and wages for *migrant labour* to South African mines.

Figs. 4.2 and 4.3 show the development of nominal wages for all wage labour from the establishment of the cattle export sector in the 1930s until the takeover of the diamond economy in the mid-1970s. This long-term perspective allows us to relate developments of the colonial cattle economy with significant changes in wage levels. We show that the unskilled labourers experienced an increase in wages throughout the cattle-led growth period. The average annual incomes of both domestic servants and agricultural workers rose from around 20 pounds in 1930 to around 70 pounds in 1965. After independence, incomes for the urban domestic workers and unskilled workers in the formal sector further increased to approximately 90 pounds. Information

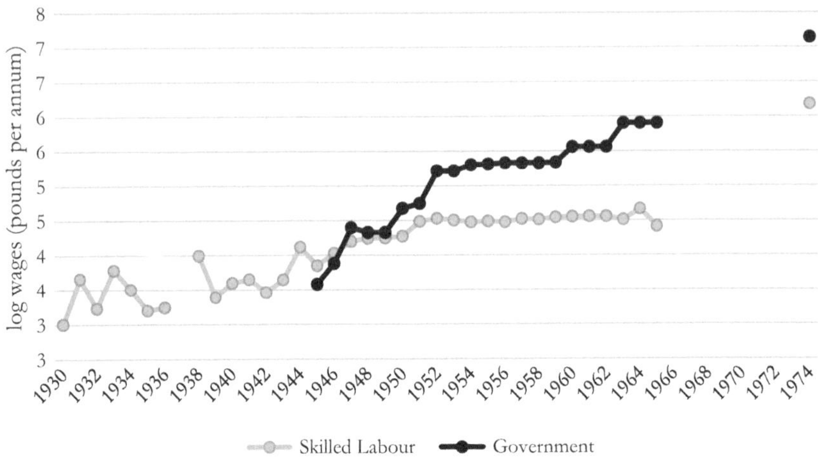

Fig. 4.3 Wage developments (logs) for skilled labour and government employees, 1930–1974 (pounds per annum). Source: Bolt and Hillbom (2015)

about the domestic mining sector is very scattered. Wages paid to the unskilled domestic miners appear to have been low throughout the colonial period, only rising with the discovery of diamonds.

Unskilled wage employment did expand not only in terms of wage levels but also in terms of numbers of individuals employed. During the 1930s, around 2,000 people, or 1 per cent of the population, were recorded as working in agriculture, and this almost doubled to around 3,500 (still making up around 1 per cent of the population) at independence (Annual Report, 1963–1965; Blue Books, 1930). Meanwhile, total employment in domestic services grew from about 1,500 halfway through the colonial period to around 2,000 in 1965. The scattered information we have on the mining sector further indicates that at its height during the cattle economy, about 600 workers worked in domestic mines (Blue Books, 1946/1947).

We move on to the category of skilled labour which includes various groups, such as shopkeepers and owners of eating houses, commercial butchers and bakers, construction workers and builders, bricklayers, mechanics, clerks, and drivers as well as exporters of ostrich feathers, ivory, skins, agricultural products, and cattle (Census, 1946; Schapera & Comaroff, 1991, p. 23). This group makes up the closest thing we have to an entrepreneurial class, although their success varied and for long the group size was limited. We do know, however, that the number of Africans employed in skilled jobs started to rise during the 1920s and within the skilled labour category, over 800 Africans were employed in 1946. This number increased to over 4,200 or around 1 per cent of the population in 1963 (Annual Reports, 1946, 1947, 1963; Blue Books, 1910/1911, 1920–1928, 1946/1947). Due to insufficient primary data, all European skilled labour has been left out of our sample.

Wages for skilled labourers rose continuously from the early 1940s until just before independence, but these developments were dwarfed by the hike in wages after 1960 (see Fig. 4.3). Annual wages paid to skilled workers increased from around 100 pounds in 1960 to between 450 and 500 pounds in 1974. For the period between the start of diamond mining in 1967 and the mid-1970s when we have argued for the structural breaking point for the diamond economy, there is a transition. During this decade we cannot disentangle the effects of diamond incomes either on growth numbers or on increasing wages. While we maintain that they are not enough to warrant being considered a breaking point, they are muddling the waters and we need to treat our numbers with care when drawing conclusions.

African government employment was limited throughout the first half of the colonial period, only to increase from the 1930s onwards. This coincided with the enhanced British colonial ambition across Africa to put more emphasis on investments and policies aimed at generating some socioeconomic development (Cooper, 2002). The number of lower-ranking Tswana government officials, working, for example, as clerks and police officers, increased to 1,050 in 1946 and 4,000 in 1963 (Annual Reports, 1946, 1947, 1963, 1965; Blue Books, 1946/1947). At the same time, wages rapidly rose during those years, again especially after 1960 (see Fig. 4.3). Wages for government employees were on average ten times as high in the mid-1960s as they had been in 1945, and tripled between 1965 and 1974 to being close to 1,250 pounds per annum. In addition, this group is likely to have been well connected to the agricultural sector via extended families, receiving some incomes in kind complementing their salaries. Again, the number of Europeans remained so small and the wage information so scattered that we have excluded them.

Finally, we turn to our fourth category, migrant labour. Labour migration has constituted an important part of Botswana's labour force, especially in the earlier colonial period, as wage opportunities within the domestic economy were very limited. There existed primarily two important reasons for the Tswana to migrate in search of employment. First, labour migration strategies constituted a way for cattle-less households and small-scale cattle holders living at or under subsistence to access cash incomes that could be saved and used to buy (additional) cattle. Second, labour migration was a way to obtain cash incomes needed to pay taxes imposed by the colonial government. From the 1930s labour migration increased (Murray & Parsons, 1990; Schapera, 1994), but, as was discussed already in Chap. 3, figures are inconsistent when it comes to defining the size of the group of migrants. This challenge is probably explained by the significant shifts in magnitude over time and that most migrants did not bother to apply for labour passes from the colonial administration. Data from a 1943 survey suggest that around 28 per cent of all adult men were working away from home. Roughly 90 per cent of them went to the Union of South Africa, and of those, around 60 per cent was employed in the mines (Salkin, 1987; Schapera & Comaroff, 1991). Yet, official figures (labour passes issued) indicate a much smaller group of around 8,000 migrant labourers. Officials note, however, that there was much unregistered labour migration (Annual Report, 1931, p. 24).

Investigations into wage levels in colonial Africa by other scholars provide us with an opportunity to give a comparative perspective on developments in Bechuanaland. Nominal wages paid to agricultural workers in the Protectorate were, more or less, on a par with nominal rural wages paid in Kenya and Zimbabwe, and a little higher when compared with Uganda and Ghana. However, wages in all countries except Ghana rose faster and ended up higher than those in Bechuanaland in the years prior to independence (Bowden et al., 2008). Meanwhile, wage levels for urban unskilled workers in Bechuanaland were relatively high, compared to both East and West Africa, at least until the 1950s (Frankema & van Waijenburg, 2012—Appendix Fig. 1A). Labour migration to South Africa working either as domestic help or in the mines was a worthwhile strategy as nominal wages were generally higher there compared to other regions in colonial Africa (Frankema & van Waijenburg, 2012). This wage difference eventually influenced domestic wages and mining wages within Bechuanaland increased from 1940 onwards, with a more rapid increase in the years after independence.

In addition to the above discussion of changes in wage levels over time, we are specifically interested in differences in wages between unskilled and skilled workers, the so-called skill premium, the reason being that the wage gap between skilled and unskilled workers is typically interpreted as the reward for the workers who possess more human capital and hence are more productive. As new growth theory argues that human capital formation is one of the most important determinants for long-term growth—the skill premium is often understood as a predictor of such a process (van Zanden, 2003). Changes in the ratio indicate the relative supply and demand for skilled versus unskilled labour, which in turn depend on demographic change, education, and accelerating skill-biased technological change (Katz & Murphy, 1992).

Figure 4.4 shows the development of both skilled and unskilled wages. The gap between them reflects the skill premium. From the figure it is clear

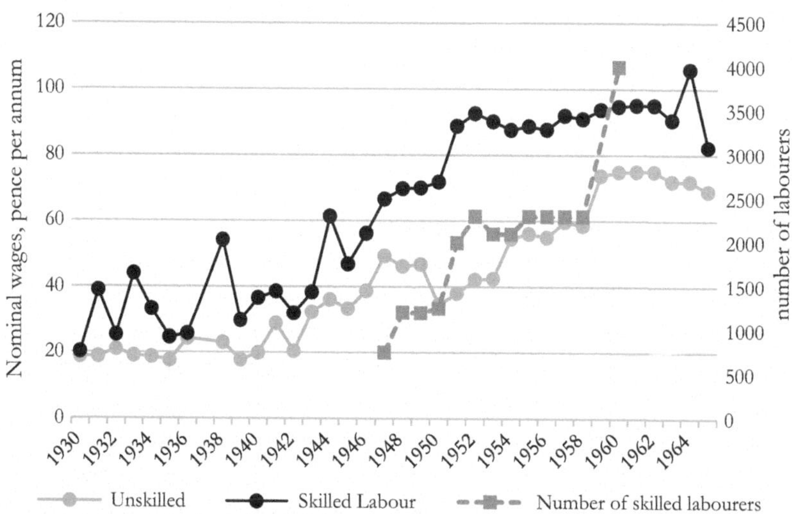

Fig. 4.4 Skill premium and number of skilled labourers, 1930–1965. Source: Bolt and Hillbom (2015)

that in Bechuanaland the skill premium takes off after the 1940s, modestly in the first half of the decade, but more rapidly increasing towards the end of the decade. In the 1950s we see a stagnation in the wage level of skilled workers and a catch-up in the wages of the unskilled, hence a shrinking skill premium. In the 1960s there is a decline in both skilled and unskilled wages as well as in the skill premium. On average, skilled workers earned 50 per cent more between 1923 and 1965 compared with their unskilled counterparts, but the size of the premium varied substantially over time. All in all, the skill premium is similar to the one found in Mauritius, but substantially below those found for most other British colonies during the same time (Frankema & van Waijenburg, 2012, p. 903).

When mapping the number of individuals employed as skilled labour over time, we see an increase that coincides with the increase in wages. Hence the increase in skill premiums does not seem to stem from a lack of supply. Instead, it reasonably reflects the low demand for skilled workers. If there would have been more demand for skilled workers, competition from employers would have pushed up skilled wages, increasing the skill premium to levels of most other British colonies. Whereas colonial reports for other countries consistently complain about the lack of skilled African workers, we have not come across a single grievance about skilled labour shortages in Bechuanaland.

The limited demand for skilled workers and the consequent modest growth in the skill premium are both explained by Bechuanaland's economic structures. The colonial government primarily aimed to exploit the Protectorate's abundant factors of production, namely, land and cattle. The setup of the cattle export sector and the subsequent expansion of the economy constituted a government response to existing geography and factor endowments conditioning in the form of a climate suitable for cattle rearing and an abundant grazing rage. These initial conditions constituted the basis for the political and economic institutions promoting and steering strategies for cattle-led economic growth. The enforcement of colonial strategies was further helped by the fact that a development of the cattle export sector resonated well with the interests of the Tswana elite. All in all, there was a lack of interest on the side of both the colonial government and the Tswana elite to diversify the economy (Colclough & McCarthy, 1980; Hillbom, 2014; Parsons & Crowder, 1988). Throughout the colonial era the economy continued to be dependent on cattle, a low value added agricultural product that demanded only a basic technology processing industry in the form of an abattoir which was only built in 1954. In addition, with no diversification of the economy, there were no other sectors that required technological advancements. Hence, the demand for skilled labour stayed modest throughout the period of cattle-led growth (Bolt & Hillbom, 2015).

Finally, to provide us with yet another perspective on occupational structures and wage levels during the cattle-led growth period we compare developments in the public and private sector, respectively. Such a comparison informs us about the relative demand and supply for different types of labour and about underlying productivity in both sectors. As technology advances, labour productivity in the private sector increases as labourers are able to use the technology to produce more with the same labour input. This could stimulate wage increases in the private sector relative to public sector wages and serve as an indication of the economic strength of the private sector (Psacharopoulos, 1984). Consequently, by capturing the public–private divide in Bechuanaland we can draw conclusions about the two sectors relative success and/or failure.

If we compare wages paid to skilled labourers to those paid to government employees, their earnings were on a par in the mid-1940s, but then

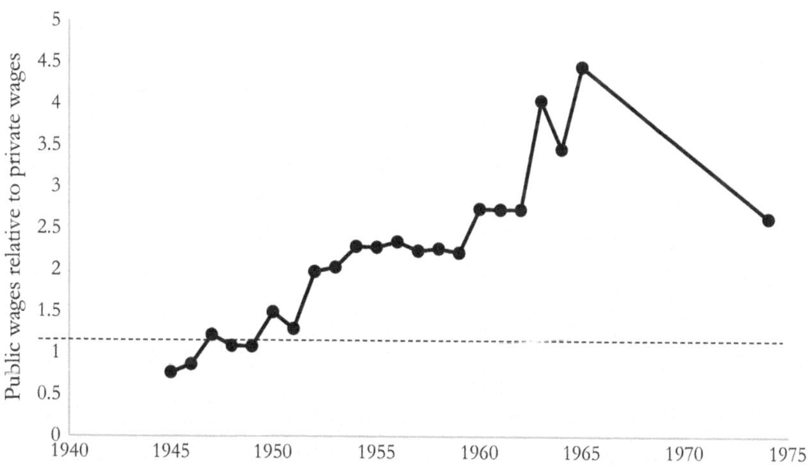

Fig. 4.5 Public–private sector wage ratio, 1945–1975. Source: Bolt and Hillbom (2015). Note: Public sector wages are government employee wages. Private sector wages are the wages paid to skilled urban labourers

the public sector forged ahead and reached a ratio of 4.5 before independence (see Fig. 4.5). After independence the private sector wages for skilled workers somewhat caught up with the government sector wages, but around the start of the diamond economy, the average government employee still earned more than 2.5 times as much as an educated skilled workers in the private sector. In terms of employment both government workers and skilled labourers remained small groups. In 1974 around 2 per cent of the population was working for the government and 1.5 per cent found employment in the private sector as a skilled worker.

The growing public–private divide was made possible by the shift in British colonial policies, which included a growing state apparatus in the African colonies. For Bechuanaland there was an increase in government revenues from two new sources: first, British grants and loans were offered, starting in the 1930s and increasing throughout the 1940s and, second, the establishment of the cattle industry provided new export revenues (see Chap. 3). As the state had more money to spend, it could employ more government officials as well as increase their salaries. The growth of the colonial administration and the relative profitability for the individual to participate in the public rather than the private sector is a phenomenon known from both colonial and independent Africa. From a long-term perspective, this has created obstacles for economic development as the public sector commonly has become overdimensioned in relation to its capacity, controlling essential resources and attracting individuals with high levels of education. Meanwhile, the private sector has stayed economically weak, generally lacking political influence and support as well as finding it difficult to attract sufficient human capital (Cooper, 2002; Freund & Rocha, 2010; Moss, 2007).

Summing up, from 1940 we see a clear wage increase in all sectors with a more rapid increase after the end of the 1950s. The increase coincides with colonial strategies to develop Bechuanaland's cattle exports and can be assumed to be explained by the cattle-led growth process. However, throughout the colonial era wage levels remained too modest to stimulate new labour-saving technologies analogous to Allen's (2009) analysis of the British economy. While a direct comparison with Britain is far-fetched, we can still expect that the principle of increasing wage levels motivating technological change, even at much more modest levels, can be the same. Instead, low-cost agricultural labour remained available throughout the colonial period and although domestic servants earned a little more than unskilled urban workers in other African regions, this was not a sector where the increased use of technology could reduce labour costs. Further, despite increases in wages and a growing wage gap between skilled and unskilled labour, the skill premium stayed modest throughout the period. Hence, this suggests that the growth period was characterized by a lack of incentives for additional human capital formation to fuel further long-term growth. Finally, the significant increase in the public–private divide clearly indicates the weakness of the private sector including lower demand for skilled labour compared to the public sector. The weak development of the private sector contributes to our inference that the cattle-led growth period was characterized by limited technology development and limited sectorial change.

4.4.2 Incomes in the Rural Informal Sector

We have seen continued, albeit sometimes modestly, rising incomes for the wage employees in Bechuanaland from the establishment of the cattle export sector right up to the period when diamond extraction takes over as the main driver of the economy in the mid-1970s. Yet, it is within the cattle sector itself where one would logically expect the greatest effect from the opening up of export markets for cattle. This is even more so given that the very large majority of Bechuanaland's population, roughly 85 per cent, was engaged in the agricultural sector, either as cattle holders or as crop farmers. As explained in Chap. 3, the establishment of the cattle export sector was driven by the search to increase government revenues. While other African colonial administrations had engaged in turning natural resources into export revenues and income-earning opportunities already at the onset of colonial state formation (Frankema & van Waijenburg, 2014), Bechuanaland was lagging behind. The only sizeable export market that was feasible to reach from Bechuanaland considering the high transaction costs due to the land-locked location of the Protectorate and the poorly developed ifrastructure was South Africa where animals were sold alive. The challenge was that South Africa had a significant beef production of its own and consequently there was not an explicite demand for additional beef.

For decades after the establishment of the Protectorate in 1885, Britain, the British South Africa Company, Rhodesia, the Union of South Africa, and the Tswana *dikgosi* struggled over who would be assigned administrative rights over Bechuanaland. Because of this insecurity the administration initially stayed passive and primarily engaged in tax collection without launching development strategies. In this political tug of war, South African authorities wanted Bechuanaland to develop into a labour reserve and they restricted cattle exports from the Protectorate causing the price for cattle to fall drastically, from £25 in 1900 to £2.5 in the early 1920s. In 1941 South Africa lifted its restrictions and both the volume of exports and domestic prices for cattle in Botswana rapidly expanded. Prices for cattle in South Africa were much higher than in Botswana, and the opportunity of selling animals for this higher price put upward pressure on the domestic cattle prices and encouraged increasing cattle exports (Parsons, 1993, p. 266) (see Fig. 4.6).

Determining the effects of the establishment of the cattle export sector for incomes and living standards of farmers is not straightforward. There are no official records available that provide information about farmers' incomes. Consequently, we had to calculate rough estimates of rural

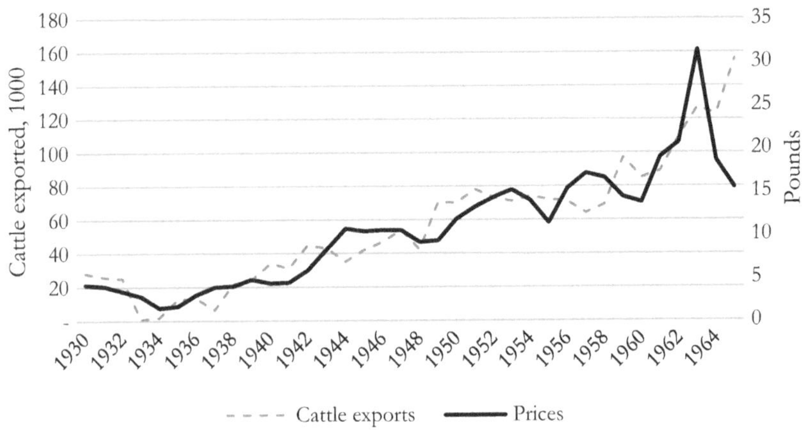

Fig. 4.6 Cattle prices and cattle exports, 1930–1965. Sources: Bolt and Hillbom (2016)

incomes based on a variety of sources. Based on anthropological sources we have divided the rural population into four income categories which we base on cattle holding and herd size: the poorest group are the *cattle-less* living at subsistence and their group increased in size from 7 to 45 per cent of the rural population during our time of investigation. Next, the *small-scale cattle holders* are defined as holding one to ten heads of cattle and their group increased from 20 to 40 per cent of the population. The *medium-scale cattle owners* owned between 10 and 50 heads of cattle, and this group declined in size from 35 to 10 per cent of the population. The *large-scale cattle owners* owned more than 100 heads of cattle and made up around 5 per cent of the population throughout the cattle-led growth period.[2]

The basis of all rural livelihoods was crop farming for household consumption. Based on the fact that historical sources provide no indications that people were falling below subsistence, we assume this production to have been sufficient although not resulting in much surplus. It appears that in the case of hardship, the existing social networks in Tswana society made sure help was provided to assure survival, but not much more than that. The calculation of subsistence levels are complicated by the fact that information on what smallholders exactly grew, the quantities grown, and the value of these products is scarce. Therefore we instead focus on the consumption value of subsistence and calculate a bare-bones subsistence basket in the tradition of the real wage literature (Allen, 2001; de Haas, 2016). This method captures how much one had to pay to buy the goods a person minimally needed to consume to stay alive. Following the work of Allen (2001) and Frankema and van Waijenburg (2012), the basket offers a little over 1900 calories and 44 grams of protein per adult per day and we include the cheapest food products that still offered the minimum required level of calories and protein. In addition, the basket includes minimal amounts of fuel, lighting, soap, and cotton/linen, and lastly, we increased the basket by 5 per cent to include housing expenditure. To arrive at the costs for a family to survive, one man's basket is multiplied by the size of a standard family consisting of a man, a woman, and a few (three) children. As women and children need less calories to survive than a man does, the single basket is multiplied by three to obtain the family basket (Allen, 2001; Frankema & Van Waijenburg, 2012). As both men and women are included in the cattle-owning social classes, it is reasonable to assume that both needed to provide income for half a family. Therefore, the costs to live at subsistence are set equal to 1.5 times the bare-bones basket.[3]

The cattle-less often possessed a few sheep, goats, or fowls from which they also obtained some in-kind income (Schapera & Comaroff, 1991). As prices for small stock were not recorded, we calculate an average animal unit per person. In addition, this group could get access to cattle through *mafisa*, a cattle-lending system described in Chap. 3. For the small-scale cattle holders there were some in-kind income opportunities as they had access to draft power, and could potentially lend out an ox to cattle-less neighbours in return for labour or foodstuff (Gulbrandsen, 1996, p. 201). Further, cattle provided some milk for those living at the cattle posts although, due to the hot climate, milk did not keep and there was no market for sales (Schapera & Comaroff, 1991, pp. 18–19).

Otherwise, incomes above subsistence primarily came from the sales of cattle and these opportunities greatly expanded with the establishment of the cattle export sector. Incomes from cattle sales were, however, not within reach of all cattle owners as they could only safely sell animals if their herd size was large enough to survive periods of disease and droughts. At the time, a robust herd size meant roughly 50 animals (Roe, 1980) and during the whole period under investigation, it was only the large-scale cattle holders who owned more than 50 heads. Based on this, we assume that the main ambition of all other groups of cattle holders was to enlarge their herds and sell as few animals as possible, only selling of beasts when forced by the need to pay for example annual taxes. We calculate the number of cattle sold by multiplying the offtake rate by the average stock held. Summing up all sales of both medium- and large-scale cattle holders gives a higher export figure than the official recorded number for live cattle exports. Yet, the official figures were probably an underestimation of total animals sold, as hides were also exported and there was also a modest domestic market (Schapera & Comaroff, 1991, pp. 15, 19). By multiplying the estimated number of cattle sold per social class by the prevailing retail price we calculate average cash income for the medium- and large-scale cattle holders.

Table 4.1 Incomes in the agricultural sector compared to both unskilled and government wages, pence per day

	1936	1946	1956	1963
Cattle-less	5	8	9	15
Small-scale cattle holders	6	12	15	17
Medium-scale cattle holders	12	34	37	50
Large-scale cattle holders	23	90	141	327
Unskilled rural wage	12	28	42	55
Government wage		37	159	282

Source: Bolt and Hillbom (2015, 2016)

For all cattle-owning social classes, livestock breeding broadened the opportunities to store wealth. To capture this, calves from each herd have been taken to represent rent or capital accumulated in the herd. Rent incomes were calculated by multiplying the average price of calves by the number of calves for every herd size. Subsequently, rent incomes were added to cash incomes for all cattle-owning social classes in all periods.

Incomes derived in the agricultural sector are summed up in Table 4.1. It shows that incomes for large-scale cattle owners rapidly increased with the establishment of the cattle export sector and that the large-scale cattle owners were the most earning group at the end of the colonial period, even surpassing the government officials who earned on average around 282 pence per day in 1963. Meanwhile, medium-scale cattle owners also saw their incomes increase, but to a much smaller extent as they provided fewer animals for exports. Their average incomes follow the trend in unskilled agricultural wages. The increasing incomes for the cattle sector were driven by a combination of new market opportunities and rapidly increasing prices for beef in South Africa (see Fig. 4.6). Meanwhile, the small-scale cattle holders and the cattle-less, that is, the two groups not profiting from the new cattle export opportunities also saw increases in their incomes, but to a modest degree. Our calculations for the agricultural economy then clearly demonstrates that the cattle-led growth period translated into substantial changes in incomes and also had a crucial impact on a stark polarization trend.

4.5 Diamond-Led Growth

Soon after the formal announcement of the discovery of diamonds in 1967 mining activities started. In 1973 the mining sector contributed already around 10 per cent to total GDP. This constituted a structural break from the previous cattle-based economy. In the following decade diamond incomes increased further and ever since the diamond sector has remained the most productive sector in Botswana's economy. In the mid-1980s, its contribution to GDP had increased to 53 per cent, after which it slowly declined to roughly 35 per cent of GDP in 2009, remaining relatively constant thereafter (Gaolathe, 1997, p. 408: Table 2; Leith, 1997a; Siwawa-Ndai, 1997; World Bank, 2017). In Sect. 4.3 and Fig. 4.1 we discussed the spectacular development of GDP per capita during the diamond-led growth period. Bearing in mind that Botswana possesses the richest diamond deposits in the world and that the country has supplied about 15 per cent of all diamonds ever produced, these remarkable growth rates are not surprising.

Global demand for diamonds has been relatively stable ever since diamonds were discovered, initially due to the demand for diamond jewellery and more recently also due to its value for industrial applications such as cutting, grinding, drilling, and polishing procedures. As a result, diamond exports have been less vulnerable to adverse market conditions compared to many other, more volatile, perishable or bulkier goods. Additionally, diamond prices have shown a rapid increase between 1960 and 2015, of around 14 per cent per year (Antwerp World Diamond Centre, 2017). With the exception of a brief downturn during the latest financial crisis, the Botswana government has been able to take advantage of its diamond resources and bridge bad market years relying on savings from good years. Given the stable, albeit recently slightly lower, global demand for diamonds, we are in this section paying limited attention to the role of demand, and instead focus on the supply side of Botswana's diamond-led growth.

In contrast to the data challenges we met when discussing the cattle-led growth period, for the diamond economy we can rely on existing national accounts to unravel economic growth. We start our discussion of the development of the diamond economy by looking at the changing role of the three main sectors in Botswana's economy during the diamond led-growth period, namely, agriculture, industry, and services. In the first section, we look at the contribution of the three sectors to economy-wide production (contribution of the sectors to total GDP). Subsequently, we focus on employment. We analyse how labour has moved between the different sectors in search of employment, and to what extent that has could have contributed to growth.

4.5.1 Sectorial Share of GDP

The switch from depending on sales of cattle to relying on diamond exports for economic growth has had radical implications for the role of the various sectors within the economy. While both cattle and diamonds are primary products, cattle farming is part of the agricultural sector while diamond mining is included in the industrial sector. In Fig. 4.7 we show the development of each of the sectors as a share of total GDP. The rapid increase of the industrial sector is nearly completely driven by diamond mining, something clearly demonstrated by the fact that the sharp increase of the industrial sector correlates perfectly with the start of the diamond mining in the late 1960s. Industry surpassed agriculture in the mid-1970s in terms of its contribution to GDP, to become the largest sector of the economy only a few years later. Even though the industrial sector started expanding rapidly right after the mining of diamonds in the late 1960s, the agricultural cattle sector continued to dominate the economy until the mid-1970s when the industrial mining sector took over and the diamond-led growth period was definitely established.

In the meantime, services have consistently represented a large share of GDP. During the cattle economy it was on par with agriculture, and consisted of mainly low-productive government services. During the height of the diamond-led growth during the 1980s and 1990s, the service sector occupied a stable second place in terms of share in total output. From the turn of the millennium this tertiary sector has actually become the largest sector of Botswana's economy. Below we break this overview down into a more detailed discussion of what is happening in terms of

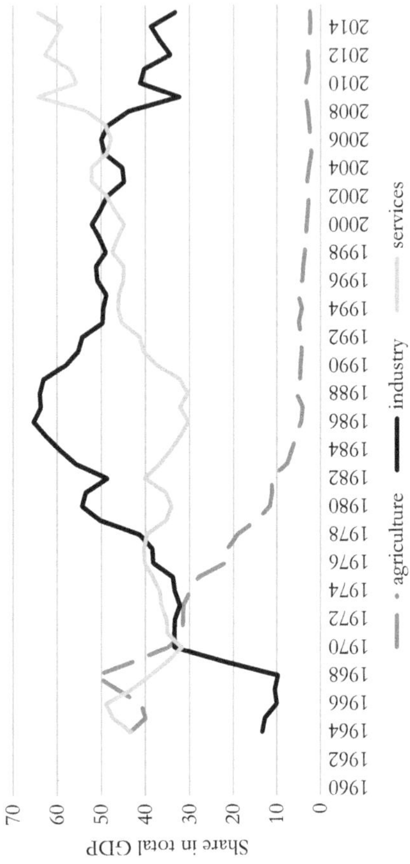

Fig. 4.7 Agriculture, industry, and service sectors, value added (per cent of GDP), 1964–2015. Source: Timmer et al. (2015), World Bank (2017)

growth, technological change, and productivity sector by sector. However, we save our critical in-depth analysis of Botswana's challenge with regard to the lack of noteworthy diversification, sectorial change, and structural transformation to Chap. 5.

Agriculture: We already know from the previous discussion on the cattle-led growth period that Botswana's economy at the time of independence was dependent on incomes from agriculture. The sector accounted for roughly 40 per cent of GDP and cattle/beef exports represented 85 per cent of government export earnings. After the turn of the millennium, its contribution to GDP had declined to less than 3 per cent. While this development represents a shift in balance in the economy as a whole, it does not mean that the agricultural sector has become obsolete. On the contrary, cattle-led growth has continued in the shadow of diamonds and in absolute numbers the value of the agricultural sector has actually increased by roughly 150 per cent. However, as total GDP increased from US$51 million at independence to over US$14 billion in 2016 due to exceptional incomes from diamond exports, the relative contribution of agriculture has declined drastically (Colclough & McCarthy, 1980, p. 32; Harvey & Lewis, 1990, pp. 78–82; Leith, 1997b, p. 530; Republic of Botswana, 2007; World Bank, 2017).

To encourage the agricultural sector, the Botswana independence government has continued the agricultural policies of its colonial predecessor with construction of water sources, subsidizing veterinary services, distributing vaccines, and building veterinary fences. In addition, it has set up the Botswana Meat Commission (BMC) as a non-profit parastatal monopsony buyer of cattle and exporter of beef (Acemoglu et al., 2003, p. 101; Lawry, 1983, p. 14). In 1975 the government negotiated favourable trade conditions from the Beef and Veal Protocol of the Lomé convention, a trade agreement between the EEC, the predecessor to the EU, and former European colonies in Africa, Caribbean, and the Pacific Islands, termed the ACP group. The intention with the trade agreement was that it would replace former colonial aid and for Botswana it contained the guarantee of a set quota of beef exports to the European market with high profits due to 90 per cent reductions in import levies. While profits were supposed to be invested in social development efforts such as infrastructure and education, a large share was instead distributed directly to primarily the large-scale cattle holders providing animals to the BMC. In 2000, the Lomé Agreement was replaced by the Cotonou Agreement, but the Lomé terms were extended until 2007. Under the Cotonou Agreement, which runs up until the year 2020, Botswana continues to gain from similar preferential trade treatment (Harvey & Lewis, 1990, pp. 78–82; Leith, 2005, pp. 70, 115; Siwawa-Ndai, 1997, p. 363).

All in all, government policies have supported and cemented existing structures rather than encouraged innovation and change. The composition of the agricultural sector has stayed the same and the livestock sector has continued to dominate, presently contributing 80 per cent to the agricultural GDP. As was the case during the colonial era, ranching remains a low-technology sector with limited technological advances since the introduction of modern boreholes and the establishment of the Lobatse abattoir in 1954. Growth is extensive in character and based on continuously increasing numbers of animals, although there have been severe setbacks in drought years. Productivity, measured by offtake rates meaning percentage of animals slaughtered out of the national stock, has been modest in an international comparison. In 1967 offtake rates were at 9 per cent and after first staying constant they declined to 7 per cent in 2007 where they have remained. This means that there was no productivity increase for four decades in the country's most important agricultural sector. To put this in an international perspective we can compare Botswana's offtake rates in 2007 with other beef-producing economies, for example, neighbouring South Africa had offtake rates at 22 per cent, Mongolia at 19 per cent and Argentina at 27 per cent (Hillbom, 2010).

According to theory, agricultural transformation happens through technological change and subsequent productivity increase in subsistence agriculture. During the transformation process there is an accumulation of capital and freeing up of labour and as these resources are transferred to industry and other capitalist sectors, structural transformation is instigated (see, e.g. Kuznets, 1973; Lewis, 1954; Mellor, 1986; Timmer, 2009). However, in the case of Botswana the agricultural sector does not have the preconditions to initiate such an agricultural transformation process. As mentioned above, the sector is characterized by low levels of technology and extensive growth with modest productivity. Institutional change primarily in the form of alterations of government policies could improve the situation, but the dry climate remains as a fundamental obstacle to sizeable agricultural growth (Republic of Botswana, 2003, pp. 178–182; Silitshena & McLeod, 1998, chapters 9 and 10). In relation to the low population numbers, land has been abundant, but only 4 per cent of the country's area is suitable for crop farming (Parson, 1984, p. 4). While the potential grazing range is extensive (as discussed in Chap. 3), cattle herding is conditioned by access to water, which continues to be the scarce agricultural resource. Polarization in cattle ownership with increasing numbers of cattle-less small-scale farmers at one end and large holders at the other has continued (Gulbrandsen, 1996, p. 3; Peters, 1994; Silitshena & McLeod, 1998, chapter 11). These inequalities will be further discussed in Chap. 6.

In the 1930s, Bechuanaland farmers grew 90 per cent of the territory's cereals consumption, but production decreased to 50 per cent of domestic consumption in the 1980s. In 1991, the Botswana government let go of its previous goal to become self-sufficient in food production and instead adopted a policy of food security (Silitshena & McLeod, 1998, pp. 88–89). Today the country is completely dependent on food imports. Meanwhile, fields and animals yielded even below the requirements for subsistence farming and many rural households became dependent on complementary off-farm incomes (Gulbrandsen, 1996, pp. 2–3). From an environmental sustainability point of view, cattle farming has become debatable as natural resources such as water and land are being heavily exploited while returns in terms of contribution to the overall economy are modest. While the limited share of GDP suggests a minor role for agriculture in the economy, the sector remains extremely important for the Botswana economy in terms of employment (see Sect. 4.5.2). Further, social status remains strongly associated with the ownership of cattle.

Industry: When the agricultural sector is failing to fill its role as the driver towards sustained growth, other more successful sectors, in the case of Botswana the mining industry, can substitute for its shortcomings in forming capital, thereby becoming the engine of continued economic progress (Gerschenkron, 1962). The general technological level of industry in Botswana, however, has stayed low and productivity has not experienced any significant increase with the exception of the mining sector.

The increase in industrial productivity has been brought about mainly by increase in factor input of capital and skilled and unskilled labour and only less than 10 per cent of growth in output during the diamond boom in the 1980s and 1990s was due to productivity increase (Leith, 1997a, pp. 29–30). Unfortunately, mining has not been complemented by other forms of industry, nor has it encouraged or contributed to technological advance, via either imported technology or domestic innovations (Gaolathe, 1997, pp. 412–413; Mpabanga, 1997, p. 373; Republic of Botswana, 2004, p. 12: Fig. 2.4). Until recently, diamonds have been exported in raw and unprocessed form. While small enterprises dedicated to cutting have been established in the last few years, it is too early to talk about linkage effects.

Under the assumption that diamonds are not forever, that is, they are not an infinite resource, alternative sectors need to be developed. The mining sector does hold additional opportunities such as the exploitation of nickel and coal, although these resources are less valuable. While this would bring a diversification of the mining sector itself, it perpetuates natural resource dependency. Instead, it would be desirable to find alternatives to primary production, primarily manufacturing and processing industries. These sections of the industrial sector are expected to be much more important as sources of technological progress and knowledge and skills generated there are expected to spread to other sectors and affect them positively by contributing to increasing their productivity. In Botswana the manufacturing sector, however, has remained modest throughout the diamond-led economy, in terms of both employment and value added. Figure 4.8 shows that while there was a significant increase in value added at the very start of diamond-led growth, numbers have stabilized after 1990 at 6 to 7 per cent of total GDP. Meanwhile, employment in manufacturing rose more slowly, but stabilized around the same time at 6 or 7 per cent of total employment (Timmer et al., 2015).

The failure to promote manufacturing is commonly seen as one of the main negative implications of resource abundance and dependency (Mikesell, 1997). In all fairness, it has to be remembered that part of the explanation for the relative weak performance of the manufacturing sector lies in the rapid growth of the economy as a whole. Total output in

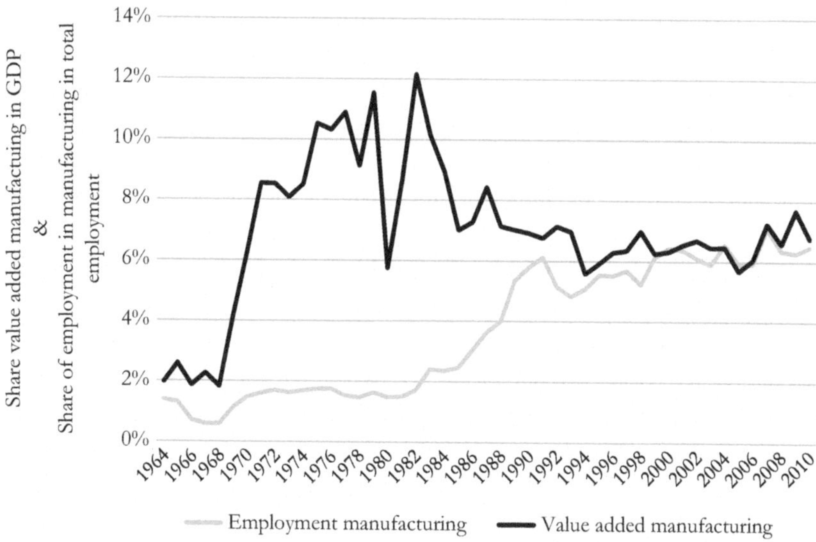

Fig. 4.8 Development of the manufacturing sector, 1964–2010. Source: Timmer et al. (2015)

manufacturing increased on average with 7 per cent per year since 1975, but coming from a very low level this means that the manufacturing sector still contributed only around 7 per cent of the total GDP in 2010. In comparison it can be noted that in South Africa, the oldest industrializing country on the subcontinent, manufacturing was 15 per cent of GDP and in Mauritius it was 18 per cent of GDP in 2010 (Timmer et al., 2015). Further, the fact that the export of diamonds in the raw continues at some 85 per cent of total export earnings is also alarming (Bank of Botswana, 2014; World Bank, 2017). While manufacturing has experienced substantial annual absolute growth, it will have to do better relative to other sectors if the Botswana economy is to maintain its growth levels and the population its current standard of living in the long run (Owusu & Ismail Samatar, 1997).

Services: Sachs and Warner (1999) have shown that there is a general trend for natural resource-rich countries to have smaller manufacturing sectors paired with larger service sectors. Botswana fits this bill perfectly. We have already discussed the limitations to the manufacturing sector and in this section we focus on the potentially oversized service sector. In Fig. 4.7 we show how the service sector in terms of share of GDP throughout the independence era has held a consistent and important position in the economy. It was the largest sector at the time of independence and while it lost out relative to industry during the most spectacular era of diamond expansion in the 1980s and early 1990s, it is at present the biggest sector representing 56 per cent of total GDP (World Bank, 2017).

The largest subsector within services in terms of value added is government services. While this represents a continuation of a trend that started with the establishment of the government sector during the colonial period, it has been further enhanced with rising government revenues during the diamond-led growth and additional financial opportunities for expansion this generated. The Botswana government has used a large part of diamond rents for investments in social development, primarily in infrastructure and human capital formation. Such investments have represented as much as 40 per cent of GDP, thereby being among the highest in Africa and on a par with developed countries such as Norway (Acemoglu et al., 2003; Leith, 2005, p. 85). In addition, the government bureaucracy itself has increased. The second largest service sector in terms of value added is trade, that is, social and personal services in the form of hotels, restaurants, shops, repairs, and so on, in the private sector (Timmer et al., 2015). The growing tourist industry, currently representing some 4 per cent of GDP, has contributed to the growth of this subsector (World Bank, 2017), but the expansion is also indirectly dependent on diamonds as the current growth period has brought general increasing surplus and consumption in the economy.

From a sustainable growth perspective the challenge with the current development is that the government sector as well as social and personal services is the least productive sector in terms of labour productivity (McMillan et al., 2014). Baumol (1967) even termed them 'stagnant services'. The increased size and importance of these stagnant sectors in the economy in terms of both value added and employment creates significant challenges for future growth. This is because the only way to continue the current high economic growth rates is to engage further in high-productive sectors, not to overexpand the low-productive services (De Vries et al., 2015; McMillan et al., 2014).

4.5.2 Occupations and Wages in the Diamond Economy

The contribution to total GDP is not the only way to evaluate the role played by the various sectors in the growth process. An alternative way of understanding growth trajectories would be to look at the composition of the labour force. Dual economy theory as developed by Lewis (1954) and Ranis and Fei (1961) predicts that when labour can migrate from the traditional sectors characterized by low labour productivity to modern sectors with much higher labour productivity, this will drive economy-wide growth. When labour starts moving out of agriculture to modern, more productive sectors such as industry this can create a positive spiral of growth. Due to higher labour productivity in the modern sectors, higher incomes are earned and a surplus is created in the economy offering opportunities for additional investments, technological advances, further productivity increases, and a full modernization of the economy (Kuznets, 1973; Lewis, 1954; Ranis & Fei, 1961).

In Fig. 4.9 we can see that while the share of labour in the agricultural sector has declined drastically from almost 90 per cent in 1964 to 38 per

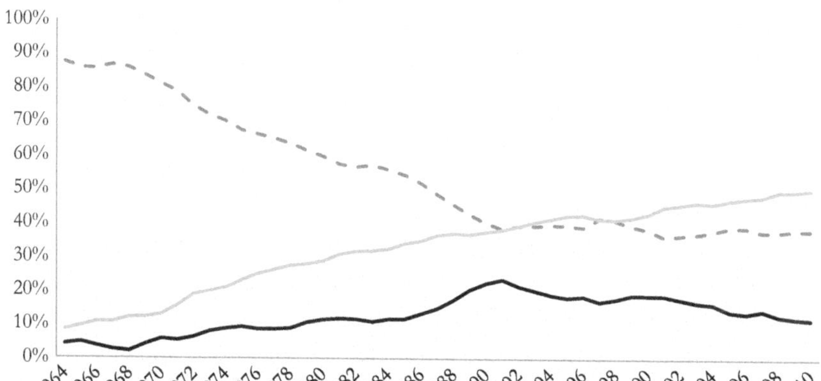

Fig. 4.9 Share of labour per sector, 1964–2010. We have no more recent information on employment shares. Source: Timmer et al. (2015)

cent in 2010, it remained the most important sector in terms of employment until the late 1980s. While its share in total employment has remained constant over the last decades it was overtaken by the service sector as the largest sector in terms of employment in the early 1990s. The service sector has been on a consistent rise during our whole period of investigation providing employment mostly in trade and government services and is now the sector harbouring the largest share of employment. Meanwhile, industry has absorbed a much smaller share of the labour force. Consequently, the major movement of the labour force takes place between the agricultural sector which is characterized by low technological progress to the service sector which in Botswana also has low labour productivity (McMillan et al., 2014). This in turn means that the theoretical prediction that increasing incomes are generated as labour moves into more productive sectors offering higher wages cannot be corroborated for the Botswana case.

Nevertheless, Botswana's long-term economic growth experience has had a remarkable impact on average incomes. Since 1975 average incomes have been raised from less than US$430 to around US$6,800 per annum (current US$) (World Bank, 2017). In the absence of technological progress, increased labour productivity, structural transformation, and modernization of the economy, this growth experience can only be explained by the rise of the diamond sector and the impact it has had on the economy as a whole. Even though only relatively few people are employed in the mining sector, the revenues it generates have created what can only be described as a wealth shock to the economy (Ismail, 2010). It means that as more resources are available, mainly due to government spending and transfers, there is room for a growing demand for goods and services, leading to rising prices resulting in upward pressures on wages also in the private sector. This conclusion for the diamond-led growth period resonates with the mechanisms identified as driving wage increase during the previous cattle-led growth. The differences do not lie in the characteristics of the two growth experiences, but in the magnitude and the general wealth derived from diamonds.

4.6 Summing Up and Moving On ...

After the establishment of the cattle sector, Botswana's economy started to expand. As national accounts and formal statistics capturing this period are largely missing, we discussed the cattle-led growth period and its effects on economic structures via mapping changes in wage levels in formal employment and computing incomes in agricultural self-employment. Overall average incomes rose modestly, but not everyone enjoyed similar increases. The small elite of government employees and large-scale cattle holders gained substantially, while most other groups only saw limited improvements or even stagnation during the growth period. The private sector remained underdeveloped, something that was reflected in the narrow demand for skilled workers, low skill premium, and lagging of private sector wages relative to the public sector.

A decade after diamonds were discovered, mining activities had taken over the role of being the prime driver of economic expansion. The resulting growth completely overshadowed the achievements of the cattle economy. It was another example of natural resource-driven growth, and the fundamental explanation for the success of the second period lay in that a low-value agricultural product, that is, cattle, had been exchanged for a high-value mineral, that is, diamonds. There was a significant increase in wages and incomes based on the staggering diamond revenues, creating a wealth chock in the economy allowing for primarily public sector expansion, but also rising wages within the private sector. Wage improvements were not, however, explained by the majority of the workforce moving into sectors with high labour productivity.

The sensational diamond-led growth provided Botswana with a window of opportunity, but in Chap. 5 we claim that the economy remains natural resource dependent, lacking diversification and development of alternative productive activities. Thus, the country is still in search for sustainable economic development that can continue after the last diamonds have been mined. The economy has been trapped in continuous natural resource dependency and although efforts have been made to break out of this diamond-coated cage, they have so far failed. In addition, the lack of an economic structural break coincides with the absence of a break in state structures and a continuation of the gate-keeping state, which has invested in social progress but not promoted inclusive, broad-based development.

Notes

1. Real GDP per capita growth, WDI (2017). The Maddison Project database (2018) suggests growth rates of 10 and 8 per cent for those decades, respectively (Maddison Project database, version 2018, Bolt et al., 2018).
2. These numbers do not add up to total rural population, as these are rough estimates based on anthropological sources. We treat the rest of the population as 'unspecified' and do not assign an income to this group. See Bolt and Hillbom (2016) for more details.
3. For a more detailed presentation of our methods and data we refer to Bolt and Hillbom (2015).

References

Acemoglu, D., Johnson, S., & Robinson, J. (2001). The colonial origins of comparative development: An empirical investigation. *The American Economic Review, 91*(5), 1369–1401.

Acemoglu, D., Johnson, S., & Robinson, J. A. (2002). Reversal of fortune: Geography and institutions in the making of the modern world income distribution. *The Quarterly Journal of Economics, 117*(4), 1231–1294.

Acemoglu, D., Johnson, S., & Robinson, J. A. (2003). An African success story: Botswana. In D. Rodrik (Ed.), *In search of prosperity: Analytic narratives on economic growth* (pp. 80–119). Princeton and Oxford: Princeton University Press.

Acemoglu, D., & Robinson, J. A. (2010). Why is Africa poor? *Economic History of Developing Regions, 25*(1), 21–50.

Albouy, D. Y. (2012). The colonial origins of comparative development: An empirical investigation: Comment. *The American Economic Review, 102*(6), 3059–3076.

Allen, R. C. (2001). The great divergence in European wages and prices from the Middle Ages to the First World War. *Explorations in Economic History, 38*(4), 411–447.

Allen, R. C. (2009). *The British industrial revolution in global perspective*. Cambridge: Cambridge University Press.

Austin, G. (2008). Resources, techniques, and strategies south of the Sahara: Revising the factor endowments perspective on African economic development, 1500–2000. *The Economic History Review, 61*(3), 587–624.

Auty, R. M. (2001). The political economy of resource-driven growth. *European Economic Review, 45*(4), 839–846.

Baumol, W. J. (1967). Macroeconomics of unbalanced growth: The anatomy of urban crisis. *The American Economic Review, 57*(3), 415–426.

Bloom, D. E., Sachs, J. D., Collier, P., & Udry, C. (1998). Geography, demography, and economic growth in Africa. *Brookings Papers on Economic Activity, 1998*(2), 207–295.

Bolt, J., & Hillbom, E. (2015). Potential for diversification? The role of the formal sector in Bechuanaland Protectorate's economy, 1900–65. *Economic History of Developing Regions, 30*(2), 95–124.

Bolt, J., & Hillbom, E. (2016). Long-term Trends in Economic Inequality: Lessons from colonial Botswana, 1921–1974. *Economic History Review, 69*(4), 1255–1284.

Bolt, J., Inklaar, R., de Jong, H., & van Zanden, J. L. (2018). Rebasing 'Maddison': new income comparisons and the shape of long-run economic development, GGDC Research Memorandum 174, Maddison Project Database, version 2018.

Bowden, S., Chiripanhura, B., & Mosley, P. (2008). Measuring and explaining poverty in six African countries: A long-period approach. *Journal of International Development, 30*(8), 1049–1079.

Colclough, C., & McCarthy, S. (1980). *The political economy of Botswana: A study of growth and distribution*. Oxford: Oxford University Press.

Collier, P., & Gunning, J. W. (1999). Why has Africa grown slowly? *The Journal of Economic Perspectives, 13*(3), 3–22.

Cooper, F. (2002). *Africa since 1940: The past of the present*. Cambridge: Cambridge University Press.

De Haas, M. (2016). Measuring rural welfare in colonial Africa: Did Uganda's smallholders thrive? *The Economic History Review, 70*(2), 605–631.

De Vries, G., Timmer, M., & de Vries, K. (2015). Structural transformation in Africa: Static gains, dynamic losses. *The Journal of Development Studies, 51*(6), 674–688.

Easterly, W., & Levine, R. (1997). Africa's growth tragedy: Policies and ethnic divisions. *The Quarterly Journal of Economics, 112*(4), 1203–1250.

Faye, M., McArthur, J. W., Schmidt-Traub, G., Kruk, M., Bahadur, C., Sachs, J., et al. (2004). Ending Africa's poverty trap. *Brookings Papers on Economic Activity, 2004*(1), 117–240.

Frankema, E. (2015). The biogeographic roots of world inequality. Animals, disease and human settlement patterns in Africa and the Americas before 1492. *World Development, 70*, 274–285.

Frankema, E., & Van Waijenburg, M. (2012). Structural impediments to African growth? New evidence from real wages in British Africa, 1880–1965. *The Journal of Economic History, 72*(4), 895–926.

Frankema, E., & van Waijenburg, M. (2014). Metropolitan blueprints of colonial taxation? lessons from fiscal capacity building in british and french africa, c. 1880–1940. *The Journal of African History, 55*(3), 371–400.

Freund, C. L., & Rocha, N. (2010). What constrains Africa's exports? *Policy Research Working Paper Series 5184*. Washington, DC: The World Bank.

Gallup, J. L., Sachs, J. D., & Mellinger, A. D. (1999). Geography and economic development. *International Regional Science Review, 22*(2), 179–232.

Gaolathe, B. (1997). Development of Botswana's Mineral sector. In J. S. Salkin, D. Mpabanga, D. Cowan, J. Selwe, & M. Wright (Eds.), *Aspects of the Botswana economy* (pp. 401–431). Gaborone, Botswana: Lentswe La Lesedi.

Garner, P. (2006, January). Economic growth in sub-Saharan Africa. Retrieved from SSRN https://ssrn.com/abstract=853184 or https://doi.org/10.2139/ssrn.853184

Gerschenkron, A. (1962). *Economic backwardness in historical perspective: In economic backwardness in historical perspective* (pp. 5–30). Cambridge, MA: The Belknap Press.

Gulbrandsen, Ø. (1996). *Poverty in the midst of Plenty: Socio-economic marginalization, ecological deterioration and political stability in a Tswana society* (No. 45). Bergen: Norse Publications.

Gylfason, T., Herbertsson, T. T., & Zoega, G. (1999). A mixed blessing. Natural Resources and Economic Growth. *Macroeconomic Dynamics, 3*(2), 204–225.

Habakkuk, H. J. (1962). *American and British technology in the nineteenth century*. London: Cambridge University Press.

Harvey, C., & Lewis, S. R., Jr. (1990). *Policy choice and development performance in Botswana*. London: Macmillan in association with the OECD Development Centre.

Hillbom, E. (2010). Agricultural development and the distribution of water resources in Kgatleng District, Botswana. *Development Southern Africa, 27*(3), 413–427.

Hillbom, E. (2014). Cattle, diamonds and institutions: Main drivers of Botswana's economic development, 1850 to present. *Journal of International Development, 26*(2), 155–176.

Hopkins, A. (2009). The new economic history of Africa. *Journal of African History, 50*, 155–177.

Ismail, K. (2010). The structural manifestation of the 'dutch disease': The case of oil exporting countries. *IMF Working Paper WP/10/103,* New York: The International Monetary Fund.

Jerven, M. (2010). Accounting for the African growth miracle: The official evidence–Botswana 1965–1995. *Journal of Southern African Studies, 36*(1), 73–94.

Katz, L. F., & Murphy, K. M. (1992). Changes in relative wages, 1963–1987: Supply and demand factors. *The Quarterly Journal of Economics, 107*(1), 35–78.

Kuznets, S. (1973). Modern economic growth: findings and reflections. *The American Economic Review, 63*(3), 247–258.

Landes, D. S. (1998). *The wealth and poverty of nations: Why some countries are so rich and some so poor.* New York: WW Norton.

Lawry, S. W. (1983). *Land tenure, land policy, and smallholder livestock development in Botswana* (No. 78). Madison: Land Tenure Center, University of Wisconsin-Madison.

Leite, C. A., & Weidmann, J. (1999). Does mother nature corrupt? Natural resources, corruption, and economic growth. *IMF Working Paper 99/85.* Washington, DC: International Monetary Fund.

Leith, C. (1997a). Growth and structural transformation in Botswana. In J. S. Salkin, D. Mpabanga, D. Cowan, J. Selwe, & M. Wright (Eds.), *Aspects of the Botswana economy* (pp. 21–35). Gaborone, Botswana: Lentswe La Lesedi.

Leith, C. (1997b). Botswana's international trade policies. In J. S. Salkin, D. Mpabanga, D. Cowan, J. Selwe, & M. Wright (Eds.), *Aspects of the Botswana economy* (pp. 529–548). Gaborone, Botswana: Lentswe La Lesedi.

Leith, J. C. (2005). *Why Botswana prospered.* Montreal and Kingston: McGill-Queen's University Press.

Lewis, W. A. (1954). Economic development with unlimited supplies of labour. *The Manchester School, 22*(2), 139–191.

McMillan, M., Rodrik, D., & Verduzco-Gallo, Í. (2014). Globalization, structural change, and productivity growth, with an update on Africa. *World Development, 63*, 11–32.

Mellor, J. W. (1986). *Agriculture on the road to industrialization.* Washington, DC: International Food Policy Research Institue l.

Mikesell, J. L. (1997). Is the retail sales tax really inferior to the value-added tax? *The sales tax in the 21st century*. In M. Murray & W. Fox (eds.), *The Sales Tax in the 21st Century*. Westport, CT: Greenwood Publishing.

Milanovic, B. (2016). *Global inequality*. Cambridge, MA: Harvard University Press.

Moss, T. J. (2007). *African development: Making sense of the issues and actors*. Boulder, CO: Lynne Rienner Publishers.

Mpabanga, D. (1997). Constraints to industrial development. In J. S. Salkin, D. Mpabanga, D. Cowan, J. Selwe, & M. Wright (Eds.), *Aspects of the Botswana economy* (pp. 369–387). Gaborone, Botswana: Lentswe La Lesedi.

North, C. D. (1981). Structure and change in economic history. *New York: Norton, 5*, 33–40.

North, D. C. (1990). *Institutions, institutional change and economic performance*. Cambridge: Cambridge University Press.

North, D. C. (2005). *Understanding the process of economic change*. Princeton: Princeton University Press.

Nurkse, R. (1953). *Problems of capital formation in underdeveloped countries*. New York: Oxford University Press.

Owusu, F., & Ismail Samatar, A. (1997). Industrial strategy and the African State: The Botswana experience. *Canadian Journal of African Studies, 31*(2), 268–299.

Parson, J. (1984). *Botswana: Liberal democracy and labor reserve in Southern Africa*. Boulder, CO: Westview Press.

Parsons, N. (1993). *A new history of Southern Africa* (2nd ed.). London: Macmillan Education Ltd.

Parsons, N., & Crowder, M. (Eds.). (1988). *Monarch of all I survey: Bechuanaland diaries 1929–37*. Gaborone, Botswana: The Botswana Society.

Peters, P. E. (1994). *Dividing the commons: Politics, policy, and culture in Botswana*. Charlottesville: University Press of Virginia.

Prados de La Escosura, L. (2012). Output per head in pre-independence Africa: Quantitative conjectures. *Economic History of Developing Regions, 27*(2), 1–36.

Psacharopoulos, G. (1984). Assessing training priorities in developing countries: Current practice and possible alternatives. *International Labour Review, 123*, 569.

Ranis, G., & Fei, J. C. (1961). A theory of economic development. *American Economic Review, 51*, 533–558.

Republic of Botswana. (2003). *National development plan 9*. Gaborone, Botswana: Ministry of Finance and Development Planning.

Republic of Botswana. (2004). *Labour statistics 2002*. Gaborone, Botswana: Government Printer.

Roe, E. (1980). *Development of livestock, agriculture and water supplies in Eastern Botswana before independence: A short history and policy analysis*. Gaborone, Botswana: Ministry of Agriculture.

Rostow, W. W. (1960). *The stages of growth: A non-communist manifesto*. New York: Cambridge University Press.

Sachs, J. D., & Warner, A. M. (1995). Natural resource abundance and economic growth. *Development Discussion Paper No. 517a*, October, Harvard Institute for International Development, Harvard University.

Sachs, J. D., & Warner, A. M. (1999). The big push, natural resource booms and growth. *Journal of Development Economics, 59*(1), 43–76.

Salkin, J. (1987). Research on employment and unemployment in Botswana. In R. Hitchcock, N. Parsons, & J. Taylor (Eds.), *Research for development in Botswana* (pp. 142–171). Gaborone, Botswana: The Botswana Society.

Samatar, A. I. (1999). *An African miracle: State and class leadership and colonial legacy in Botswana development*. Portsmouth, NH: Heinemann.

Schapera, I. (1994). *A handbook of Tswana law and custom*. Münster: LIT Verlag.

Schapera, I., & Comaroff, J. L. (1991). *The Tswana* (Revised ed.). London: Kegan Paul International.

Silitshena, R. M. K., & McLeod, G. (1998). *Botswana: A physical, social, and economic geography* (2nd ed.). Gaborone, Botswana: Longman Botswana Ltd.

Siwawa-Ndai, P. D. (1997). Industrialisation in Botswana: Evolution, performance and prospects. In J. Salkin et al. (Eds.), *Aspects of the Botswana economy* (pp. 335–367). Gaborone, Botswana: Lentswe La Lesedi.

Timmer, C. P. (2009). *A world without agriculture*. Cambridge, MA: AIE Press.

Timmer, M. P., de Vries, G. J., & de Vries, K. (2015). Patterns of structural change in developing countries. In J. Weiss & M. Tribe (Eds.), *Routledge handbook of industry and development* (pp. 65–83). London: Routledge.

Van der Ploeg, F. (2011). Natural resources: Curse or blessing? *Journal of Economic Literature, 49*(2), 366–420.

Van Zanden, J. L. (2003). Rich and poor before the Industrial Revolution: A comparison between Java and the Netherlands at the beginning of the 19th century. *Explorations in Economic History, 40*(1), 1–23.

Van Zanden, J. L. (2009). The skill premium and the 'Great Divergence'. *European Review of Economic History, 13*(1), 121–153.
Weil, D. N. (2013). *Economic growth*. Boston, MA: Pearson Education Ltd.

Internet Sources

Antwerp World Diamond Centre. (2017). Retrieved October, 2017, from https://www.awdc.be/
Bank of Botswana. (2014). *Annual report*. Gaborone, Botswana: Bank of Botswana. Retrieved October, 2017, from http://www.bankofbotswana.bw/assets/uploaded/BoB%20AR%202014%20WEB%20MAIN.pdf
Republic of Botswana. (2007). Trade statistics. Table 3A: Export by principal commodities. Gaborone, Botswana: Central Statistics Office. Retrieved September 28, 2007, from http://www.cso.gov.bw/
World Bank. (2017). World development indicators. Washington, DC. Retrieved August, 2017, from http://databank.worldbank.org/data/reports.aspx?source=world-development-indicators

Archive Material

Annual Report of the Bechuanaland Protectorate. Issues 1921–1938; 1946–1965. London School of Economics Library.
Blue Books of Statistics. Issues 1904–1925. UK National Archives, CO/567.
Blue Books of Statistics. Issues 1926–1947. UK National Archives, DO/26.
Bechuanaland Protectorate Government Census 1946, London School of Economics Library.
CSO (Central Statistics Office). 1965. Ministry of Finance and Development Planning, Population and Housing Census 1964. Gaborone, Botswana.

5

Trapped by Diamonds, c. 1975–Present

5.1 Introduction

In the previous chapter we discussed Botswana's two growth periods led by cattle and diamonds, respectively. Although the diamond-led growth period has been much more spectacular and successful than the cattle-led growth period, the country has continuously profited from its natural resource abundance. At the same time, the economy has failed to diversify, either through supply-driven processes and government investments or through demand-driven processes based on increasing incomes. During the cattle economy, it was probably not realistic to expect that export revenues would cater for a development of the broader economy, as growth during that period remained too modest. However, the staggering growth record of the diamond economy that generated significant export revenues for the independence government provided a concrete window of opportunity for diversification and achieving sustained growth.

In this chapter, our focus is on the diamond economy, and we argue that while Botswana has managed long-term economic *growth*, it has failed to initiate sustainable inclusive economic *development*. One of the

E. Hillbom, J. Bolt, *Botswana – A Modern Economic History*, Palgrave Studies in Economic History, https://doi.org/10.1007/978-3-319-73144-5_5

most interesting aspects of Botswana's growth miracle is how the government, in contrast to many other natural resource-abundant developing countries, has succeeded to stay clear of the natural resource curse via good management of diamond incomes. Nevertheless, we maintain that the economy is caught in a natural resource trap, being consistently dependent on natural resource revenues. The government has been unable to stimulate the development of complementary or alternative high-productive sectors that potentially could take over as the new growth engines the day diamonds run out. We examine the mechanisms that have led to the country becoming trapped in a long-term state of successful export-led growth based on natural resource abundance, as well as what effects that has had on inclusive broad-based development.

We situate our discussion in the theoretical distinction between economic growth and economic development. While economic growth captures the expansion of the economy in terms of increasing value of production, this process is not necessarily based on technological change, improved productivity, and a diversification of the economy. In many resource-dependent economies, growth is a result of increased exploitation of resources, which often requires only limited technological development and stimulates restricted diversification. In such economies, growth processes are vulnerable to busts, as growth is connected to, for example, price developments in the global market. When prices for commodities go down, economies dependent on those commodities suffer. In addition, these natural resources are not endless; eventually they will run out. In contrast, economic development has significant economic growth as a base, but it is paired with technological change and diversification of the economy resulting in long-term sustainable inclusive growth and social development. We will show the importance of this distinction and claim that while Botswana has experienced rapid long-term economic growth, it has been without sustainable economic development.

While the core of economic development or modern economic growth (in Kuznets terms) is primarily the transformation of the economy, it also includes social change. With the structural transformation of the economy, alternative productive sectors are developed which generate income-earning opportunities for an increasing share of the population, making use of their capabilities and human capital. Paired with technological development and increasing productivity, this leads to sustainable government revenues that can be used as the basis for the development of a welfare state. Indeed, the government of Botswana has invested a significant share of diamond revenues in social development and the political system has matured. Nevertheless, we argue that in its most fundamental structure, the state in Botswana remains a gate-keeping state, albeit a development-oriented one, which has not been capable of launching inclusive strategies for broad-based socioeconomic development. Instead, we see the creation of a dual society with persistent poverty and inequality in the midst of plenty. In this respect, Botswana follows the expected pattern of a small economy dominated by a high-value natural resource.

This chapter starts with a theoretical discussion on the differences between economic growth and sustained development. We then move on to describe the initial conditions at the onset of the diamond economy, the effects these had on the management of diamond incomes, and the resulting diamond dependency. In the subsequent section we discuss the concept of the resource trap and show how Botswana is caught in such a trap. Next we examine the political, social, and economic aspects of Botswana's development-oriented gate-keeping state and we discuss through what mechanisms the lack of transformation has resulted in the development of a dual economy and society. In the last section we sum up and introduce the themes discussed in Chap. 6.

5.2 Technology, Sectorial Change, and Structural Transformation

The theoretical framework of Chap. 4 focused on institutions and geography/factor endowments as drivers of economic growth and these basic factors will continue to play an important role in our analysis. However, we now broaden the analysis to also include the issues of sustainability of growth from a structural change perspective. We use it to analyse what would be required for diamond incomes to be turned into sustained inclusive socioeconomic development. However, let us first consider the link between natural resource abundance and growth. The fact that Botswana has managed to turn its diamond resources into long-run growth is not an obvious outcome. Many natural resource-rich developing countries have failed to use their resources productively, and have often displayed rather poor growth performances (Sachs & Warner, 1995). This might seem surprising given that resource abundance in theory constitutes a factor conducive to growth as natural resources represent valuable assets to economies in addition to labour and capital, and when traded they generate wealth for the economy. However, when poorly managed, resources do not provide such a wealth windfall.

Therefore, the quality of institutions is often considered the link between resource abundance and subsequent economic growth. When institutions are good and resources are managed well, they can broadly benefit the economy. Conversely, when institutional quality is low, the abundance of resources often give rise to rent-seeking activities leading to political instability with low levels of economic growth or even crisis and collapse (Auty, 2001; Gylfason, Herbertsson, & Zoega, 1999; Leite & Weidmann, 1999; Sachs & Warner, 1999; van der Ploeg, 2011). Botswana is commonly hailed for its high institutional quality and good management of diamond resources. Nevertheless, as will be discussed below, despite some efforts the Botswana government has not managed to use revenues from these resources to stimulate technological and sectorial change for the purpose of achieving a diversification of the economy. Hence, even though there has been political stability and a good management of diamond resources, this has not been enough to achieve a structural transformation of the economy and sustained economic growth (Hillbom, 2008, 2014).

In his seminal paper from 1973, Kuznets argued that modern economic growth marks a distinct economic epoch of sustained and inclusive growth and development. Sustained economic growth can be distinguished from premodern, or preindustrial, growth based on six characteristics: (1) high rates of economic growth per capita paired with high population growth; (2) high rates of productivity growth; (3) structural transformation of the economy; (4) rapid changes in social and ideological structures; (5) participation in a globalized economy; and (6) a minimum level of modern technology. Growth thus comes from the development of new sectors with modern technology and increasing labour productivity. What Kuznets was trying to capture was of course a stylized description of industrialization, but his ideas could be applied more generally to diversification into any alternative sectors with higher labour productivity.

While modern economic growth requires a new economic structure, it also commonly contains the continuation of old trends, although in an accelerated form. This makes the identification and analysis of the structural break between the premodern and the modern complicated. Initial efforts such as an encouraging infant industry may well make up a potential starting point of industrialization and modernization of the economy. However, it is not until some time has passed that one is able to determine whether the change has been broad and inclusive enough to gain its own momentum and become sustainable. Depending on its causes and characteristics, different growth periods can be more or less likely to stimulate such processes of structural change. Consequently, many growth periods and development efforts can offer a window of opportunity, but whether or not they are followed by structural change is another matter. Botswana's diamond-led growth is a prominent example of a growth period providing an opportunity for sustained growth by generating revenues to be invested in diversification and technological development. However, diversification has not yet taken off and the economy remains trapped in consistent premodern growth (Hillbom, 2008, 2014).

From the discussion above, it seems that structural transformation processes all have certain uniform traits. At the same time, there are several different pathways within the process itself. Building on Kuznets, Adelman and Morris (1997) argue that all processes of economic development are multifaceted and non-linear. There are many possible development trajectories that economies can go through while still sharing a common end goal. In their categorization, Botswana falls into a typology of agricultural, primary export-oriented, sharply dualistic, and land-abundant countries. Within this group the characteristics of existing natural resource endowments and degrees of government autonomy from tribal domestic elites and colonial powers determine patterns and sequence of structural change. In this chapter we will identify these legacies, both precolonial and colonial.

Technological change leading to increasing labour productivity is the key to sustained growth. While Kuznets (1955, 1973) envisioned technological progress in industry and agriculture, today we can also include the new opportunities of the service sector, primarily through digitalization (Milanovic, 2016). Applicable to all of the three overarching sectors, Lewis (1954, 1979) theorized about the importance of the movement of labour from low- to high-productivity sectors. He stipulated as his starting point a closed economy where the population is large relative to natural resources and capital, and due to low levels of technology, seasonality, and so on, there is an unlimited supply of labour. As this labour leaves the subsistence sector where the marginal productivity is negligible, zero, or even negative and moves into the capitalist sector with significantly higher productivity, structural change and economic modernization are realized. The industrialization process is at the heart of the capitalist sector, but it also includes capitalist agriculture and Lewis was concerned with raising agricultural productivity in order to prevent the creation of a dual economy. Today we also add the service sector to the original model.

The core of sustainable growth is then a development of numerous sectors with high labour productivity and employment absorption capacity. It is desirable at the macroeconomic level because diversification and efficiency enhancement make the economy less vulnerable to external shocks and increasing employment opportunities enable a large section of society to participate. With the involvement of different sectors a broad-based cumulative process of inclusive growth and structural transformation is achieved. In this process there are ways for the state to shape or guide development efforts to be more or less inclusive or equitable. It can be via political and economic institutional structures developed to stimulate and guide the diversification process, or through the creation of social security for the most vulnerable in society (Piketty, 2014). As economic growth raises income levels, a modernized institutional structure can stimulate broad improvements in living conditions for the broader segments of society via the redistribution of resources and incomes. An alternative way of expressing it is that inclusive economic development is by its very nature incompatible with Lewis dual economy where only a limited modern sector benefits from the expansion of the economy. Based on the above categorization of inclusive economic development it is possible to claim that the goal of economic progress is broad-based social development.

With the demanding definition outlined above there is only a limited group consisting primarily of Pacific Asian countries that have transformed into developed economies since World War II. For the African continent, we add Mauritius to this category claiming that the country has come far in achieving sectorial change and modern economic growth, albeit it is not yet a high-income country with a developed welfare state (Meisenhelder, 1997; World Bank, 2017). Even if the bottleneck for joining the group of countries that have achieved economic development is narrow, it is an important lesson from the last 50 years that economic development for developing countries is possible (Adelman, 2003). In a few decades we will be able to add several more countries to our list, but we question if Botswana will be one of them.

5.3 Initial Conditions and Governance

As discussed in depth in Chap. 4, geography and factor endowments have played a decisive role for Botswana's growth trajectory. The most obvious resource in this respect has been the abundance of diamonds. It is difficult to imagine that the growth miracle could have happened without the discovery of diamonds, a natural resource that has turned out to be advantageous in several ways. First, diamonds are extremely valuable and therefore they can constitute the basis for substantial economic growth. Further, they are easily storable as they do not perish and do not take up space. This means that if you have the financial management to build an economic buffer you can at low costs hold back exports in times of low world market prices and then re-enter the market as prices go up again. Third, with a high value per weight unit diamonds are cheap to transport, removing the disadvantage Botswana has as a landlocked country. Finally, they are exported to the global market, nullifying any negative effects of overwhelming regional competition like the one Botswana has had in relation to South Africa. On the global market there is also a long-term consistent high demand and consequently few and short-lived slumps in prices (Hillbom, 2008, 2014).

All diamond producers share the above-mentioned potential advantages, but in the case of Botswana there is another important geographic advantage that makes the extraction of its diamonds different than the extraction of so-called blood diamonds in, for example, Liberia and Sierra Leone. Diamond resources in Botswana are located in the ground and can only be extracted through deep mining requiring large-scale investments. In West Africa, diamonds are found in the surface layers and can be washed from riverbeds thereby becoming an open access for any interested party to extract using basic technology, something that invites conflict between agents. The placement of Botswana's diamond resources has meant that extraction has been in the hands of the state in its capacity of being one of very few players that have had the financial resources to set up the deep mining endeavours.

This specific setup of the mining activities and the central role in the extraction of diamonds played by the government leads us to discuss the quality of state institutions, that is, if the state is capable of managing the advantageous initial conditions or not. The standard explanation for Botswana's successful management of incomes from its diamonds has some compulsory elements. First, there is the 50–50 partnership with the South African mining company De Beers that led to the creation of the jointly owned company Debswana in 1969. Through this partnership, the government has both extracted diamonds wisely and secured significant incomes for the country.

Second, the government has shown great prudence in the management of diamond incomes keeping expenses consistent in boom years in the global market and even building up foreign exchange reserves, thereby being able to compensate for years with declining prices. This strategy combined with proper management of the exchange rate has also meant that real exchange rate appreciations have been under control, which has been positive for the export sector. Through fiscal policies, the government has avoided external debt problems and has maintained a stable growth rate over time (Hill, 1991). There is a consensus on the shrewdness of the government, both in building international reserves and in using its diamond revenues for investments in key sectors such as infrastructure, education, and health care.

Third, and in some sense being the precondition for the two first, the institutional framework is regarded to be of overall high quality. In terms of accountability of the government, regulatory quality, and government effectiveness, Botswana is at similar levels as various OECD countries. In terms of political stability and control of corruption, the country features in the top group worldwide (Worldwide Governance Indicators, 2016). Some scholars trace the roots to these good contemporary political institutions back to precolonial structures, particularly the *kgotla* system (see Chap. 2) (Acemoglu et al., 2003; Acemoglu & Robinson, 2010; Robinson & Parsons, 2006). These precolonial institutions allegedly created a tradition of openness, accountability, and dialogue between the citizens and their leaders, laying the foundation for the good quality of today's political institutions.

Finally, in an African comparison Botswana's leaders have been regarded as honest and with the first president, Sir Seretse Khama, at the forefront the 'wise leaders explanation' is a common one (Masire, 2006). It is, however, also an explanation that appears to have been more appropriate for the time period close to independence, but less so for the last couple of decades. Makgala (2006), for example, points out that while elite corruption was rare until the 1990s it has since become increasingly common. Indeed, even though the control of corruption is still perceived as very high and among the world's best, the performance in this area has been deteriorating slowly (Worldwide Governance Indicators, 2016).

With advantageous initial conditions and good financial management of diamond incomes, it is no surprise that diamonds have dominated the economy. As shown in Fig. 5.1, the mining sector has under our current period of investigation contributed considerably to the national economy and government revenues. Diamonds have contributed, on average, around 50 per cent of the total GDP from 1975 until the 2010, although with the relative growth of the service sector, mining now contributes a little over 30 per cent of GDP. Additionally, 85 per cent of contemporary export incomes and 50 per cent of government revenues are generated by the diamond sector (Bank of Botswana, 2014; Republic of Botswana, 2003, p. 28: Table 3.1, 205: Table 11.1, 206: Table 11.3; World Bank, 2017). With these figures the long-term diamond dependency is confirmed beyond any doubt.

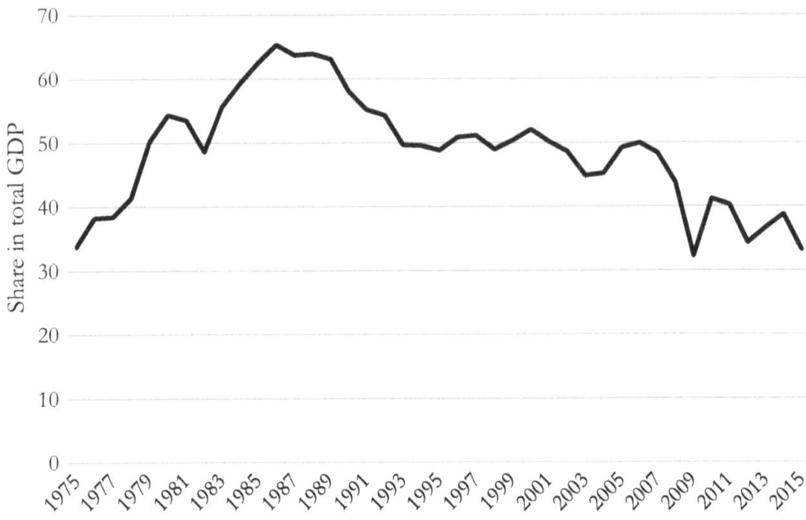

Fig. 5.1 Share of the mining sector in total GDP, 1975–2015. Source: World Bank (2010); Timmer et al. (2015)

5.4 The Natural Resource Trap

Taking advantage of one's natural resources for securing export revenues has been a common strategy for many countries and the role of natural resources typically increases with the value of the resources. Hence, there are many economies in the world that are completely dominated by point-source resources such as oil, gas, and diamonds, or valuable agricultural produce such as cocoa. As revenues from such exports raises wealth and purchasing power, this allows for increasing imports and investments in modern technology and human capital as well as in alternative productive sectors. Such developments could stimulate the rise of various productive economic sectors as well as raise overall labour productivity. While some countries have managed to use the export-led growth based on valuable natural resources to instigate endogenous growth, others appear to be caught with vulnerable economies dominated by natural resources. Many of those have even experienced paradoxical economic stagnation or crisis in the midst of natural resource abundance. Just as the long-term outcome of agricultural transformation is the decline of the agricultural sector in relative terms (Timmer, 2009), natural resource-based transformation requires that other sectors take over as drivers of the economy from valuable natural resources. The temptation is strong, however, to stay with the goose laying the golden egg and it is challenging to motivate investments away from the economy's most profitable sector.

5.4.1 Crowding Out and Institutional Quality

When natural resources start to hinder growth instead of boosting it, the abundance of natural resources can become a hindrance for economic development instead of an opportunity. In Botswana, for example, the dominance of diamonds has resulted in a crowding out of industrialization efforts. This effect was first described in the case of the discovery of natural gas in the Netherlands in 1959; hence it has been named the 'Dutch Disease'. The basic mechanisms of these processes are that as an economy starts exporting valuable natural resources, foreign exchange starts flowing in leading to a higher demand for domestic currency. Without intervention, this results in the appreciation of the domestic currency, making the country less competitive on the export markets. The loss of competiveness leads to lower sales and shrinking export sectors, causing a loss of economic activities in other sectors than the natural resource sector, hence deindustrialization. Because the Dutch Disease concept is originally based on the experience of an already industrialized economy, it is commonly used to describe the crowding out of existing industrial sectors. In the case of Botswana, however, there never existed a proper industrial sector which could be undermined and therefore the crowding out is more accurately related to potential industrialization efforts that were never realised. Nevertheless, the basic mechanisms have been the same and due to them, Botswana, just as many other developing countries, has ended up in a situation wherein the high revenues from the natural resource sector in combination with the loss of competitiveness have hindered incentives to start industrialization efforts instead of fuelling them.

Around the world and throughout history we can find a great variation in how different countries have handled the challenges of combining the abundance of valuable natural resources with the sustainment of alternative productive sectors. There exist various examples of countries that have experienced both natural resource abundance and export dependency without the crowding out of other sectors. For example, while Norway's discovery of abundant oil resources in the 1970s and the subsequent 40 years of oil extraction have constituted the basis for the country becoming one of the richtes countries in the world, other productive sectors have simultaneously been developed and the economy has diversified (Gylfason, 2001).

Meanwhile, other countries have instead experienced economic crisis and collapse in the midst of exploiting and exporting their abundant resources. When the crisis has developed into extreme cases of crowding out and there is more or less a collapse of the economy as a whole, the situation has even been termed a 'natural resource curse'. An example of such a curse is Nigeria when the country in the middle of the oil crises in the 1970s, when most oil producers secured significant export revenues, managed to combine being a major oil exporter with having a severe economic crisis (van der Ploeg, 2011). What sets the success stories and the failures apart appears to be their institutional quality. Consequently, this aspect has been given a prominent place in any natural resource curse analysis. Taking it to its extreme, it could be argued that the resource curse is only present in countries with high value resources and poor institutional quality (Brunnschweiler, 2008; Brunnschweiler & Bulte, 2008; van der Ploeg, 2011).

Botswana's half-century of independent rule characterized by exceptional economic growth, significant social development, and political stability would not have been possible without good institutional quality. It is clear that the state has been capable of developing a rule of law including secure property rights as well as a high regulatory quality while keeping levels of corruption modest. High institutional quality is therefore often mentioned as the key explanation for Botswana's growth miracle. The claim is also often made that the origin of this good institutional quality is to be found in precolonial institutional structures and that colonial influence, potentially corrupting these structures, was limited. Specifically it is the tradition of public meetings, so-called *kgotla* meetings, where all male Tswana members in the community had the opportunity to be heard by the chief as well as institutionalized negotiations between the traditional elite and their subjects that are commonly hailed as the basis for political stability, accountability, and social development (Acemoglu et al., 2003; Acemoglu & Robinson, 2010; Masire, 2006; Robinson & Parsons, 2006). To fully appreciate what has safeguarded Botswana from becoming the victim of the natural resource curse we should, however, emphasize the broader explanations instead of focusing on the phenomenon of the *kgotla* specifically. At the structural level it is the initial cultural homogeneity of the population together with the overall precolonial Tswana tradition of centralized governance and state capacity, which we discuss in Chap. 3, that has been an important basis for developing lasting and stable political institutions.

That being said, we need to remember that there is also well-founded critique against the institutional structure of the Botswana state in regard to elite capturing, high levels of inequality, discrimination against minorities, inability to battle the HIV/AIDS epidemic, and passivation of the poor. (For this literature, see, e.g. Allen & Heald, 2004; Good, 1993; Gulbrandsen, 1996; Heald, 2005; Hillbom, 2008; Lekoko & van der Merwe, 2006; Makgala, 2006; Nthomang, 2004; Phaladze & Tlou, 2006.) We will return to and elaborate further on these aspects of the success story as we discuss the development-oriented gate-keeping state in the following section and in Chap. 6, where we focus on long-term trends of inequality. For now, however, we focus on the more narrow issue of the management of the diamond resources and in this regard the government has shown great prudency and political institutions have served this purpose well.

The prudent management of diamond incomes does not, however, erase the challenge inherent in the economy having a dominating and lucrative tradable natural resource sector that is supporting a growing non-tradable service sector while the tradable manufacturing sector is relatively economically weak (World Bank, 2017). The greater the income from natural resource exports the higher the demands for the non-tradable sector leaving less capital and labour available for the manufacturing sector (Corden & Neary, 1982; Iimi, 2006, p. 5). As already mentioned, what sets Botswana apart from the typical Dutch Disease syndrome is the fact that manufacturing has never taken off, neither during colonial nor during independence eras, and, consequently, there was nothing to be ruined with a reallocation of capital and labour to other sectors. However, the wealth of the diamond sector limited incentives and opportunities for diversification and development of manufacturing. The prevention of industrialization efforts in the midst of successful natural resource-led growth is central for our claim that Botswana currently is caught in a so called "natural resource trap". The term has previously been used by other scholars, for example, Collier (2008), and in our argument it signifies the inability of Botswana to diversify its economy and break out of the profitable natural resource dependency.

Summing up, it appears that, while being the 18th largest resource exporter in the world (Iimi, 2006, p. 6), Botswana has managed to avoid the natural resource curse in the sense of civil conflict, authoritarianism, and rent seeking. The explanations for this are found in a tradition of well-functioning political institutions that cater for a sound long-term plan for the extraction of natural resources and good policies for continued national growth (Hill, 1991; Iimi, 2006). This achievement makes Botswana a member of a very exclusive group of developing countries (Sachs & Warner, 1995). Meanwhile, the country is demonstrating the characteristics of both natural resource abundance and export dependency. As long as diamonds continue to dominate government revenues there are few incentives for diversified industrialization and the development of alternative productive sectors.

5.4.2 Challenges of Diversification

As we saw in Chap. 4, Botswana's both growth periods have been driven by the exploitation of single natural resources and throughout the economy has consistently been a mono-product natural resource-dependent economy with a lack of diversification. So far, limited industrial growth has primarily been driven by the post-independence expansion of the mining sector, that is, diamond production. This is what can be expected based on existing scholarly literature telling us that in a small economy dominated by a high-value natural resource there are generally few linkages to other productive sectors or to the economy at large (Auty, 2001; Hirschman, 1958). Botswana and its diamond wealth constitute a very clear example of how resource dependency often reduces incentives to diversify, thereby hindering sustainable economic development. Until a few years back, diamonds were only exported unprocessed, but today there is an infant cutting industry establishing itself. Nonetheless, mining has of yet not contributed to any significant technological advances in the wider economy outside the sector itself.

Further, diamond production engages only a small workforce of roughly 8,000 paid employees, which corresponds to around 2 per cent of the total labour force. Overall, the growth miracle has never provided any substantial employment opportunities (Gaolathe, 1997; Republic of Botswana, 2004, p. 24: Table 2.1; World Bank 2014). Table 5.1 shows the shares of the population working in the three main sectors of the economy: agriculture, industry, and services. In 1975, at the start of our period of investigation in this chapter, income opportunities were still mainly to be found in the agricultural sector and they consisted primarily of self-employment, but formal employment in the service sector was increasing. Especially government services and community and personal

Table 5.1 Percentage of total employment in agriculture, industry, and service

	1975% (share)	1985% (share)	1995% (share)	2005% (share)	2010% (share)
Agriculture	68	54	39	39	38
Mining	3	4	3	2	2
Manufacturing	2	2	6	6	6
Utilities	0	1	1	1	1
Construction	4	5	8	5	3
Industry	9	12	18	14	12
Trade, transport finance	4	6	12	17	22
Finance	1	2	5	5	7
Government services	9	14	18	19	17
Community and personal services	9	11	7	5	4
Services	23	34	42	47	50

Sources: Timmer et al. (2015)

services provided employment opportunities in the mid 1970s. Over the years services has taken over as the main sector for employment with continuous growth in government and trade. Agriculture is now in second place. However, both agriculture and the traditional services like government services and trade are generally characterized by low labour productivity, only generating limited economic growth (McMillan et al., 2014). As discussed also in Chap. 4, the development of labour-intensive manufacturing activities or manufacturing activities in general have been lacking throughout the history of Botswana. Within the industrial sector, manufacturing activities actually generate half of the jobs within the sector, and yet only 6 per cent of the population is working in manufacturing.

When it comes to expanding beyond the traditional and well-established sectors, and away from natural resource dependency, Botswana has exposed itself as resembling other African countries, from which it is generally set apart (Hillbom, 2008). Efforts have been made to identify explanations for Botswana's paradox of having successful macroeconomic management coexisting with government failure to implement policy instigating private sector development. The puzzle is even more interesting as the government from the start of the independence era has signalled its awareness of the importance of diversification. Over the years a number of schemes to support entrepreneurial activities have been launched. The National Development Bank (NDB) was established in 1965 to provide loans to small-scale entrepreneurs in general and within the agricultural sector in particular. Botswana Development Corporation (BDC) was a venture capital company set up in 1970 to further complement the commercial banks. Both banks were owned 100 per cent by the Botswana government. The most high-profile incentive programme was the Financial Assistance Policy (FAP) running 1982–2001, which was projected to promote and expand employment-intensive and non-traditional businesses. Unfortunately, these and other government schemes aimed at encouraging private entrepreneurship became subject to increasing abuse by both government employers and recipients, and subsequently they failed to meet with initial expectations (Leith, 2005). In an effort to explain their failure Conteh (2008) claimed that the policy programmes of the last decades of the twentieth and early years of the twenty-first century had been far too fragmented and, in some cases, even contradictory. There has, simply, been a lack of an overarching ambition and a comprehensive, consistent strategy from the government.

A recent effort was the launching of the Economic Diversification Drive (EDD) running over the years 2011–2016. With this policy intervention the government recognized the continued challenges with diversifying the economy generally and particularly developing the private sector. The short-term strategy was that the state would actively support actors within the private sector to target specific sectors within local production and consumption, thereby achieving quick wins through the harvesting of low-hanging fruits. In the medium and long term the strategy was aimed to promote diversification of the economy by encouraging the development of globally competitive enterprises in need of limited or no concrete support by the state. Again, the focus was on the private sector developing goods and services that constituted an alternative to mining, and it was envisaged that the cumulative growth of the private sector would breed a culture of entrepreneurship (Botswana Government, 2011). As of now, there are no indications of significant results from this strategy, but we will have to wait before we can judge what will be the long-term outcome.

Finally, we move away from efforts relating to the supply side, that is, the encouragement of entrepreneurial initiatives to start new businesses, and instead turn towards the demand side. What could be said about opportunities for demand-driven manufacturing constituting a basis for a diversification of the economy? If incomes grow substantially, consumption and investment increase as a result. This could lead to higher demand for domestically produced goods resulting in diversification and potentially sustained growth. To what extent can we expect such a development to take place in Botswana? To answer this question we have to consider poverty and living standards during the diamond economy. First, during the whole independence era there has been an increase in estimated GDP per capita of roughly 1,300 dollars to over 15,000 dollars in 2016 (PPP, 2011 dollars). Poverty levels have declined from 59 per cent in 1986 to 19 per cent in 2012 (World Bank, 2017). In Chap. 4, we also discussed the overall increase in wage levels during the diamond economy. Taken together this means that there has been an impressive increase in standards of living and the ability to consume. However, there are as of yet few signs that these opportunities have benefitted domestic production.

With a population as small as that of Botswana (2.3 million) and the country's overall modest levels of incomes and continued substantial levels of poverty, the domestic market for basic consumption goods such as processed food, textiles, and domestic utensils remains limited. Broadening the scope, it has to be recognized that regional competition constitutes an additional real challenge for the manufacturing sector and the persistence of the natural resource trap. Being the neighbour of South Africa, Africa's primary industrial economy, Botswana's domestic production has consistently been under heavy pressure from foreign competition and processed foods and manufactured goods are primarily imported. While this presents a real hindrance for the development of alternative productive sectors, we do not believe that it rules out all opportunities for diversification in terms of, for example, developing processing industries in relation to natural resource extraction, that is, agriculture and mining, or local manufacturing. In addition, an increasing number of developing countries are taking advantage of the technical revolution in digitalization offering capitalist services such as call centres and banking services and this alternative holds the advantage of reducing Botswana's challenges of being land locked.

We find that a compelling explanation for the continued natural resource dependency can be found in the consistency in the political and economic elite. During the diamond economy the cattle-holding elites and their associates have in addition to controlling the traditional authorities also increased their hold on the independence government, including being connected to the leading bureaucrats (Good, 1994, p. 499; Good & Taylor, 2008). Their income basis broadened from relying on beef exports to also profiting from diamond revenues. For almost a century there has been a lack of committed strategies to encourage the private sector and flawed attempts to diversify the economy. Instead the government sector has dominated the economy and in the last couple of decades it has become exposed to an increasing degree of elite capturing (Hillbom, 2008, 2012; Makgala, 2006). Despite this critique it should be emphasized that current leaders have been brought up in a tradition of accountability and prudent economic management and so far they have preserved a mostly well-functioning political institutional structure.

5.5 The Development-Oriented Gate-Keeping State

Throughout the post-World War II era we have seen an ongoing debate on the potential success as well as the distortion due to state-led development efforts. The discussion has come in many shapes and forms. Some such as Gerschenkron's (1962) theories on catch-up processes, Myrdal's arguments for a strong state-led development in *Asian Drama* (1968), and Sachs' (2005) call for an end to poverty in our time have argued for top-down solutions. At the other end of the scale we find examples such as Hayek's (1944) conviction of the need for bottom-up change and Easterly's (2014) recent protest against the tyranny of experts. Whichever side you take in these debates it is clear that the role the state takes on in development processes is imperative for the shaping of the development process. Arguably, it also dictates the outcome.

Since the 1930s until the present, Botswana's economic growth has depended on government revenues from monopolized natural resource exports, first cattle and then diamonds, and a consequence of the dominance of the state's economic activities has been that development efforts have primarily been state-led. Potentially by indirect necessity rather than by direct choice, economic policies have followed a liberal tradition of promoting openness and market orientation. In Chap. 3 we introduced the argument that the colonial era saw the establishment of the gate-keeping state. Its policies lay behind the establishment of the cattle export sector and thereby it instigated the first export-led growth spurt. While some have characterized the Botswana state after independence as a developmental state (Mbabazi & Taylor, 2005; Meisenhelder, 1997; Mkandawire, 2001), we instead claim that the gate-keeping state structures have persisted, albeit there have been significant efforts to provide basic needs and social development to the majority of its citizens (Hillbom, 2012).

With all its benevolent intentions the outcome of this development-oriented gate-keeping state is that for all intents and purposes, the Botswana of today is a dual economy and society in Lewis' (1955) characterization. The basic explanation for this situation is the same as the one for the lack of sustained growth—the inability to break away from the dependency on an extremely valuable natural resource such as diamonds to instead instigate sectorial change and inclusive development, especially the establishment of labour-intensive and labour-productive wage sectors offering employment. Duality is then not a sign of the failure of the gate-keeping state per se, but the failure to get rid of the gate-keeping state structures and exchange it for a more inclusive development process. This duality contains political, economic, and social aspects, and we will discuss them one by one starting with the political aspects as they set the scene for economic and social development.

5.5.1 Political Aspects

In Chaps. 2 and 3 we argued that while the early colonial period saw limited colonial influence, there is cause to talk of colonial legacies as the development of the cattle export sector in the later colonial period has had a significant and lasting impact. Throughout the period of British rule Bechuanaland stayed a peasant colony, where modest European presence combined with colonial investments aimed at further developing the cattle sector primarily benefitted the Tswana cattle elite. The Indirect Rule system left the indigenous elite in charge of administrating the respective *merafe* throughout the colonial era, thereby reinforcing their political power, and as large-scale cattle holders they gained substantial incomes from the cattle export sector. When the time came for independence, the British intentionally transferred political control over the new nation into the hands of the elite by appointing its members to leading positions and supporting their political ambitions. The history of how the economic and political elite stayed one and the same and the path dependency in the political leadership and social structures of the precolonial, colonial, and postcolonial periods are well documented and uncontested (see, e.g. Acemoglu et al., 2003; Colclough & McCarthy, 1980, chapter 1; Good, 1993; Good & Taylor, 2008; Peters, 1994; Wylie, 1990).

Through tribal organizations and in cooperation with the British administration, the Tswana elite was actively involved in suggesting and executing development efforts in the Protectorate during the late colonial period. When the time came to prepare for independence in the early 1960s, the British supported the Botswana Democratic Party (BDP) because they deemed their leaders that were themselves large-scale cattle holders, most likely to continue colonial policies supporting the livestock sector. This included the future presidents Sir Seretse Khama and Quett Masire. The peaceful transition of power to the independence government was conducted with the explicit ambition to ensure political stability and continuity in economic policies, to cement existing social structures, and to hinder radical political elements (Good & Taylor, 2008). Considering that the BDP has won every election since 1965 and the government has stayed true to a Western-style capitalist economic system centred on management of diamonds and supporting the livestock sector, it is clear that these ambitions were successful.

Following the British tradition, Botswana uses a first-past-the-post electoral system where the party with the most representatives at the constituency level also controls parliament. While the BDP has stayed in power, its political dominance has been increasingly challenged and the share of competitive constituencies has consistently increased. With the diamond incomes allowing for investments in social development the BDP has stayed popular, but another explanation for continuity is that the opposition has found it hard to organize itself. After independence the more radical Botswana People's Party (BPP) increasingly lost influence, and from the 1980s into the 1990s the opposition consolidated behind the Botswana National Front (BNF). In 1998 the BNF, however, imploded, resulting in the additional creation of the Botswana Congress Party (BCP). With economic and social change over the decades the composition of the opposition's voters has changed. When the country was still primarily agrarian, opposition came from the limited urban centres, some tribal leaders, and non-Tswana groups. With increasing urbanization as well as the development of the mining and service sectors the opposition has found new and increasing support in the growing groups of urban dwellers, the more educated middle classes and the struggling private sector (Poteete, 2012). With the BDP maintaining a strong connection to the old elites and the rural areas it is linking the large-scale cattle holders to both the agricultural/cattle sector in general and the state institutions and bureaucracy managing the country's diamond revenues (Good, 1994). Meanwhile, groups representing alternative economic interests to cattle and diamonds are still waiting to rule the country.

Some scholars have argued that continuity in political leadership and the harmonizing between political and economic interests has been advantageous, or even a primary explanation for the economic success, as it has ensured political stability and consensus around development strategies (Acemoglu et al., 2003; Masire, 2006). Located in a region containing many examples of dictatorship, civil wars, and other types of political unrest, Botswana has stood out, because of both the peacefulness characterizing the independence era and the democratic system in the form of open multiparty elections. It has also been pointed out that the BDP's consistency in gaining a majority in parliament has allowed for the party to launch long-term pro-growth strategies (Poteete, 2009b). For others the elitist top-down structure of the government is a sign of Botswana never developing beyond being a minimalist democracy (Good & Taylor, 2008). The elitist structure is not only about the ruling party, but also about the position of the president himself. Since the late 1990s increasing power has been invested in the presidency and there are growing numbers of reports of authoritarianism and presidentialism coming from within BDP, the opposition parties, labour unions, and the media. This increasing authoritarianism has made it even harder for alternative forces to influence government policies (Good & Taylor, 2008; Makgala, 2006; Poteete, 2009a).

The potentially most interesting and important political break with the old order during independence has been the transfer of political power and natural resources from tribal to state institutions. This includes the transfer of administration of land, nationalization of mineral resources, and subordination of tribal authorities. The reforms were championed by Sir Seretse Khama and part of his conscious nation-building strategies. Especially the decision to give the government rather than the *mefare* control over mineral resources turned out to be decisive both for the management of the growth miracle and for opportunities to use diamond incomes for nationwide social development. In the current constitution eight distinct Tswana *merafe* are recognized. While each one is directly represented by its *kgosi* in the House of Chiefs, an advisory body to the parliament, they are no longer autonomous but incorporated into the centralized state. In addition to restricting the influence of the *merafe* the government has generally promoted ethnical and racial neutral policies providing rural development, infrastructure, health care, and schooling to some extent to all Batswana citizens (Poteete, 2009a).

The theory on modern economic growth implies that growth should lead to shifts in the economic position of various groups attached to particular production sectors. Hence, that old economic elites have to be challenged and transformed or replaced in order for new production sectors to appear, together signifying a break with old economic and social structures (Kuznets, 1973). We argue that in Botswana the status quo remained which allowed the political and economic elite to build socio-economic systems protecting their own financial interests in the form of continued support to the cattle and diamond sectors rather than investing in sectorial change. Lack of political change and continuity in elites have also resulted in limiting government efforts to restrict inequality through taxation and transfers of resources. From a structural perspective the colonial gate-keeping state lives on with new leaders at the realm. While they have proved to be 'development oriented' in the sense that they have managed growth and provided social development they are not motivated to initiate the break with existing economic, social, and political structures needed to achieve inclusive and sustainable economic development (Hillbom, 2008, 2012). In a situation such as this, elites acting to promote their own self-interest is only what can be expected (Kaufmann & Kraay, 2002).

5.5.2 Economic Aspects

In the spirit of structural economists such as Kuznets and Lewis, growth is primarily valued not because it further enriches the already well-off, but because it gives an opportunity to significantly and lastingly transform the economy to ensure continued sustained growth. This allows for improved standards of living for the majority, including the poor. For a country to achieve the characteristics of economic development it is a requirement that poverty is alleviated, income levels are considerably improved, and resources and opportunities are more equally distributed by a modern state in order for all segments of society to benefit and contribute (Adelman, 2003, pp. 17–18). Such an inclusive process is not possible only through government transfers to those in need, but it also requires increased labour productivity and employment opportunities that come with modern economic growth. Unequal distribution of resources and incomes and a dual economy with discriminated sectors and groups are then part of a definition of a society prior to modern economic growth.

Overall, the sub-Sahara African region is hard hit by prevailing poverty. World Bank data show that in 2012, 42.4 per cent of its population was living in extreme poverty defined as less than US$1.90 per day, which is much higher than the world's average of 14.9 per cent (World Bank, 2017). In Botswana there has been both a trickling down from the wealthier segments of society and a political consciousness regarding the need to fight high poverty rates. As a consequence, poverty in terms of income levels have been significantly improved from 59 per cent of individuals living below the national poverty line in 1985 (Jefferis, 1997, p. 484: Table 2) to 19 per cent in 2012 (World Bank, 2017). Notwithstanding, there have also been reports of prevailing and even increasing rural poverty, at least in certain parts of the country (see, e.g. Gulbrandsen, 1996; Wikan, 2004).

Botswana's poverty reduction may stand out in a regional context, but from a critical perspective it opens up for two comments: First, it is less impressive if we relate it to the diamond-led growth miracle and substantial improvements in GDP per capita. In Mauritius, the other

African growth miracle, less than 5 per cent of the population lives under the global poverty line of US$1.90 a day. This is substantially less than the approximately 20 per cent of poor in Botswana today. Second, attitudes towards inequalities and poverty are rooted in normative values and distribution of resources and incomes are subject to conscious government policies. Government policy on distribution of wealth in Botswana has mainly been the equivalent of a basic needs approach, giving support to the poor via food-for-work programmes that have been running during droughts since 1965 (Colclough & McCarthy, 1980, p. 133; Lekoko & van der Merwe, 2006; Nthomang, 2004) as well as providing health care and education free of charge until recently. While these transfers are applaudable we claim that a diversification of the economy and development of labour-intensive sectors offering employment paired with increasing salaries based on improved labour productivity would have a more radical effect on poverty reduction. In essence, the latter type of poverty reduction is the pathway of Mauritius.

At the core of the duality is the divide between the modern urban sector and the underdeveloped rural areas. In many African countries rural development is taking on a much broader role than agricultural growth as a majority of smallholders are net consumers of agricultural products and diversify their incomes into off-farming and non-farming. In the stagnating rural areas in Botswana, however, agriculture still constitutes the main opportunity to secure a living as there are few alternative economic activities. Regarding the agricultural sector, poverty is more a matter of access to resources than of income levels and since the smallholders are mainly subsistence farmers their standards of living may be difficult to estimate. A minimal access to resources is generally guaranteed within the traditional property rights systems where key resources such as water and land have a strong public goods dimension (Carlsson, 2003, pp. 101–107). Nevertheless, the Tswana farmers are vulnerable and prone to poverty due to vulnarable climatic and soil conditions and recurring droughts. This weakness of the agricultural sector has implications for poverty reduction on a national level. As discussed in Chap. 4, roughly 40 per cent of the labour force is currently found in agriculture, but some studies estimate that the traditional agriculture is only able to support a quarter of the labour force. This means that people currently engaged in traditional subsistence farming are underemployed. In order to reduce poverty there is pressure on other sectors to offer employment and labour incomes (Jefferis, 1997; World Bank, 2017). While internal migrants in Botswana appear to maintain their contacts with their home-based households and urban to rural remittances have constituted a welcome addition to rural households, remittances have not had a significant effect on the ability of rural households to maintain a reasonable standard of living (Campbell, 2010).

Meanwhile, the wealthiest segments of society have claimed most of the economy's incomes. The richest 10 per cent of society earned more than 40 per cent of total incomes up until the turn of the twenty-first century (World Bank, 2017). After that, it declined somewhat to around 35 per cent. A widening divide between the richest and the poorest groups in society may in itself not be a severe reason for concern from a strictly economic point of view. Today we see increasing inequality in many developing countries such as the USA and Pacific Asian countries. These processes of increasing within-country income inequality in the rich part of the world are primarily driven by the stagnating incomes of the lower middle class and increasing incomes and wealth in the small group of the super-rich (Milanovic, 2016). The economies involved continue to be successful, although there are political consequences that lie outside the scope of our current discussion. What is disturbing in the case of Botswana is that the income divergence is combined with high unemployment, continued high poverty rates, and discrimination of certain groups, specifically the Basarwa (see, e.g. Curry, 1987; Good, 1993; Nthomang, 2004). Together this reflects an institutional inequality where government policies tend to favour elites in various ways while denying the majority of the population equal opportunities (Engerman & Sokoloff, 2002; World Bank, 2006, pp. 107–108). Contemporary inequalities appear to be inherent in the socioeconomic structure going back in history (see, e.g. Good, 1994, p. 205; Peters, 1994; Wylie, 1990) and in Chap. 6 we will elaborate more on long-term inequality trends.

5.5.3 Social Aspects

The spectacular diamond-led economic growth during the independence era has allowed for the Botswana government to put much effort into social development. It has spent as much as 40 per cent of GDP yearly on infrastructure and human capital (Acemoglu et al., 2003, p. 85; Leith, 2005, p. 85: Fig. 3.9). This has led to impressive results. In 1966, for example, there were only 12 kilometres of paved roads (Acemoglu et al., 2003, p. 80) while today this figure is around 9,000 kilometres. There are four international airports, 3.3 million mobile phones, 870,000 Internet users, and 96 per cent of the population has access to improved water sources (World Bank, 2017). The British considered education to be a tribal responsibility and at independence there were less than two dozen Batswana who had received university education and 100 who had completed secondary school (Acemoglu et al., 2003, pp. 80–83; Colclough & McCarthy, 1980, p. 28). Today adult literacy rates are 88 per cent and 23 per cent of the population has enrolled in tertiary education (World Bank, 2017).

While health indicators improved after independence due to government investments they have been severely negatively affected by the rampant HIV/AIDS epidemic that struck the country in the 1980s. Botswana is one of the worst hit countries in the world with a 22 per cent prevalence rate in the group of adults aged 15–49 (UNAIDS, 2017). In principle, these high numbers could be expected to be a serious obstacle to economic progress, but there is little evidence that HIV/AIDS has had a detrimental effect on diamond-led growth. The explanation lies in the fact that the diamond sector, the growth engine of the economy, employs a limited number of workers and as is indicated by the high 18 per cent unemployment rates, there is a significant excess of labour. While the societal costs and health expenses for the government have been high, growth has persisted (World Bank, 2017).

It is a paradox that a well-functioning state as the one in Botswana in spite of recognizing the epidemic at an early stage and starting programmes and emergency plans to control further spread already in the late 1980s, has been unsuccessful in its fight against HIV/AIDS. Much effort has been put into information and testing campaigns, encouraging the use of condoms, and so on. However, the necessary change of lifestyles and gender relations has not yet happened and the government is unable to meet its targeted 1 per cent incidence rate (Allen & Heald, 2004; Heald, 2006; Republic of Botswana, 2015). Notwithstanding, the spread of cheaper anti-retroviral medicines has managed to turn some of the negative trends from the 1990s and while life expectancy at birth fell from close to 63 in 1989 to 48 in 2001, it recovered to 64 years in 2014 (World Bank, 2017).

Duality is clearly demonstrated in the divide between the modern, wealthier urban areas relying on diamond incomes and the poor rural sector lacking agricultural development. Botswana has been urbanizing quickly for the last four decades and has moved from 4 per cent living in urban settlements at independence (Gulbrandsen, 1996, p. 19) to around 60 per cent presently (World Bank, 2017). Urbanization increased especially rapidly during the 1980s, the period when the diamond economy was at its height (see Chap. 4 and Fig. 5.1). Meanwhile, since the early 1990s a serious unemployment problem has been registered with rates hovering around 18 per cent since 2000 (World Bank, 2017). As long as the industry and service sectors are not expanding the figure will probably not improve significantly. Despite high urban unemployment rates, individuals continue to migrate to the urban areas (see Fig. 5.2).

Urbanization can be viewed as a sign of structural change, but although it entails a profound reorganization of the population and has implications for various aspects of human development, it is not per definition equal to growth of either the industrial or the capitalist sectors wherein high productivity is found. Lewis' (1954) original model is often misunderstood and quoted as an argument for economic development evolving around a process of labour moving from agriculture to industry and of industrialization equalling urbanization. However, the focus is actually on labour transfer from traditional/subsistence to capitalist sectors and any sector (agriculture, industry, and services) can become capitalist as long as there is technological change and sufficiently increasing labour productivity. Meanwhile, the subsistence sector is primarily associated with premodern agriculture, but it is a common feature in devel-

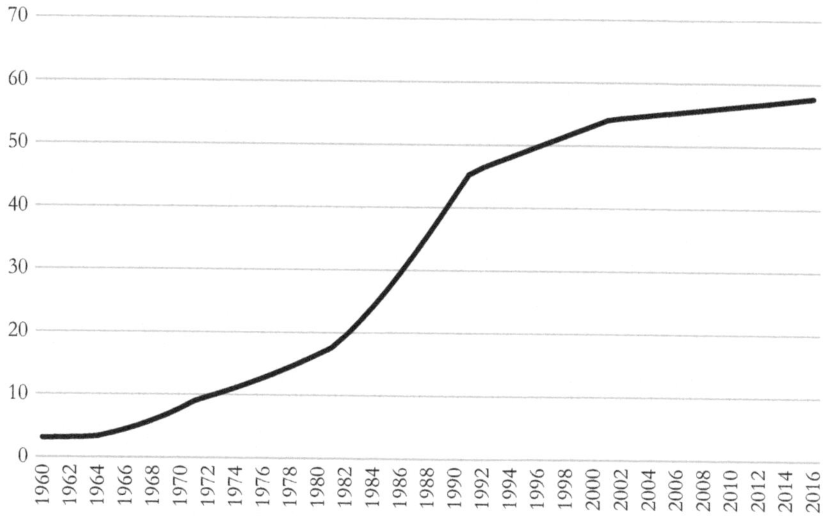

Fig. 5.2 Increase in urban population as percentage share of total population, 1960–2016. Source: World Bank (2017)

oping countries that subsistence sectors are expanding also in urban areas, the most evident example being informal self-employment. Botswana's prime engine of growth, the diamond sector, is neither located in the urban areas nor does it have significant links to other sectors of industry. The urban settlements are instead attracting labour that finds employment within the government administration, service sector, household employment, trade, and so on. Some of the employment opportunities are in the formal sector but many are in the informal sector. Thus, labour is to a significant degree moving from subsistence agriculture to non-capitalist urban sectors and becoming yet another indicator that economic development is absent in the midst of a social transformation due to urbanization.

Lipton (1977) pointed out that the most important class conflict in developing countries is that between the rural poor and the urban groups experiencing improvements in living standards and human capital. There is an urban bias favouring the larger cities and industry at the expense of the countryside and agriculture and it is driving a process creating dual economies. It is damaging because it leads to a sub-optimal allocation of resources and distribution of incomes. As long as the majority of the poor are located in rural areas and the agricultural production is characterized by low levels of technology and productivity compared to the urban sector, the highest returns will be on investments made in the rural sector. Urban bias is then slowing down both growth and development. In Botswana most of agriculture has been in the private sector and the government has merely provided a framework of infrastructure, administration, education, and utilities. While government spending on agriculture has historically been small compared to urban areas (Harvey & Lewis, 1990, pp. 252–253), private investments have not succeeded in compensating for the lack of government involvement.

5.6 Summing Up and Moving On ...

In this chapter, we have discussed why the diamond-led growth miracle has not been a success story from the point of view of achieving inclusive sustainable economic development. Despite extraordinary export incomes from diamond mining and prudent financial management of these resources, gains have not been invested in alternative high-productive and employment-creating sectors, neither by the government nor by individuals and companies in the private sector. One could argue that a lack of sectorial change is not the worst development challenge that resource-rich developing economies have experienced and that Botswana has avoided the natural resource curse, and enjoyed both spectacular growth and political stability. Consistent government revenues and significantly improved standards of living for the population at large have been welcome but also, for the lack of a better word, pacifying. The natural resource dependency that characterized the colonial cattle economy has persisted as the exceptional diamond-led growth rates and structural status quo have not generated incentives to change. The result is an economy trapped by its own natural resource wealth.

An important reason to define the diamond-led growth period as a success story is that growth has been paired with political stability and social development. While this is true, the lack of political will and economic dynamics to drive a transformation process means that the fundamental political and economic structures of the colonial gate-keeping state remain. There is nothing in the principles of the gate-keeping state that prevents it from instigating and forwarding selective and targeted development. It was actually one of the fundamental ambitions of the colonial era. What it does not have, though, are the structures and dynamics for inclusive, broad-based, and comprehensive transformation of the economy and society. The result is a dual society where poverty and exclusion exist in the midst of plenty and modernity.

If being caught in a natural resource trap is inconsistent with an inclusive structural transformation process, and the same is true for consistent high levels of inequality, which we will focus on in the next chapter. Sub-Saharan Africa is one of the most unequal regions in the world, and Botswana with a current Gini of roughly 0.6 belongs to the top of the list, even in a regional comparison. In the African context, analyses of long-term trends in inequality in relation to sectorial change are missing because we only have relatively consistent, though shaky, information about inequality for the independence era. For Botswana we have, however, constructed income Ginis from the 1920 onwards and when pairing them with independence statistics we can create a 'super Kuznets curve', which will allow us to discuss inequality trends stretching over almost a century.

References

Acemoglu, D., Johnson, S., & Robinson, J. A. (2003). An African success story: Botswana. In D. Rodrik (Ed.), *In search of prosperity: Analytic narratives on economic growth* (pp. 80–119). Princeton and Oxford: Princeton University Press.

Acemoglu, D., & Robinson, J. A. (2010). Why is Africa poor? *Economic History of Developing Regions, 25*(1), 21–50.

Adelman, I. (2003). Global Institutions and Economic Development—What have we learned? In M. Andersson & C. Gunnarsson (Eds.), *Development and structural change in Asia-Pacific—Globalising miracles or end of a model?* (pp. 17–47). London: Routledge.

Adelman, I., & Morris, C. T. (1997). Editorial: Development history and its implications for development theory. *World Development, 25*(6), 831–840.

Allen, T., & Heald, S. (2004). HIV/AIDS policy in Africa: What has worked in Uganda and what has failed in Botswana? *Journal of International Development, 16*(8), 1141–1154.

Auty, R. M. (2001). The political economy of resource-driven growth. *European Economic Review, 45*(4), 839–846.

Brunnschweiler, C. N. (2008). Cursing the blessings? Natural resource abundance, institutions, and economic growth. *World Development, 36*(3), 399–419.

Brunnschweiler, C. N., & Bulte, E. H. (2008). The resource curse revisited and revised: A tale of paradoxes and red herrings. *Journal of Environmental Economics and Management, 55*(3), 248–264.

Campbell, E. K. (2010). The role of remittances in Botswana: Does internal migration really reward sending families? *Population, Space and Place, 16*(2), 151–164.

Carlsson, E. 2003. *To Have and to Hold: Continuity and change in property rights institutions governing water resources among the Meru of Tanzania and the BaKgtala in Botswana; 1925–2000*. Lund Studies in Economic History, 28. Stockholm: Almqvist & Wiksell International.

Colclough, C., & McCarthy, S. (1980). *The political economy of Botswana: A study of growth and distribution*. Oxford: Oxford University Press.

Collier, P. (2008). *The bottom billion: Why the poorest countries are failing and what can be done about it*. New York: Oxford University Press.

Conteh, C. (2008). Rethinking Botswana's economic diversification policy: Dysfunctional state–market partnership. *Commonwealth & Comparative Politics, 46*(4), 540–554.

Corden, W. M., & Neary, J. P. (1982). Booming sector and de-industrialisation in a small open economy. *The Economic Journal, 92*(368), 825–848.

Curry, R. L. (1987). Botswana's macroeconomic management of its mineral-based growth: It used mining revenues for development and services but must now broaden the beneficiaries. *American Journal of Economics and Sociology, 46*(4), 473–478. https://doi.org/10.1111/j.1536-7150.1987.tb01995.x

Easterly, W. (2014). *Tyranny of experts*. New York: Basic Books.

Engerman, S. L., & Sokoloff, K. L. (2002). Factor endowments, inequality, and paths of development among new world economics. *Economia, 3*(1), 41–108.

Gaolathe, B. (1997). Development of Botswana's mineral sector. In J. S. Salkin, D. Mpabanga, D. Cowan, J. Selwe, & M. Wright (Eds.), *Aspects of the Botswana economy* (pp. 401–431). Gaborone, Botswana: Lentswe La Lesedi.

Gerschenkron, A. (1962). *Economic backwardness in historical perspective: In economic backwardness in historical perspective* (pp. 5–30). Cambridge, MA: The Belknap Press.
Good, K. (1993). At the ends of the ladder: Radical inequalities in Botswana. *The Journal of Modern African Studies, 31*(2), 203–230.
Good, K. (1994). Corruption and mismanagement in Botswana: A best-case example? *The Journal of Modern African Studies, 32*(3), 499–521.
Good, K., & Taylor, I. (2008). Botswana: A minimalist democracy. *Democratization, 15*(4), 750–765.
Gulbrandsen, Ø. (1996). *Poverty in the midst of Plenty: Socio-economic marginalization, ecological deterioration and political stability in a Tswana society* (No. 45). Bergen: Norse Publications.
Gylfason, T. (2001). Nature, power and growth. *Scottish Journal of Political Economy, 48*(5), 558–588. https://doi.org/10.1111/1467-9485.00215
Gylfason, T., Herbertsson, T. T., & Zoega, G. (1999). A mixed blessing. Natural resources and economic growth. *Macroeconomic Dynamics, 3*(2), 204–225.
Harvey, C., & Lewis, S. R., Jr. (1990). *Policy choice and development performance in Botswana*. London: Macmillan in association with the OECD Development Centre.
Hayek, F. A. (1944). *The road to serfdom*. London: George Routledge & Sons.
Heald, S. (2006). Abstain or die: The development of HIV/AIDS policy in Botswana. *Journal of biosocial science, 38*(1), 29–41.
Hill, C. B. (1991). Managing commodity booms in Botswana. *World Development, 19*(9), 1185–1196.
Hillbom, E. (2008). Diamonds or development? A structural assessment of Botswana's forty years of success. *The Journal of Modern African Studies, 46*(2), 191–214.
Hillbom, E. (2012). Botswana: A development oriented gate keeping state. *African Affairs, 111*(442), 67–89.
Hillbom, E. (2014). Cattle, diamonds and institutions: Main drivers of Botswana's economic development, 1850 to present. *Journal of International Development, 26*(2), 155–176.
Hirschman, A. (1958). *The strategy of economic development*. New Haven: Yale University Press.
Iimi, A. (2006). Did botswana escape from the resource curse? *IMF Working Paper 06/138*. Washington, DC: International Monetary Fund.
Jefferis, K. (1997). Poverty in Botswana. In J. S. Salkin, D. Mpabanga, D. Cowan, J. Selwe, & M. Wright (Eds.), *Aspects of the Botswana economy* (pp. 469–499). Gaborone, Botswana: Lentswe La Lesedi.

Kaufmann, D., & Kraay, A. (2002). Growth without governance. *Economica, 3*(1), 169–229.
Kuznets, S. (1955). Economic growth and income inequality. *The American Economic Review, 45*(1), 1–28.
Kuznets, S. (1973). Modern economic growth: Findings and reflections. *The American Economic Review, 63*(3), 247–258.
Kuznets, S., & Murphy, J. T. (1966). *Modern economic growth: Rate, structure, and spread* (Vol. 2). New Haven: Yale University Press.
Leite, C. A., & Weidmann, J. (1999). Does mother nature corrupt? Natural resources, corruption, and economic growth. *IMF Working Paper 99/85*. Washington, DC: International Monetary Fund.
Leith, J. C. (2005). *Why Botswana prospered.* Montreal & Kingston: McGill-Queen's University Press.
Lekoko, R. N., & Van Der Merwe, M. (2006). Beyond the rhetoric of empowerment: Speak the language, live the experience of the rural poor. *International Review of Education, 52*(3–4), 323–332.
Lewis, A. (1955). *The theory on economic growth*. London: Allen & Unwin.
Lewis, W. A. (1954). Economic development with unlimited supplies of labour. *The Manchester School, 22*(2), 139–191.
Lewis, W. A. (1979). The dual economy revisited. *The Manchester School, 47*(3), 211–229.
Lipton, M. (1977). *Why poor people stay poor: A study of urban bias in world development*. London: Maurice temple Smith Ltd.
Makgala, C. J. (2006). *Elite conflict in Botswana: A history*. Pretoria: African Institute of South Africa.
Masire, Q. K. (2006). *Very Brave or very foolish? Memoires of an African democrat.* Gaborone, Botswana: Macmillan Botswana Publishing Co (Pty) Ltd.
Mbabazi, P., & Taylor, I. (2005). *The potentiality of 'developmental states' in Africa*. Botswana and Uganda Compared, Dakar: CODESRIA.
McMillan, M., Rodrik, D., & Verduzco-Gallo, Í. (2014). Globalization, structural change, and productivity growth, with an update on Africa. *World Development, 63*, 11–32.
Meisenhelder, T. (1997). The developmental state in Mauritius. *The Journal of Modern African Studies, 35*(2), 279–297.
Milanovic, B. (2016). *Global inequality*. Cambridge, MA: Harvard University Press.
Mkandawire, T. (2001). Thinking about developmental states in Africa. *Cambridge Journal of Economics, 25*(3), 289–314.

Myrdal, G. (1968). *Asian drama, an inquiry into the poverty of nations.* New York: Pantheon Books

Nthomang, K. (2004). Relentless colonialism: The case of the Remote Area Development Programme (RADP) and the Basarwa in Botswana. *The Journal of Modern African Studies, 42*(3), 415–435.

Peters, P. E. (1994). *Dividing the commons: Politics, policy, and culture in Botswana.* Charlottesville: University Press of Virginia.

Phaladze, N., & Tlou, S. (2006). Gender and HIV/AIDS in Botswana: A focus on inequalities and discrimination. *Gender & Development, 14*(1), 23–35.

Piketty, T. (2014). *Capital in the 21st century.* Cambridge and London: Harvard University Press.

Poteete, A. R. (2009a). Defining political community and rights to natural resources in Botswana. *Development and Change, 40*(2), 281–305.

Poteete, A. R. (2009b). Is development path dependent or political? A reinterpretation of mineral-dependent development in Botswana. *The Journal of Development Studies, 45*(4), 544–571.

Poteete, A. R. (2012). Electoral competition, factionalism, and persistent party dominance in Botswana. *The Journal of Modern African Studies, 50*(1), 75–102.

Republic of Botswana. (2003). *National development plan 9.* Gaborone, Botswana: Ministry of Finance and Development Planning.

Republic of Botswana. (2004). *Labour statistics 2002.* Gaborone, Botswana: Government Printer.

Republic of Botswana. (2015). *Progress report of the national response to the 2011 declaration of Commitments on HIV and AIDS.* Gaborone, Botswana: National Aids Coordination Agency.

Robinson, J. A., & Parsons, Q. N. (2006). State formation and governance in Botswana. *Journal of African Economies, 15*(AERC Suppl 1), 100–140.

Sachs, J. (2005). *The end of poverty: How we can make it happen in our lifetime.* London: Penguin.

Sachs, J. D. (2012). Government, geography, and growth: The true drivers of economic development. Foreign Affairs, September/October 2012.

Sachs, J. D., & Warner, A. M. (1995). Natural resource abundance and economic growth. *Development Discussion Paper No. 517a.* October, Harvard Institute for International Development, Harvard University.

Sachs, J. D., & Warner, A. M. (1999). The big push, natural resource booms and growth. *Journal of Development Economics, 59*(1), 43–76.

Timmer, C. P. (2009). *A world without agriculture.* Cambridge, MA: AIE Press.

van der Ploeg, F. (2011). Natural resources: Curse or blessing? *Journal of Economic Literature, 49*(2), 366–420.

Wikan, G. (2004). The level of living in rural Botswana re-studied. *Norsk Geografisk Tidsskrift-Norwegian Journal of Geography, 58*(1), 1–10.
World Bank. (2016). *Development goals in an era of demographic change*. Washington, DC: IBRD/World Bank.
Wylie, D. (1990). *A little god: The twilight of patriarchy in a Southern African chiefdom*. Hanover, NH: Wesleyan University Press.

Internet Sources

Bank of Botswana. (2014). *Annual report*. Gaborone, Botswana: Bank of Botswana. Retrieved October, 2017, from http://www.bankofbotswana.bw/assets/uploaded/BoB%20AR%202014%20WEB%20MAIN.pdf
Botswana Government. (2011). Economic diversification drive: Medium and long-term strategy, 2011–2016. Ministry of Trade and Industry. Retrieved from https://unfccc.int/files/adaptation/groups_committees/adaptation_committee/application/pdf/20151002_botswana.pdf
UNAIDS. (2017). UNAIDS data. Retrieved August, 2017, from http://www.unaids.org/en/regionscountries/countries/botswana
World Bank. (2017). World development indicators. Washington, DC. Retrieved August, 2017, from http://databank.worldbank.org/data/reports.aspx?source=world-development-indicators
Worldwide Governance Indicators. (2016). Retrieved October, 2017, from http://info.worldbank.org/governance/wgi/#home

6

Inequality of Incomes and Opportunity, c. 1920–Present

6.1 Introduction

The question of why incomes, resources, and opportunities are so much more unevenly distributed in some countries than in others has been central in economics and economic history for more than half a century. Central to the debates is the relationship between economic growth and income distribution, and to what extent and in what way the exclusion of large sections of society through poverty and unequal opportunities, affects long-term economic development. In relation to our aim to understand the opportunities and hindrances for Botswana achieving inclusive sustainable economic growth (as discussed in Chaps. 4 and 5), we argue that high levels of inequality are both an indication of failing inclusive development and a preventer of future sustainable growth. We do that by investigating long-term inequality trends and analysing them in relation to Botswana's lack of sectorial change and structural transformation.

Despite continued scholarly attention, we remain without clear and encompassing answers as to how inequality impacts long run

E. Hillbom, J. Bolt, *Botswana – A Modern Economic History*, Palgrave Studies in Economic History, https://doi.org/10.1007/978-3-319-73144-5_6

development. One reason for this is the limitation of empirical scope in most scholary work until recently. Most studies were concerned with inequality trends in the developed world during and after industrialization (Kuznets, 1955; Lindert, 1986). Thereby the preindustrial era was left outside the theoretical model and there was no empirical evidence for the larger share of the world's populations living outside Europe and North America. The Eurocentric focus did not, however, prevent the results being implicitly assumed to be applicable to the world as a whole. The main reason explaining the lack of attention was that the information necessary to investigate the missing time periods and geographic regions is very patchy and scattered or altogether missing. In the case of Africa, for example, we know very little of inequality trends during the colonial era and therefore we cannot systematically explain what caused regional inequality levels to be among the highest in the world at the time of independence in the 1960s (World Bank, 2017). Recently, however, a growing body of literature is adding empirical evidence on the factors driving inequality both in regions outside the developed world and for time periods prior to when countries started to industrialize.

Inequality has played an important role in Botswana's economic history and contemporary Botswana remains one of the most unequal countries in the world. Commonly, high levels of inequality are seen as the rule rather than the exception in developing countries dependent on exports of high-value natural resources (van der Ploeg, 2011). In Botswana, however, income inequality was already very high at the time of the establishment of the diamond economy in the mid-1970s. The implication is that it is not enough for us to pay attention to post-independence inequality levels to understand why gains from the more recent and spectacular growth period have not been more equally distributed. We need to trace Botswana's contemporary high levels of inequality back to the cattle economy to understand what factors drove the initial rise in inequality. In an African comparative perspective, the experience of Botswana is not unique. Many countries came out of the colonial era as natural resources-dependent economies (minerals and/or agriculture) with high levels of inequality and today several of the most unequal countries in the world are located in this region (World Bank, 2017).

There is, however, a lack of research tracing the roots of these inequality trends. We propose that our in-depth long-term analysis of the Botswana case will contribute to a better regional and global understanding of drivers of long run inequality.

While inequality in the diamond economy has been consistently high, it has not increased much further, but rather stagnated or recently even slightly declined. This resonates with claims by Sala-i-Martin and Pinkovskiy (2010) who state that several African countries experienced a peak of income inequality in the mid-1990s and since then there has been some signs of declining inequality in the region. As the labour force in Botswana is primarily moving from the agricultural to the service sector, this potential bend of the inequality curve cannot be explained by sequencing of sectorial change and industrialization that characterized the European experience. Instead, government transfers and the move of labour into the service sector play a decisive role in recent inequality developments. Meanwhile, institutional continuity, societal duality, and economic exclusion indicate persistent inequality of opportunity.

We start this chapter with a presentation of the theoretical literature on the relationship between long-term trends in inequality and processes of structural transformation. This is followed by a discussion about the theoretical predictions on the timing of changes in inequality trends, the sequencing of structural transformation and the role of institutional inequality. Subsequently we chart income inequality in Botswana's preindustrial era based on social tables. In the fourth section we analyse income inequality in the diamond economy investigating changes in Gini coefficients and wage levels. We then move beyond income inequality turning our attention to inequality in resource distribution and income-earning opportunities. Finally, we sum up and move ahead.

6.2 Drivers of Long-Term Inequality Trends

For understanding changes in long-term inequality trends within countries, the workhorse model of most economists and economic historians has been the Kuznets model. In 1955 Kuznets put forward his influential 'inverted U hypothesis', arguing that as an economy starts to develop it will first experience a rise in inequality. As development continues, inequality at some point will start to decline, a trend that is depicted as an inverted U shape in a graph where development is on the horizontal axes and inequality is on the vertical axes. The main explanation of both the upward and the downward sloping segment of the inverted U curve are the relative changes in a nation's sectoral employment. Kuznets argued that income inequality was influenced by the reallocation of workers from the agricultural sector to non-agricultural sectors. This argument resonates with the Lewis (1954) theory on the 'unlimited supply of labour' where workers move from the traditional, commonly equated with the rural agricultural sector but actually meaning the sector of low labour productivity, to the capitalist, or urban and industrial, sector with higher productivity and better-paying jobs.

Both Kuznets and Lewis argue that this transfer of labour to sectors with higher labour productivity initially increases inequality primarily due to wage differences between the agricultural/traditional sector and the industrial/capitalist sector (between-sector inequality). Moreover, as the variance of incomes in the industrial sector is larger than in the traditional agricultural sector due to skill premiums, inequality is further increased (within-sector inequality). As economic development continues, inequality is at some point expected to decline again as more and more people find employment in the modern sectors. Then the influence of between-sector inequality decreases as only a limited number of people are still working in the agricultural sector. As more people are working in the modern sectors, skill premiums decrease and within-sector inequality is lower. Between-sector migration is expected to continue until the labour surplus in the agricultural sector is depleted and technological change has also transformed the agricultural sector to being capitalist with high labour productivity (Kuznets, 1955; Lewis, 1954).

In his seminal paper Kuznets (1955) stated that his model was based on 95 per cent theoretical reasoning and only 5 per cent empirical evidence. Since then the bulk of empirical evidence has grown substantially and it has become possible to critically scrutinize long-term inequality trends. Over the decades scholars seem to have identified some stylized facts that fit with Kuznets' classic model of inequality and growth for the contemporary period, although these results are highly debated. Using a cross-sectional approach, various studies indeed find lower-income inequality in poor agricultural-based economies, high-income inequality in growing and transitioning economies, and lower-income inequality again in wealthy modern economies (Ahluwalia, 1976; Todaro & Smith, 2009). At the same time, there are contradicting studies finding no evidence to support the inverted U curve relationship between development and inequality for the recent period (Atkinson & Brandolini, 2001; Bowman, 1997; Desbordes & Verardi, 2012). Whether supporting or refuting Kuznets' main assumptions, however, this literature only investigates the two end points of the Kuznets hypothesis—the correlation between per capita income and inequality. It tells us very little about the process or the drivers of the trends as it does not include, for example, relative employment shares as an explanation (Anand & Kanbur, 1993; Kanbur, 2000, 2012).

Ignoring the processes, however, takes the field of research on inequality away from what we consider to be the lasting contribution of Kuznets' work—the fundamental question probing into what is the long-term relationship between trends in inequality and sectorial change. While remaining with this theoretical focus there are four limitations of Kuznets' original model that we would like to highlight—the timing of both increase and decline in inequality; the sequencing of sectorial change; the assumed end point of the Kuznets curve; and the lack of a discussion on unequal distribution of resources and opportunities as the underlying basis for income inequality.

Starting with the issue of timing, there is rapidly growing empirical evidence calling into question Kuznets' hypothesis for the preindustrial period as one characterized by low and stagnant levels of inequality. Instead, changes in inequality are also found during absence of structural employment changes, limited economic growth, and even during periods of economic decline. Several scholars have pointed out that increasing inequality can already start with preindustrial economic development, that is, without the reallocation of employment. To capture long-term inequality trends van Zanden (1995) suggests the creation of 'super Kuznets curves', starting in the early modern era and stretching over a longer period of time than proposed by Kuznets. In contrast, Reis (2017) demonstrates how early modern phases of economic contraction in Portugal led to diminishing levels of inequality, and Alfani and Ryckbosch (2016) show that inequality in various other regions in early modern Europe also tended to rise in the absence of economic growth or during periods of economic decline. Further, there is also a growing literature suggesting a number of non-economic explanations, such as epidemics, wars and other major natural or political dislocations, as factors driving long-term inequality trends in preindustrial and industrial economies (Alfani, 2010, 2015; Herlihy, 1978; Scheidel, 2017). With the addition of a larger number of empirical case studies providing extended time horizons we expect that we can move beyond contradicting results and eventually be able to identify a variety of globally equally relevant pathways.

Moving on to the sequencing of sectorial change, we know that contemporary developing economies, both in Africa and elsewhere, do not adhere to the sequencing of agriculture–industry–services that we have been taught to expect in the industrialized countries of Europe, North America, and Pacific Asia (de Vries et al., 2015; McMillan et al., 2014). Instead, they commonly experience a very limited industrialization while instead the service sector consistently takes over from agriculture as the main contributor to GDP. In addition, and more importantly from the Kuznets model perspective, labour moves from agriculture to services, but without passing through the highly productive industrial sector. In the 1950s when Kuznets presented his model this complication was not observed, but it has substantial consequences for the applicability of the original model. As opposed to industry, the service sector contains relatively productive activities such as in the financial sector, but also very low-productive activities such as government administration and personal services. This makes the service sector as a whole difficult to place within the dichotomy of, on the one hand, a traditional/rural/agricultural sector and, on the other hand, a capitalist/urban/industrial sector. With the occurrence of low-productive self-employment common in contemporary African cities urbanization does not automatically constitute a modernization in economic terms (see Chap. 5). The spread of productivity within the sector also means that there is an even greater variety of incomes compared to both agriculture and industry and this affects both between- and within-sector inequality.

In addition, the assumption that industrialized countries would automatically arrive and stay at low levels of inequality, implying that there is an end point to the process, must be questioned in view of recent trends. Developed economies in Europe and North America that only remain with a small share of their labour active in agriculture are experiencing a substantial increase in inequality. The increasing openness to global trade and rapid economic growth experienced by the countries in Pacific Asia have gone hand in hand with recent increases in within-country inequality (Milanovic, 2016; Stiglitz, 2012). Milanovic (2016) argues that the current upswing in within-country inequality constitutes a second Kuznets curve driven by the structural transformation into the tertiary economy. Rather than settling on having a single inverted U-shaped curve he argues that we should think of Kuznets waves as made up of consecutive curves. Driving this recent increase in inequality is again the reallocation of labour, but now it moves from the relatively homogeneous manufacturing sector to the skill-heterogeneous service sector resulting in within-sector inequality driving up within-country inequality. Thinking of inequality trends in terms of Kuznets waves also provides an opportunity to include the previously discussed inequality swings in pre-industrial societies. It does not, however, settle the question of whether movements are driven by economic factors or by epidemics and war in the absence of economic growth and rising mean incomes.

Finally, the literature that we have been referring to above is primarily concerned with income inequality and while this is an important measurement it can be argued that it is an outcome rather than the essence of inequality. The equity literature instead argues that the proof of the pudding of whether or not an economy has the structures needed to achieve sustainable economic development lies in the distribution of access to productive resources and opportunities. It is stated that not only is there an inseparable link between equity and avoidance of absolute deprivation (World Bank, 2005, pp. 18–19), but it also plays an important role in promoting development as it frees people from the poverty trap and strengthens political institutions. For example, access to agricultural resources and improved incomes enable the rural poor to turn away from being risk minimizers to becoming utility optimizers contributing to the economy with their human capital capacities, raised productivity, and market interaction (Lipton, 1968). Equitable, or inclusive, institutions invite all individuals into the development process, but increased capabilities of individuals also result in higher demands for well-functioning economic and political institutions (Acemoglu & Robinson, 2012; World Bank, 2005, chapter 6).

6.3 Income Inequality in the Cattle Era, c. 1920–1975

The first official figures we have for income inequality in Botswana are World Bank numbers reporting a Gini of 0.6 in 1974 (Chernikovsky et al., 1985; World Bank, 2017). From that, we can conclude that levels were already high at the onset of the diamond economy, and, therefore, they must have already started increasing during the cattle economy. Consequently, to understand imperative factors driving increasing inequality of incomes and to trace the timing of the increase we need to work our way as far back in time as we can based on available archival and secondary sources. We dedicate this section to such a historical analysis covering as much as we can of the time before the diamond economy, thereby adding the preindustrial era to a super Kuznets curve for Botswana. We have been able to estimate inequality for six consecutive decades from 1921 to 1975, thereby covering the time period from the decades leading up to the cattle-led growth period as well as that growth period up until the structural break into the diamond economy.

6.3.1 Capturing Colonial Income Distribution

Given that information on individual wages and occupations becomes increasingly scarcer when we go back in time, we rely on social tables for calculating the distribution of incomes. The first scholar to develop this method was Gregory King who computed incomes and expenses for families in the late seventeenth century in England (see Lindert & Williamson,

1983). Subsequently, social tables were used by economic historians to estimate both national accounts 'from below' and inequality. The literature on various preindustrial Western European economies is the most extensive (see, e.g. Alfani, 2010, 2015; Alfani & Ryckbosch, 2016; Alvarez-Nogal & Prados de la Escosura, 2004, 2007, 2013; Lindert & Williamson, 1983, 2016; Milanovic et al., 2011; Reis, 2017). However, there is also an expanding number of studies done on developing countries, for example, van Zanden (2003) and Lopez Jerez (2014) for Asia as well as Berry (1990), Rodríguez Weber (2015), Bértola, Camou, Maubrigades, and Melgar (2008), and Prados de la Escosura (2007) for Latin America.

In the case of colonial sub-Saharan Africa, Bigsten (1987) computed income distribution and growth in Kenya for 1914–1976, and recently Alfani and Tadei (2017) produced inequality measures for Senegal, Cote d'Ivoire, and the Central African Republic during the colonial period. Both studies focus on the formal urban sector, and treat the indigenous rural sector as one unit. To us this constitutes an insufficient scope in relation to what we are aiming to achieve as is puts the large majority of the population, roughly 85 per cent in the case of Bechuanaland, in one and the same income group. We have therefore chosen a different route and by combining official colonial records with anthropological studies, we have managed to diversify within the agricultural self-employment sector and measure income inequality for the Bechuanaland economy as a whole.

Constructing social tables entails dividing the population of a society or country into various more or less homogeneous groups, also termed social classes or income classes. For each social class the number of individuals or households within that group together with the average wage is required. In combination with the total population of the country, population shares and income shares can be computed which provide the ingredients for the calculations of Gini coefficients (Milanovic et al., 2011; Bolt & Hillbom, 2016). As social tables capture between-class and not within-class income differences the method is especially useful for analysing societies where class structures are easily identified and differences in incomes between classes are significant (Milanovic et al., 2011). We are well aware that this is not the case for Bechuanaland where income spans overlapped and we cannot always assume that all individuals within a higher social class were wealthier than those in a lower social class. Nevertheless, relying on colonial archives and anthropological literature, we still manage to create eight relatively homogeneous social classes distinghuising different groups within both the formal and the informal sectors. The second set of income classes is especially important as it represents the large majority of the preindustrial economy. Either this bulk of the population is commonly left out of inequality calculations or they are treated as a homogeneous group awarded a joint average income instead of being divided up into income classes and granted some variation.[1]

We present our four social classes involved in self-employment in the agricultural sector first and then move on to the additional four income classes in formal wage employment. For both categories we start with the most well-off groups and work our way down the ladder. As we have to some extent discussed our division of social classes and their incomes in Chap. 4 when analysing the cattle-led growth period, this might be slightly repetative. However, we consider a short discussion of our social classes here imperative for a good understanding of our approach and our results. We present our four social classes involved in self-employment in the agricultural sector first and then move on to the additional four income classes in formal wage employment. For both categories we start with the most well-off groups and work our way down the ladder.

The Tswana agro-pastoral system of production dominating the agricultural sector in Bechuanaland was characterized by economic wealth, social status, and political influence depending on the ownership and control of cattle. Consequently, we base our identification of income classes within agricultural self-employment on the size of cattle herds. At the top of the ladder we find the *large-scale cattle holders and landed elite*. This privileged group primarily consisted of the tribal elites, *dikgosi* together with a few others, residing on communal land in the Native Reserves (see Map 2.2). We define this group as those holding a minimum of 100 heads of cattle, but we know that the largest herds could be made up of as many as 5,000 cattle or more. In addition, there was a limited number of Europeans with privately owned farms on either Crown Lands or land under company rule. The majority of these were large-scale cattle holders, but a small number specialized in commercial crop production. Before the development of the cattle export sector in the 1930s, native large-scale cattle holders primarily sold a few animals to cover expenses such as taxes and schooling. With an expanding export sector, members of this group were given new opportunities to turn their cattle wealth into cash incomes. Consistently, throughout our time period, this group represented roughly 5 per cent of the population (CSO, RIDS 1974/1975; Gulbrandsen, 1996, p. 79; Schapera, 1994; Schapera & Comaroff, 1991, p. 17).

The next income group is the *medium-scale cattle holders*. Members of this group held herds consisting of between 10 and 100 heads of cattle with average sizes fluctuating over time. They were using their cattle wealth to generate incomes to pay, for example, annual taxes. While they represented some 30–35 per cent of population up until the mid-1940s (Schapera & Comaroff, 1991, p. 17) there was later a continuous shrinking of the group size and in the mid-1970s, they only made up around 10 per cent of the total population (Colclough & McCarthy, 1980, p. 113; Good, 1992, 1993, 1994; Oommen et al., 1983, p. 38, Table 3.3.).

Prior to the mid-1940s, around 18 per cent of the population held less than ten heads of cattle, but the size of this income class of *small-scale cattle holders* increased to 40 per cent in the 1970s (Colclough & McCarthy, 1980; CSO, RIDS 1974/1975). Our 'ten-head-per-herd' distinction is important as this size is accepted as the minimum of any herd to yield an annual disposable income (Schapera & Comaroff, 1991, p. 17). Notwithstanding, this group both possessed wealth embodied in their cattle and acquired limited incomes in kind from their animals in the form of milk, primarily for family members staying at the cattle posts. In addition, they had access to draft power, which was important for their crop farming activities (Gulbrandsen, 1996, p. 201).

Meanwhile, the poorest members of the agricultural society were the *cattle-less*, living at subsistence level and relying primarily on incomes from rain-fed crop farming and holding some small stock such as goats and sheep. In contrast to the small-scale cattle holders they controlled no wealth and received no incomes in kind from cattle of their own. However, with the emphasis in Tswana society on patron–client relationships, extended families, and the cattle-lending system of *mafisa* (discussed in detail in Chap. 2), they were kept from falling below subsistence levels as they could rely on assistance from those better off. In the mid-1930s, 7–11 per cent of the population belonged to this income class (Schapera & Comaroff, 1991, p. 17). An important subgroup within this income class was bonded labour, a group that we cannot explicitly categorize as self-employed. It is impossible to say exactly how many, but significant numbers of primarily Basarwa were kept in slave-like labour control systems living at subsistence levels and being paid only with food and housing. This was most common in the Western communities where chiefs held individuals as *malate*, or serfs, for tasks such as crop farming, hunting, and herding livestock. They were not free to move away and their masters could lend them out to work for someone else. Although this type of servitude was de jure abolished by the colonial administration, it de facto remained as a blatant example of social inequality (Schapera & Comaroff, 1991, pp. 22, 31). The share of the population living as *malata* slowly decreased during the colonial period, but the number of the cattleless increased from 14 per cent of the population in the early years of our time period, to around 36 per cent in the 1970s (Bolt & Hillbom, 2016, Appendix 2, Table A2.6).

Moving on to formal wage employment, we in this section dicuss all employment recorded in the colonial statistics. While all of these groups gained more or less from the growth of the cattle economy and thereby increased their incomes, the income class that gained the most was the *European government administrators and officials*. In the initial phase of colonialism, roughly a dozen European government administrators and officials together with a restricted number of European police officers were active in Bechuanaland. While this group increased over time as colonial administration expanded in size with export sector developments and increasing taxation efforts, it never represented more than a small fraction of the total population.

Meanwhile, the lower-ranking *African government administrators* were also part of the public sector, but because there are significant differences in incomes compared to their European colleagues, we consider them as a separate social class. With the expansion of the administration, the number of African government officials increased and in 1974 they made up around 2 per cent of the population. Members of this group were likely to be well connected to the rural areas and the agricultural sector via extended families, receiving some incomes in kind from agriculture even when primarily residing in urban settlements.

Referring back to Chap. 4 and our discussions about the public–private divide we have already established that in terms of incomes and monetary incentives the public sector was forging ahead while the private sector was not encouraged and had a modest development trajectory during the cattle economy. Representing part of the formal private sector, *skilled labour* makes up the closest thing we have to an entrepreneurial class. Traders ran stores providing imported household goods and there was a growing number of commercial butchers, bakers, and eating houses in the larger villages. This group also controlled the export of ostrich feathers, ivory, skins, agricultural products, and, most importantly, cattle (Schapera & Comaroff, 1991, p. 23). From being almost non-existent at the start of our period this group increased substantially in absolute numbers, but in 1974 they still only represented less than 2 per cent of the population.

Our last income class is unskilled *labourers* and consists of miners, construction workers, farm hands, and domestic help either staying in Bechuanaland or going as temporary migrants to neighbouring territories, especially South Africa. Labourers were primarily recruited from rural households with little or no cattle and many used their incomes to complement their agricultural activities and to invest in cattle upon their return home (Morapedi, 1999; Schapera & Comaroff, 1991). While the share of population represented by every income class is difficult to compute, the fact that information about the numbers of labour migrants is very inconsistent makes this group particularly problematic. The official share of labourers in population doubled from around 3.5 per cent in the 1920s to around 7 per cent at independence (Bolt & Hillbom, 2016).

Based on the information that we have about our various income classes we have estimated the average yearly income for each group. Based on these incomes and the population shares of each social class we calculated the distribution of incomes in the economy as a whole. By repeating the exercise for six consecutive decades from the 1920s to the 1970s, we are able to trace changes in the relative size of each social class, their average income levels, and trends in overall income inequality. Our results show that the initial rise in income inequality in Botswana can be traced back to the period between 1930 and 1940, that is, the takeoff of the cattle-led growth period. As discussed in Chap. 4, during this era two groups saw their incomes increase substantially, namely, the large-scale cattle holders and the government officials. It was their forging ahead of the rest of the population that drove the increase in income inequality in the cattle economy.

6.3.2 Gini Coefficients for the Cattle Economy

As the Gini coefficient is one of the most common ways to measure the distribution of incomes within societies, we have calculated Ginis for every decade between 1920 and 1970, using our social tables. As mentioned above, the ideal case for estimating inequality based on social tables is one where there are clearly defined social groups for which the differences in mean incomes are substantial (Milanovic et al., 2011, p. 259). In the case of Botswana's cattle economy, however, income spans between our social classes sometimes overlapped. Further, as income groups encompass more varied types of employment over time, incomes earned within groups might become more varied. Calculating a Gini based on average wages per group in such instances underestimates overall inequality as it accounts only for between-group inequality.[2] However, we can roughly gauge within-class inequalities by calculating a Gini that incorporates the maximum within-class inequality that is still compatible with the mean incomes from our social tables.

We present our results in Fig. 6.1. Income inequality was relatively low in the early parts of the colonial period with a Gini of 0.25 and 0.27 in

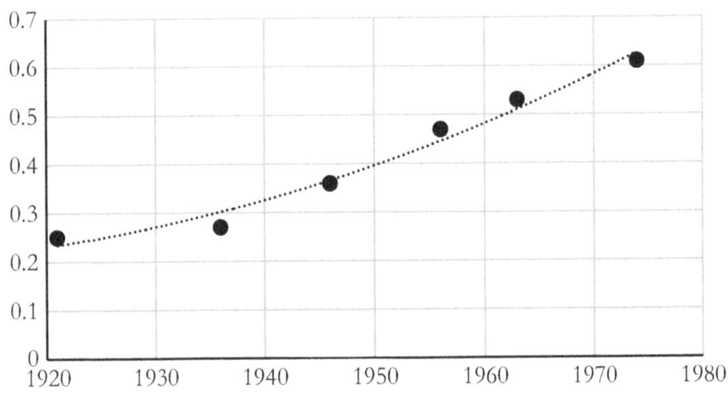

Fig. 6.1 Income Ginis for Botswana's cattle economy, 1921–1974. Source: authors' own calculations based on primary material. For details see Bolt and Hillbom (2016)

1921 and 1936, respectively. After the 1930s, though, inequality rose to 0.36 in 1946, 0.53 in 1963, and 0.61 in 1974. The timing of the increase coincides with the takeoff of the cattle-led growth period. Incorporating some within-group inequality does indeed increase inequality, especially for the year 1946, but for other years the lion's share is driven by between-group inequality. For the independence era the World Bank reports a Gini of 0.6 for 1974 and this gives us a valuable point of reference (Chernikovsky et al., 1985). Although much can be said about the reliability of the official data, which we scrutinize it in the upcoming section when discussing the diamond economy, we take the almost perfect match as a reassurance that our social tables approach is reliable and if anything it tends to underestimate inequality.

Putting our results into a comparative perspective, inequality in the early colonial period in Bechuanaland seems very low in relation to other preindustrial societies. Referring to the preindustrial Ginis presented by Milanovic, Lindert, and Williamson (2011, p. 263, Table 2), our result for Bechuanaland in 1921 is only comparable to their 0.24 Gini for China in 1880. Their Ginis for other preindustrial economies in Asia and Latin America range from 0.32 in Java in 1924 to 0.64 in Chile in 1861. Kenya is the only African territory in their sample and it has a Gini of 0.33 in 1914. Before concluding that Bechuanaland prior to the 1940s is a relatively equal society it is, however, important to remember that the Gini measures income inequality specifically. Prior to the establishment of the cattle-led growth period in the 1930s and 1940s, the Tswana elite, that is, the large-scale cattle holders, had limited opportunities to turn their assets into incomes, and they, like everyone else, depended mainly on subsistence farming while storing their significant wealth in cattle. At the same time, the 'pre-cattle export' economy entailed substantial inequality in wealth, social status, and political influence all of which directly and indirectly depended on herd size.

The changes in Gini coefficients tell us about the magnitude of increasing income inequality as well as the timing of the takeoff in relation to various other events, but not the mechanisms behind the movements. In other words, we do not learn which groups in the economy are gaining or losing their positions and to what extent changes in incomes are actually caused by the cattle-led growth. By analysing our social tables which provide information about incomes and the size of social classes, we gain more insights into who benefitted from the cattle-led growth and which groups were losing out. There are two groups that we identify as the winners in the cattle economy and whose incomes are forging ahead—it is the large-scale cattle holders who control an increasing share of a growing national herd and benefit from rising prices on cattle and the government officials whose salaries are increasing in tandem with cattle-led growth and improved government revenues.

Throughout the colonial era Bechuanaland repeatedly experienced droughts as well as outbreaks of foot-and-mouth disease. Such external shocks, for example, in the 1930s and 1960s, took high tolls eradicating substantial parts of the national herd. In between, however, numbers recovered, and as we can see in Fig. 3.5, the national herd increased from around 550,000 heads in 1936 to a bit below 1.5 million in 1964. In the midst of these external shocks, the large-scale cattle holders could endure a significant relative loss of cattle and still remain with robust herds. By increasingly controlling the boreholes as permanent water sources, a process whose mechanisms we discussed in depth in Chap. 3, they were better protected against droughts and, in fact, their average herd size increased over time.

Meanwhile, the average herd size of the medium- and small-scale cattle holders decreased and this made their herds more vulnerable (Good, 1993; Roe, 1980). The medium-scale holders lost ground in their strife towards the minimally robust herd size of 50 heads and many instead joined the group of small-scale holders. Many small-scale cattle holders saw their herds erased or were left with one to two animals instead of the ten needed for a disposable income. Some gave up, sold their last animal(s), and became labour migrants. After the drought of 1966, 75 per cent of the national herd was left in the hands of 15 per cent of the population (Colclough & McCarthy, 1980). The increasingly uneven control of water sources and subsequent access to grazing in combination with pressure from external shocks led to a cumulative process of increasing polarization within the cattle sector. This spilled over into determining who could participate and to what extent they could benefit from the expanding export sector. On top of that, cattle prices rose rapidly between 1930 and 1966 (see Table 4.6 for details) further increasing the advantages for the commercialized cattle holders. Given that export volumes were almost completely concentrated in the hands of large-scale cattle owners, this group also profited the most from price improvement.

Another group that was increasingly well off during the cattle economy was the group of government officials. As we showed in Chap. 3, the second half of the colonial era was a time when Bechuanaland benefitted from increasing colonial aid and increasing trade-tax revenues. This allowed the colonial adminstration to substantially increased their spending on public sector salaries. African government administrators also experienced a continuous increase in wages and, in addition, this group grew in relative numbers. Eventually they constituted a group that controlled a substantial share of total income. Although they never represented more than 0.5 per cent of the total population throughout the period, they earned between 13 and 58 times more than if incomes had been distributed evenly. At the same time, incomes earned by labourers and traders within the private sector remained low and stable. This discrepancy led to a substantial increase in the public–private divide, the implications of which we discussed in Chap. 4.

6.4 Diamonds and the End of Increasing Income Inequality, c. 1975–Present

The presence of high-value natural resources in an economy is often associated with an unequal distribution of incomes. Resources or mining rights are often in the hand of a selected few, and the mining of such resources generally requires little labour. In 1958, Hirschman had already stated that in a small economy dominated by a valuable natural resource, growth usually has few linkages to other sectors. In effect, the benefits from the exploitation do not automatically find their way into the broader economy via, for example, increasing employment and rising wages. While both high-value natural resources and high income inequality are present in Botswana, we showed in the previous section that the mining of diamonds was not the cause of the initial increase of income inequality. Instead, inequality started rising during the period of cattle-led growth and hence can be traced back to the premodern economy.

At the time the economy switched to relying on diamonds in the mid-1970s, inequality was already very high with a Gini of roughly 0.60. In this and the following section we analyse the developments of inequality in Botswana during the diamond economy. We scrutinize the Gini trend and put Botswana's trend in a regional perspective. Finally, we study what inequality has meant for the distribution of incomes and prevalence of poverty. We then move on to discuss how the economic transformation process from agriculture to industry and services has evolved in Botswana, and what this might tell us about future inequality.

6.4.1 Scrutinizing the Gini Trend

The substitution of cattle for diamonds as the driver of the economy has not had a noticeable effect on the levels of income inequality. When coming out of the economic period dominated by cattle, levels of inequality were already very high, and they have stayed high until the present. While the diamond economy was not responsible for the initial increase in the unequal distribution of incomes, it has also not brought inequality down. Despite some fluctuations in Gini coefficients over the years, they all broadly indicate a stagnating trend in inequality from the mid-1970s onwards. Only the last observation available for Botswana, the Gini for 2010, suggests that inequality could be starting to decline (see Fig. 6.2). If that turns out to be the case, Botswana would be supporting Sala-i-Martin and Pinkovskiy's (2010) recent research suggesting that high levels of income inequality in the African region have started to decline since the mid-1990s. It is, however, too soon to draw any definite inferences. What we do know is that when comparing inequality trends for the rural and urban areas, respectively, the overall decline in inequality in Botswana can be traced to welfare improvements in rural areas, while in the meantime inequality has increased in the cities (Assessment Report, 2015).

The interpretation of these official individual Gini observations for the independence era should be done with care for a number of reasons. First, an outcome measure can only be as good as the underlying data. For various African countries we know that statistical capacity is low, and

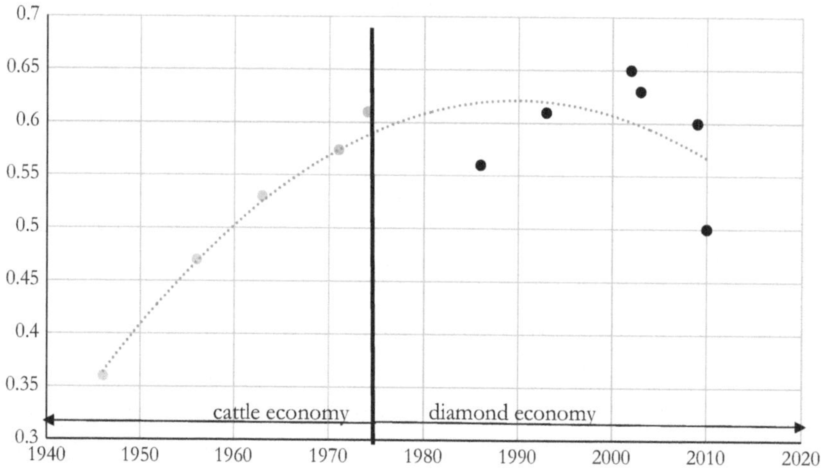

Fig. 6.2 Income inequality in Botswana, 1970–2010. Sources: 1946, 1956, 1964, 1974: Bolt and Hillbom (2016). 1986, 1993, 2002, 2003, 2009, 2010 from the UNU-Wider Inequality database. The Ginis included in that database are based on various sources. We have used the Gini for the whole population instead of rural or urban Ginis

therefore the data available for constructing Gini coefficients are patchy or unavailable (Jerven, 2013). Additionally, the available information is not always easy to access. Therefore, the information used to calculate inequality differs between various studies, reducing comparability. For Botswana, indeed, the quality of the statistical information has been questioned, although it has improved in more recent years (Jerven, 2010). The second reason to be careful while interpreting single observations, or to directly compare Gini coefficients, is that there can be differences in the coverage of the income data underlying the various measures. While some studies focus only on the rural population, others only include the urban population. In the context of sub-Saharan Africa, where many economies remain agricultural based and urbanization is still at low levels by an international comparison, any measure that does not include the rural areas cannot be taken as representative of the whole population. Therefore, in Fig. 6.2 we have only included Gini measures that refer to the whole population.

Given that Botswana is resource abundant, it is not obvious that its inequality development is representative of a broader inequality trend in Africa. By comparing inequality trends between both resource-rich and resource-scarce economies, we can compare Botswana's experience with a continent-wide perspective (see Table 6.1). For all of these African countries there are quite distinctly different Gini coefficients available and, unfortunately, it is not always clear where these differences come from or how we are to make an informed decision of preferring one rather than the other. We have again only selected Gini coefficients based on official international sources that include the whole population.

Our partial comparison in Table 6.1 shows something that is also clear when investigating the Africa region in its totality, namely, that countries in Southern Africa are more unequal in terms of the distribution of incomes than countries in the rest of the region. Resource-rich countries like Botswana, South Africa, and Zambia feature in the top group of most unequal countries together with resource-scarce countries such as Malawi and Lesotho. Meanwhile, incomes in some resource-rich countries in other regions, such as Nigeria, appear more equally distributed. This pattern indicates that a straightforward link between resource dependency and high levels of income inequality is not always there.

Table 6.1 Income inequality levels in selected post-independence African countries

Years	Botswana	Malawi	South Africa	Zambia	Mauritius	Nigeria	Cote d'Ivoire	Ghana	Uganda
1970–1974	0.61		0.51	0.57		0.58			0.40
1975–1979		0.52	0.47	0.59	0.42				
1980–1984		0.57	0.49		0.46	0.43			
1985–1989	0.56	0.60	0.47		0.40	0.49	0.44	0.48	0.44
1990–1994	0.61	0.62	0.59	0.61	0.37	0.52	0.39	0.46	0.45
1995–1999		0.66	0.61	0.61	0.39	0.53	0.44	0.43	0.43
2000–2004	0.63	0.40	0.58	0.54	0.37	0.40	0.41		0.45
2005–2010	0.60	0.46	0.63	0.56	0.36	0.49	0.43	0.43	0.44

Source: UNU-Wider Inequality database 2017. Not all countries in the text are included in the table but can all be found in the UNU-Wider database

If the very slight downturn in the latest Gini measurement continues and becomes a trend, Botswana could be a case supporting the Sala-i-Martin and Pinkovskiy (2010) argument of declining African income inequality, but generally we cannot detect any overall current trend in the countries we are looking at. Instead, South Africa has experienced a clear increase in inequality since the 1970s and several other countries show increase in inequality since the early 2000s. It is important to keep in mind though that for a number of countries and years, there are conflicting Gini coefficients available, and how we choose between them in some cases can profoundly affect the trends we find. One way of trying to deal with the mixed messages that we get from the Gini coefficients is to complement them with alternative measures of the distribution of incomes. We therefore turn our attention to the movements over time of different income groups as we continue to investigate the mechanisms driving income inequality in Botswana.

6.4.2 Poverty and Income Distribution in the Diamond Economy

Indicators that display the share of total income earned by different groups of people provide more details about which parts of society have lost out at least in relative terms during times of increasing inequality. To construct such indicators, all individuals in society need to be ranked from poor to rich, after which the population needs to be divided into five (quintiles) or ten (deciles) equally sized groups. To determine what share of total incomes earned in the economy is attributable to, say, the poorest group in society, all incomes earned by the poorest group should be divided by the total income earned in the economy as a whole. This can be done for all separate income groups, providing an overview of how total economy incomes are distributed over different income groups. For Botswana this information is available for four years between

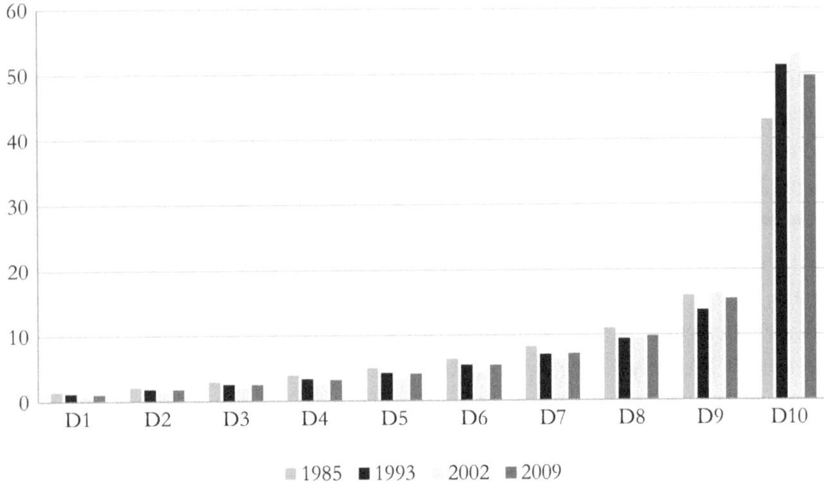

Fig. 6.3 Distribution of incomes per deciles in Botswana, 1985–2010. Source: UNU-Wider Inequality database (2017). D indicates the deciles. D1 reflects the poorest decile; D10 the richest 10 per cent

1985 and 2010 and we present the numbers in Fig. 6.3. The survey years are nicely distributed over this period, allowing us to follow changes over more than three decades. Interestingly, it covers the period when Botswana according to the Gini coefficients experienced a peak in income inequality and potentially also a subsequent decline. During the period of investigation, the poorest 10 per cent of society earned on average a meagre 1.2 per cent of total income. Its income share declined from 1.43 per cent in 1985 to 0.83 per cent in 2002, the year the Gini peaked at 0.65. After that, the share of income earned by the poorest segment of society increased slightly to just over 1 per cent. In contrast, the richest 10 per cent of the population earned around 48 per cent of total income throughout the period 1985–2010. In the year that inequality peaked, more than half of total income accrued to the top group.

After 1985, all income groups except the richest 10 per cent saw their income share decline over time. Thus growth clearly benefited the top incomes of society disproportionally. In 1985, the richest 20 per cent received 58 per cent of all incomes; in 2002 this had increased to over 70 per cent. In the last few years, this trend seems to have been halted or even partly reversed. The income share of the top group declined for the first time while the middle-income groups saw their income shares increase modestly between 2002 and 2009. This change in distribution is reflected in the decline of the Gini since 2002. It is important to emphasize that even though the gains from the rapid diamond-led growth have clearly not been distributed evenly across society, this does not necessarily imply that the poorest segments of society have experienced a decline in their absolute incomes.

At times of rapid economic growth, it can be that the total shares of income earned by the lower-income groups decline although the nominal incomes they received every month actually improves. When all incomes in the economy move up, but wages of the rich increase even faster than the incomes of the poor, inequality levels still escalate. In 1974, the government of Botswana installed a minimum wage and since the introduction, the level has been rising. However, as prices also increased due to the economic boom, in real terms the people earning a minimum wage did not experience an improvement in living standards (Leith, 2005, pp. 89, 90). Nevertheless, poverty levels have fallen during the era of the diamond economy. The share of the population living below the global poverty line of US$1.90 a day has drastically declined from 43 per cent in 1985 to 18 per cent in 2009 (PovCalnet, 2017). Associated with the poverty decline, real consumption per capita increased by more than 13 per cent between 2002/2003 and 2009/2010 (World Bank, 2015). At the same time, the World Bank has warned that around 30 per cent of the population still live just marginally above the poverty line and with even a minor downward turn in incomes they are at risk of falling back into severe poverty (World Bank, 2015).

Increase in agricultural incomes and consumption explains much of the significant poverty reduction. While rural areas are catching up and the fast urbanization trend continues poverty is no longer a primarily rural issue, it is also becoming an urban concern. There are several factors explaining the observed decline in poverty prevalence. One is a classic trickle-down story with economic growth pushing up not only prices but also incomes, and in that sense the 2000s' economic growth has been pro-poor. Further, there is a convergence between urban and rural areas as well as between the wealthier south-east and north-east regions and the rest of the country. There is also a demographic dimension as the number of children per household amongst the poor has declined, which has resulted in improved standards of living. Finally, the social development agenda pursued by the government during independence including investments in health care, education, and targeted poverty alleviation programmes has had a significant impact (Selolwane, 2013; World Bank, 2015). Still, as discussed in Chap. 5, the gap between the rich and the poor has not been closed and Botswana's society remains highly dual in character.

6.5 Inequality of Opportunity

In the previous sections we focused on income inequality, which is the common outcome measurement capturing distribution of welfare and standards of living. It can, however, be argued that income inequality is a somewhat superficial measurement and that it only constitutes an indication of a more profound inequality in economic and societal structures. The major prerequisite for the success of an economy is not that incomes are equally divided, but that resources and opportunities for securing incomes are accessible for all members of society. Giving the larger share of the population, the opportunity to fulfil their potential and thereby contribute to their own welfare as well as the wealth of society is the optimal outcome and the essence of inclusive development. While it can be argued that equal opportunities is a utopia, a state can actively promote an institutional framework where there is no formal discrimination of any groups as well as enforce policies for a more equal distribution of resources and opportunities. In this section we no longer discuss the two growth periods seperately; instead, we discuss changes in access to resources and income-earning opportunities throughout all sectors, agriculture–industry–services, during both cattle- and diamond-based growth periods.

6.5.1 Polarization in the Agricultural Sector

In the cattle-based economy the agricultural sector was so dominant that it is possible to generalize and state that access to and allocation of agricultural resources was the primary underlying driver of inequality trends. During the more recent decades after the shift to diamonds, the contribution of the agricultural sector to GDP has declined to around 2–3 per cent, but it continues to be a key sector. Independent of the growing importance of industry and the service sector, the development of the agricultural sector remains indispensable for poverty reduction. The sector provides employment for around 38 per cent of the labour force and the rural areas harbour almost half of the population. Even though poverty is becoming more urbanized during more recent years, still the majority of the people living in poverty are rural inhabitants. Throughout, agriculture has been a sector characterized by high levels of inequality and an investigation into changes in the distribution of agricultural resources is highly relevant for understanding inequality trends during both growth periods (World Bank, 2015, 2017).

The core theme in the literature on the distribution of agricultural resources is a focus on the distinction between small- versus large-scale farming units. It does not always explicitly address inequality as, depending on the availability of land, systems of production characterized by either small- or large-scale units in theory can both be part of systems with equal or unequal distribution. Implicitly, though, there is an understanding that agricultural systems in agricultural-based societies containing large-scale units are also characterized by unequal division of land with large land holdings existing in the midst of smallholders or landless agricultural workers. Subsequently there has been an ongoing debate on how to understand the relationship between land size and agricultural growth. Are these large-scale units characterized by poor land productivity hampering agricultural growth, or are they in an advantaged position with privileged access to modern technology, financial capital, and superior skills? The camp arguing for smallholder-led agricultural growth sees a causal relationship between equitable distribution of agricultural resources, on the one hand, and agricultural development, on the other hand. Thus, a more equitable distribution of agricultural lands results in pro-poor agricultural growth leading to rising incomes and improved living standards for the rural population. (For this literature, see, e.g. Berry & Cline, 1979; Collier & Dercon, 2014; Cornia, 1985; Deininger & Squire, 1996; Griffin et al., 2002; Kay, 2001.)

The empirical foundation on which this literature is based mostly contains empirical evidence collected from the plantation sectors in the Asian and Latin American regions where crop farming systems are characterized by highly unequal distribution of land resources leading to both slow growth and political instability (Engerman & Sokoloff, 2002, 2005; Griffin et al., 2002). Meanwhile, the trajectory for Africa has been different as the region has historically been characterized by land abundance and labour scarcity, and only a minority of the colonized territories, for example, South Africa, Southern Rhodesia, and Kenya, had significant settler populations. In these settler colonies the European minority over time amassed prime agricultural land while the political institutional structure restricted the indigenous populations' access to agricultural resources. In peasant economies, such as Bechuanaland, however, limited European settlement and the persistence of indigenous property rights systems are said to have led to low levels of inequality. However, since roughly the 1950s land/labour ratios have started changing in the African region and there has been a continuous shift from open to closed access to land. This has potentially caused increasing inequality in the agricultural sector and the economy at large in all countries experiencing substantial population increase, as also in the former peasant economies (Austin 2008; Mosley, 1983).

The above arguments primarily pertain to crop farming systems with private property rights to land in the form of ownership or user rights. How well do they resonate with cattle-based systems of production relying on a communal grazing range? There are studies from sub-Saharan Africa providing some answers and they indicate that the same types of causal relationships that have been identified in crop farming systems in Asia and Latin America also are at play in the African smallholder cattle sector. For example, investigations among smallholders on communal land in Zambia show a significant positive causal correlation between secure access to land, fixed investments, and productivity increase in cattle husbandry (Smith, 2004). Further, a study from South Africa indicates that herds on the communal grazing range that have secure access to additional natural resources also have a higher productivity rate (Mapiye et al., 2009). This leads us to suggest that the equity argument—that ensuring small-scale producers' control of agricultural resource leads to agricultural growth—is also of relevance for the African context and for cattle producers relying on a communal grazing range.

While land has historically been abundant in Botswana the primary obstacle for expanding the cattle sector has been access to permanent water sources in the drier areas of the grazing range. As described in Chaps. 2 and 3, cattle holders were initially depending on more or less seasonal natural open waters and shallow hand-dug wells. Then in the 1920s and 1930s both native authorities and the colonial administration started drilling modern boreholes which they handed over to individuals and syndicates deemed affluent enough to cater for maintenance and running costs. Effectively, based on these considerations only the large-scale and some middle-scale cattle holders were given permanent water points. Despite the authorities' efforts, the supply of new boreholes was consistently too low to satisfy demand. Poorer relatives and clients not considered viable as borehole caretakers struggled to secure positions at the boreholes as hirers (paying for water) or dependants (with free access but at the mercy of the patron). The selective distribution of boreholes and patron–client relationships determining access to permanent water resulted in an increasingly unequal division of water points (Hillbom, 2010; Peters, 1994, p. 58; Schapera, 1980, pp. 22–23). With the area vulnerable to droughts, accessing permanent water in turn had a profound effect on the survival of animals and the changes in size of cattle herds. In addition, controlling scarce water resources also meant controlling the abundant grazing range surrounding the water point and the polarized access to water translated to an unequal control of the grazing range. Finally, increasingly uneven distribution of water and land, that is, the opportunities for keeping cattle, resulted in a polarization of cattle holding itself.

Some scholars have argued that the property rights system within the Tswana agro-pastoral system of production granting private ownership to animals is an important ingredient in the argument of the 'good precolonial political institutions' (Acemoglu et al., 2003). Conversely, we believe that contemporary structural inequalities in Botswana's agricultural sector have their roots in the precolonial and colonial indigenous redistributive system, which gave an elite privileged access to agricultural resources and cattle (Carlsson, 2003; Good, 1994; Gulbrandsen, 1996; Peters, 1994; Wylie, 1990). Within the institutional framework of customary property rights systems, two parallel processes can be detected. There is a willingness to protect the poor and vulnerable by being lenient with free-riders among syndicate members as well as permanent hirers and to keep dependants at the boreholes. Because of the special quality of water being a life-supporting resource and imperative for the rural population making their livelihood from agriculture and cattle rearing, it appears that the principles guiding access to water resources are particularly forgiving (Carlsson, 2003; Hillbom, 2010). In this way the negotiability within the customary property rights system is possibly slowing down the process of exclusion (Berry, 2002; Odgaard, 2003). In parallel, negotiability is part of the process of increased exclusion and polarization of water resources while there is lenience with non-paying syndicate members, dependants, and temporary hirers. In a socioeconomic system increasingly driven by monetary interests the former clients are consistently being excluded and their water rights are increasingly being amassed in the hands of a cattle/water elite resulting in a more unequal distribution of water points (Hillbom, 2010).

The process of amassing resources by taking advantage of opportunities offered by the precolonial institutional structures is not unique to Botswana and its cattle sector. It is a general trend in the sub-Saharan African region that the present elites for their own benefit have continued supporting and maintaining the customary institutional systems. This is in turn resulting in considerable and growing inequality, that is, there is an ongoing polarization process within the framework of prevailing customary property institutions (Carney & Farrington, 1998; Platteau, 1996; Ribot, 2000).

In the precolonial agro-pastoral system of production, the majority of animals were already concentrated in the hands of the traditional chiefs and their relatives, but over the years this large-scale cattle-holding elite have amassed an increasing share of the national herd (Colclough & McCarthy, 1980, p. 22; Lawry 1983, p. 6). In the 1940s Isaac Schapera found that only 10 per cent of households in Bechuanaland held no livestock (Hesselberg, 1985, p. 182). During the first decade after independence the national herd expanded significantly, but at the same time many rural households lost their livestock and the numbers of cattle-less smallholders increased. An agricultural survey in 1983 reported that 40 per cent of all rural households now owned no cattle while 4 per cent of households owned 30 per cent of the national herd (Arntzen & Silitshena, 1989, p. 162). By 1993/1994 the share of cattle-less households in the rural areas had increased to 57 per cent, while 5 per cent of the families owned 50 per cent of the national herd (Gulbrandsen, 1996, p. 3). Further, 35 commercial farms, representing 0.6 per cent of cattle holders, held above 4,000 head on average and 19 farms even held more than 10,000 (Good, 1993, pp. 223–224; Silitshena & McLeod, 1998, p. 127).

6.5.2 Income-Earning Opportunities

Access to secure income-earning activities in the formal sector, whether that is through self-employment or wage labour, can play a decisive role for individuals' and households' opportunities to improve their standards of living. Studies into poverty structures in contemporary Botswana clearly identify a strong positive correlation between unemployment and inactivity, on the one hand, and poverty, on the other hand. Yet, employment is of course not a guarantee against living in poverty (World Bank, 2015). While Chaps. 4 and 5 contain further analysis of occupation structures and their relevance for analysing growth and sectorial change, here we discuss employment from the perspectives of poverty reduction and equality in access to opportunities.

During the colonial era, employment opportunities outside of self-employment in the agricultural sector were limited and never involved more than 15–20 per cent of the total population. Especially, the domestic formal sector stayed consistently small and contained few dynamic activities with potential for expansion. Increasing government revenues during the cattle economy did, however, eventually allow for some expansion in absolute numbers of employees as well as of public sector wages. In 1905, there were 15 European officials and 51 European police officers employed by the colonial government. The number of officials (excluding the police force) employed increased with more ambitious colonial strategies, for example, tax collection and export sector development, to 30 in 1906, 42 in 1915, over 80 in 1930, 120 in 1936, and 224 in 1947 (various Blue Books and Annual Yearbooks). Further, in 1946, 1,700 Africans were working for the government service, of which 153 worked for the police; in 1958 the number of people working for the government had increased to 2,500, and in 1963 4,000 were registered as government employees (various Blue Books and Annual Yearbooks). In the meantime, skilled labour in the private sector represented an even more limited group. In 1921, only 50 individuals were recorded to work in trade, increasing to up to around 800 in 1946 while the number of traders increased to 2,300 in 1956 and 4,250 in 1963 (various Blue Books and Annual Yearbooks). In Table 6.2 we present the shift in these income groups in terms of their share of the population.

Table 6.2 Allocation of the labour force, 1936–1964

	Percentage of the population			
	1936	1946	1956	1964
Agriculture				
Farm hands	1	1	1	1
Total (including cattle owners)	71	70	69	69
Industry				
Mining		1.2		0.1
Mines, South Africa	2	2.4	3.2	5.1
Skilled labour	0.01	0.2	0.5	0.8
Total	2.01	3.9	3.7	6
Service sector				
Domestic	0.03	0.4	0.4	0.4
African government officials		0.5	0.5	0.7
European government officials	0.01	0.06	0.05	0.04
Total	0.04	0.96	0.95	1.14
Unspecified	25.9	25.1	26.4	24.3
Total population	315,137	382,602	478,090	549,510

Source: updated from Hillbom and Bolt (2015, Table 3)

With domestic opportunities for formal employment being so limited, the more common strategy for the Tswana to secure wage employment was to look for opportunities outside of Bechuanaland, working as miners, farm hands, and domestic help in the neighbouring territories in Southern Africa particularly in South Africa. Anthropological sources indicate that migration was eventually of such magnitude that labour became a scarce factor of production in the Protectorate itself, to the point that it affected agricultural production negatively. Population was still at a low 265,000 in the mid-1930s (Blue Books, 1936/1937), and in many areas in the south, it was reported that as much as half of the productive population might have been absent in the 1920s and 1930s (Parsons, 1993; Ramsay et al., 1996, pp. 206–208, 211; Schapera, 1994). Most of this labour migration, however, was never recorded, and the official numbers, which are what we report in Table 6.2, are much smaller. Notwithstanding the discrepancy between sources, it is still a fact that before the cattle export sector took off at the end of the 1930s, migrant labour constituted the main source of cash incomes for the Tswana and that migrant labourers earned substantially above subsistence.

With the significant growth record of the diamond economy, formal wage employment in Botswana eventually took off. As we have also discussed in Chap. 5, the diamond-led growth period led to shifts between sectors offering employment. While the agricultural sector lost its dominant position in the economy and is currently only employing around 38 per cent of the population, most of the labour force has moved to services as an effect of both the government sector and trade expanding significantly. After independence roughly 2 to 3 per cent of the labour force was working for the government, but this number rapidly increased to 20 per cent around 2000. Meanwhile, in the early 1990s around 6 per cent was working in the trade sector consisting of trade, restaurants, and hotels, increasing to 20 per cent around 2010. In contrast, the industrial sector absorbed very little labour. Mining, however, the sector driving the growth miracle, has never provided more than 4 per cent of total employment, while construction, utilities, and manufacturing together on average employed only around 3 per cent of the labour force.

While the increase in formal employment during the diamond-led growth period was positive, the number of people without formal employment in Botswana remains substantial. If having formal employment is positively correlated with getting out of poverty, then being unemployed increases the risks of living in poverty. In addition, unemployment rates are an important signal about the health of an economy. A high unemployment rate means that large sections of society are struggling to secure incomes and instead depend on transfers from the government for incomes. When that is not available they depend on informal sector activities to scrape together their means for survival. The unemployed are often vulnerable to being trapped in poverty, unable to improve their living conditions and potentially stay permanently outside of formal employment (Quibria, 2002). Therefore, a lack of employment opportunities is one of the most important obstacles for the poor to participate in the productive economy thereby raising their incomes and reducing income inequality (World Bank, 2015).

Estimates suggest that in 1985 a quarter of the labour force was unemployed, and nearly 40 per cent of the youth were unable to find a job. Measuring unemployment is, however, difficult because not all instances of unemployment are recorded. Many unemployed may not inform the authorities and this unemployment goes unnoticed. Additionally, many people especially in the informal sector are underemployed, something that is also not captured in these statistics. Consequently, we use our figures only as indications. Nevertheless, the conclusion is clear that despite the successful macroeconomic environment throughout the diamond-dominated era, unemployment figures did not improve. In 2010, around one in every five people in the labour force was registered as unemployed, and still four out of ten young people were without a formal job. As long as the mining sector does not generate enough jobs, the only way forward to more and better jobs is by developing a dynamic and productive private sector. Inequality and poverty cannot be expected to fall significantly unless there is continued, broad-based employment growth (World Bank, 2015).

6.5.3 Institutional Inequality

The role of political institutions is an intricate part of the various processes driving inequality in opportunities discussed above. Connecting to the political economy and political science debate on the failed contemporary African state and the current poor quality of political institutions preventing economic development (Bates, 2005, 2008; van de Walle, 2001), there is a strand of literature seeking historical explanations for the role of long-term institutional development in relation to economic failure. Acemoglu, Johnson, and Robinson (2002) and Acemoglu and Robinson (2012) have argued that the primary determinants of contemporary inequality and levels of economic development are to be found in political institutions and they in turn have their roots in colonial strategies of either inclusion (being development oriented) or extraction (hindering development). At a first glance, this could be deemed relevant also for Africa since the region as a whole has historically been significantly affected by colonial extraction, through both the slave trade and territorial conquest, and is now experiencing poor economic growth. These theoretical assumptions are not, however, applicable when searching for explanations for within-region differences in postcolonial inequality trends and development trajectories between former settler and peasant colonies (Frankema et al., 2016).

Meanwhile, the factor endowment debate for both Latin America and Africa also suggests that colonial political institutions have had an impact on trends in economic development and inequality. Rather than discussing the setup of inclusive or extractive institutions, this literature argues that the key factor has been access to agricultural land. In settler economies land was reserved for Europeans, whereas in peasant economies land was accessible to African farmers and more equally distributed (Austin, 2008; Bowden et al., 2008) and inequality is assumed to have been higher at the time of independence in settler than in peasant colonies. Our result showing increasing income inequality during the colonial cattle economy in Bechuanaland, however, calls such an assumption into question. In addition, Aboagye and Bolt's (2018) recent study of colonial Ghana, which was also a peasant economy, indicates that inequality started to increase during the colonial period, especially in the cash crop growing areas as a result of the restrictions on participating in cash crop production. The relationship between colonial legacies and contemporary political institutional inequality appears to be complex and multiphased. Clearly, more research is needed before we can properly identify the various pathways shaped by the colonial experience.

Following up on the Acemoglu et al. argument, there are contemporary studies identifying political institutions as the primary determinants of the successful management of abundant natural resources, including whether government revenues are invested for a more equal and broad-based development process (Bourguignon & Morrisson, 1990). Good institutional quality is also generally recognized as the key explanatory factor for Botswana's successful and prudent management of diamond incomes. Albeit it is clear that these institutions are not an outcome of the creation of development-enhancing institutions during the colonial era. Instead, their origin has commonly been traced to precolonial institutional structures, for example, the emphasis of negotiation and compromise in the *kgotla* (Acemoglu et al., 2003; Acemoglu & Robinson, 2010; Beaulier & Subrick, 2006; Masire, 2006; Robinson & Parsons, 2006). In Chap. 3 we, however, emphasized the importance of not underestimating the lasting legacies of the late colonial era and the establishment of the cattle export sector. Notwithstanding this recognition of colonial legacies having a profound effect on economic institutions, we do not refute the inference that precolonial political institutional structures persisted into the independence era. What we do is to problematize their legacy and we claim that precolonial institutions have contributed not only to the prudent management of diamond incomes but also to contemporary structures of institutional inequality.

Our own study showing increasing income inequality and amassment of agricultural resources and polarization of cattle holding in the midst of precolonial institutions is supported by a strain of critical literature stating that Botswana's contemporary institutional inequality and increasing recent elite capturing has far-reaching historical roots. (For this literature, see, e.g. Good, 1992, 1993, 2008; Good & Taylor, 2008; Gulbrandsen, 1996; Hillbom, 2008, 2014; Makgala, 2006; Wylie, 1990.) This literature calls into question several aspects of inequality in the midst of Botswana's successful development trajectory.

Here we briefly remind the reader of three issues of inequality inherent in the country's political institutions that we have throughout the book consistently commented on. First, going back until the time of the very settlement of the Tswana in their current area there is the issue of the treatment of the Basarwa population. Their opportunities to continue their lives as hunters and gathers were constrained and instead many were kept as *malata*, bonded labour, in the Tswana cattle system of production. During the independence era they have repeatedly been forcefully relocated when large diamond deposits have been discovered in areas they occupy. Currently many Basarwa live as rural destitute surviving only on government handouts. Second, in the socioeconomic dual society (see Chap. 5), not only the Basarwa, but the rural inhabitants have generally been left behind during the progress paid for by the growth miracle and the rural areas have constituted pockets of poverty in the midst of plenty. The duality is worsened by the continued polarization in the agricultural sector with the politico-economic elite, primarily within the Botswana Democratic Party (BDP), remaining entrenched with the large-scale cattle holders. Finally, there is a growing critique of the political system becoming captured by the elites and increasingly characterized by authoritarianism, with the political power being concentrated in the office of the president.

6.6 Summing Up and Moving On ...

At the time of independence, income inequality was already high in Botswana suggesting that inequality started to rise already in the cattle economy. A common problem for investigating long-term trends in inequality in developing regions is that data are scarce. We therefore started this chapter with estimating Ginis for the colonial era. We constructed social tables for the period 1920–1974, dividing the population into income classes and calculating their average incomes and share of population. Using social tables for capturing income inequality in preindustrial economies is not unusual, but often it is only the formal sector that is captured while we incorporate the whole population. Our results show that income inequality rose sharply from the 1940s and was an outcome of cattle-led growth providing new opportunities for colonial expansion as well as for large-scale cattle holders to turn existing wealth into incomes. The process was driven by a polarization in the control of agricultural resources and ownership of cattle leading to amassment in the hands of the cattle elite as well as increasing salaries for government employees paid for by rising government revenues.

Subsequently we turned to the diamond economy. Reported Ginis are sometimes inconsistent and contradictory, but taken as an average they show a stagnation of income inequality at Gini levels of around 0.6 for the diamond-led growth period. There are also some recent estimates indicating the start of a slight decline, but this trend is not clear although it could potentially be part of a broader sub-Saharan Africa story of a break with historical high levels of inequality. Further, we investigated changes in income distribution in the recent decades, and we conclude that, again, it is the well-established elite that is gaining the most from growth.

Finally, we have argued that while income inequality is a valuable measurement of inequality trends, it is an outcome rather than a driver of said trends. To properly capture the mechanisms behind changes in income inequality we need to turn to socioeconomic structures governing the principles for distribution of access to productive resources and income-earning opportunities. A look at the whole period of investigation indicates that agriculture has been Botswana's most important sector, providing the basis for the cattle economy and until recently harbouring the majority of the population. Consequently, we pay special attention to the distribution of agricultural resources. With the growth of industry and services, formal employment has become increasingly important for income-earning opportunities, but the economy consists of few labour-intense sectors and cannot absorb surplus labour. This manifests itself in high levels of unemployment and potentially forced self-employment and has repercussions for inequality. At the end of the day, and especially in a country like Botswana with a heavy emphasis on the public sector, development strategies are driven by the state and therefore political institutions matter. We therefore end the chapter with a critical discussion on the long history of institutional inequality and contemporary elite capturing.

This brings us to the end of our analysis of the economic history of Botswana and for the last chapter all that remains is to sum up the conclusions. We do that by identifying six main takeaways from the book connecting back to our overarching analytical approaches presented in the introduction and the three topics for the thematic chapters. Finally, we return to the most fundamental challenges for the future—restructuring the economy towards diversification and sectorial change while freeing it from natural resource-driven growth in order to ensure continued economic progress, and initiating inclusive strategies for sustainable development. We argue that to take on these challenges there is need for a rise of alternative economic and social interests and a break with the old order.

Notes

1. For in-depth presentations of our data and methods for calculating incomes, shares of population, and welfare ratios we refer to Bolt and Hillbom (2015, 2016).
2. Based on a log-normal distribution, correcting for overestimation.

References

Aboagye, P., & Bolt, J. (2018). Economic inequality in Ghana, 1891–1960: Who gained from the cocoa boom? *African Economic History Network Working Paper* 38.

Acemoglu, D., Johnson, S., & Robinson, J. A. (2002). Reversal of fortune: Geography and institutions in the making of the modern world income distribution. *The Quarterly Journal of Economics, 117*(4), 1231–1294.

Acemoglu, D., & Robinson, J. A. (2010). Why is Africa poor? *Economic History of Developing Regions, 25*(1), 21–50.

Acemoglu, D., & Robinson, J. A. (2012). *Why nations fail: The origins of power, prosperity, and poverty*. New York: Crown Business.

Ahluwalia, M. S. (1976). Inequality, poverty and development. *Journal of Development Economics, 3*(4), 307–342.

Alfani, G. (2010). Wealth inequalities and population dynamics in early modern northern Italy. *The Journal of Interdisciplinary History, 40*(4), 513–549.

Alfani, G. (2015). Economic inequality in northwestern Italy: A long-term view (fourteenth to eighteenth centuries). *The Journal of Economic History, 75*(4), 1058–1096.

Alfani, G., & Ryckbosch, W. (2016). Growing apart in early modern Europe? A comparison of inequality trends in Italy and the low countries, 1500–1800. *Explorations in Economic History, 62*, 143–153. https://doi.org/10.1016/j.eeh.2016.07.003

Alfani, G., & Tadei, F. (2017). *Income inequality in colonial Africa: Building social tables for pre-independence Central African Republic, Ivory Coast, and Senegal.* African Economic History Working Paper 33/2017, African Economic History Network.

Alvarez-Nogal, C., & De La Escosura, L. P. (2007). The decline of Spain (1500–1850): Conjectural estimates. *European Review of Economic History, 11*(3), 319–366.

Álvarez-Nogal, C., & De La Escosura, L. P. (2013). The rise and fall of Spain (1270–1850). *The Economic History Review, 66*(1), 1–37.

Anand, S., & Kanbur, S. R. (1993). The Kuznets process and the inequality-development relationship. *Journal of Development Economics, 40*(1), 25–52.

Arntzen, J. W., & Silitshena, R. M. K. (1989). Access to land and farm income in Botswana. In K. Swindel, J.M Baba & M.J. Mortimore (Eds.), I*nequality and Development: Case Studies from the Third World* (pp. 158 – 188), London: Macmillan Publishers Ltd.

Assessment Report. (2015). Washington, DC: World Bank.

Atkinson, A. B., & Brandolini, A. (2001). Promise and pitfalls in the use of "secondary" data-sets: Income inequality in OECD countries as a case study. *Journal of Economic Literature, 39*(3), 771–799.

Austin, G. (2008). Resources, techniques, and strategies south of the Sahara: Revising the factor endowments perspective on African economic development, 1500–2000. *The Economic History Review, 61*(3), 587–624.

Bates, R. H. (2005). *Markets and states in tropical Africa: The political basis of agricultural policies.* Berkeley: University of California Press.

Bates, R. H. (2008). *When things fell apart: State failure in late-century Africa.* Cambridge: Cambridge University Press.

Beaulier, S. A., & Subrick, J. R. (2006). The political foundations of development: The case of Botswana. *Constitutional Political Economy, 17*(2), 103–115.

Berry, A. (1990). International trade, government, and income distribution in Peru since 1870. *Latin American Research Review, 25*(2), 31–59.

Berry, S. (2002). Debating the land question in Africa. *Comparative Studies in Society and History, 44*(4), 638–668. https://doi.org/10.1017/S0010417502000312

Berry, R. A., & Cline, W. R. (1979). *Agrarian structure and productivity in developing countries: A study prepared for the International Labour Office within the framework of the World Employment Programme*. Baltimore: Johns Hopkins University Press.

Bértola, L., Camou, M., Maubrigades, S., & Melgar, N. (2008). Human Development and Inequality in the 20th Century: the Mercosur Countries in a comparative perspective, IFC Working papers in Economic History, 2008-4.

Bigsten, A. (1987). *Income distribution and growth in a dual economy: Kenya, 1914–1976*. Gothenburg: Gothenburg University, Department of Economics.

Bolt, J., & Hillbom, E. (2015). Potential for diversification? The role of the formal sector in Bechuanaland Protectorate's economy, 1900–65. *Economic History of Developing Regions, 30*(2), 95–124.

Bolt, J., & Hillbom, E. (2016). Long-term trends in economic inequality: Lessons from colonial Botswana, 1921–1974. *Economic History Review, 69*(4), 1255–1284.

Bourguignon, F., & Morrisson, C. (1990). Income distribution, development and foreign trade: A cross-sectional analysis. *European Economic Review, 34*(6), 1113–1132.

Bowden, S., Chiripanhura, B., & Mosley, P. (2008). Measuring and explaining poverty in six African countries: A long-period approach. *Journal of International Development, 30*(8), 1049–1079.

Bowman, K. S. (1997). Should the Kuznets effect be relied on to induce equalizing growth: Evidence from post-1950 development. *World Development, 25*(1), 127–143.

Carlsson, E. (2003). *To have and to hold: Continuity and change in property rights institutions governing water resources among the Meru of Tanzania and the BaKgtala in Botswana; 1925–2000*. Lund Studies in Economic History, 28. Stockholm: Almqvist & Wiksell International.

Carney, D., & Farrington, J. (1998). *Natural resource management and institutional change*. London and New York: Routledge.

Chernikovsky, D., Lucas, R. E., & Mueller, E. (1985). *The household economy of rural Botswana: An African case*. World Bank staff working paper no. 715.

Colclough, C., & McCarthy, S. (1980). *The political economy of Botswana: A study of growth and distribution*. London: Oxford University Press.

Collier, P., & Dercon, S. (2014). African agriculture in 50 years: Smallholders in a rapidly changing world? *World Development, 63*, 92–101.

Cornia, G. A. (1985). Farm size, land yields and the agricultural production function: An analysis for fifteen developing countries. *World Development, 13*(4), 513–534. CSO, RIDS 1974/1975.

Deininger, K., & Squire, L. (1996). A new data set measuring income inequality. *The World Bank Economic Review, 10*(3), 565–591.

Desbordes, R., & Verardi, V. (2012). Refitting the Kuznets curve. *Economics Letters, 116*(2), 258–261. https://doi.org/10.1016/j.econlet.2012.03.010

Engerman, S. L., & Sokoloff, K. L. (2002). Factor endowments, inequality, and paths of development among new world economics. *Economia, 3*(1), 41–108.

Engerman, S. L., & Sokoloff, K. L. (2005). *Colonialism, inequality, and long-run paths of development*. https://doi.org/10.1093/0195305191.003.0003

Frankema, E., Green, E., & Hillbom, E. (2016). Endogenous processes of colonial settlement. The success and failure of European settler farming in Sub-Saharan Africa. *Revista de Historia Economica-Journal of Iberian and Latin American Economic History, 34*(2), 237–265.

Good, K. (1992). Interpreting the exceptionality of Botswana. *The Journal of Modern African Studies, 30*(1), 69–95.

Good, K. (1993). At the ends of the ladder: Radical inequalities in Botswana. *The Journal of Modern African Studies, 31*(2), 203–230.

Good, K. (1994). Corruption and mismanagement in Botswana: A best-case example? *The Journal of Modern African Studies, 32*(3), 499–521.

Good, K. (2008). *Diamonds, dispossession & democracy in Botswana*. Boydell and Brewer. Retrieved from http://www.jstor.org/stable/10.7722/j.ctt1bh2kzv

Good, K., & Taylor, I. (2008). Botswana: A minimalist democracy. *Democratization, 15*(4), 750–765.

Griffin, K., Khan, A. R., & Ickowitz, A. (2002). Poverty and the distribution of land. *Journal of Agrarian Change, 2*(3), 279–330.

Gulbrandsen, Ø. (1996). *Poverty in the midst of Plenty: Socio-economic marginalization, ecological deterioration and political stability in a Tswana society* (No. 45). Bergen: Norse Publications.

Herlihy, D. (1978). *The social history of Italy and Western Europe: 700–1500* (Vol. 84). London: Variorum.

Hesselberg, J. (1985). *The third world in transition: The case of the peasantry in Botswana*. Uppsala: Scandinavian Institute of African Studies.

Hillbom, E. (2008). Diamonds or development? A structural assessment of Botswana's forty years of success. *The Journal of Modern African Studies, 46*(2), 191–214.

Hillbom, E. (2010). Agricultural development and the distribution of water resources in Kgatleng District, Botswana. *Development Southern Africa, 27*(3), 413–427.
Hillbom, E. (2014). Cattle, Diamonds and Institutions: Main drivers of Botswana's economic development, 1850 to present. *Journal of International Development, 26*(2), 155–176.
Hillbom, E., & Bolt, J. (2015) Changing Income Inequality and Structural Transformation: The Case of Botswana 1921–2010. WIDER Working Paper 2015/028. Helsinki: UNU-WIDER.
Jerven, M. (2010). Accounting for the African growth miracle: The official evidence–Botswana 1965–1995. *Journal of Southern African Studies, 36*(1), 73–94.
Jerven, M. (2013). *Poor numbers: How we are misled by African development statistics and what to do about it.* Ithaca, NY: Cornell University Press.
Kanbur, R. (2000). Income distribution and development. *Handbook of Income Distribution, 1*, 791–841.
Kanbur, R. (2012). Does Kuznets still matter? In S. Kochhar (Ed.), *Policy-making for Indian planning: Essays on contemporary issues in honor of Montek S. Ahluwalia* (pp. 5–128). New Delhi: Academic Foundation Press.
Katz, L. F., & Murphy, K. M. (1992). Changes in relative wages, 1963–1987: supply and demand factors. The Quarterly Journal of Economics, *107*(1), 35–78.
Kay, C. (2001). *Asia's and Latin America's development in comparative perspective: Landlords, peasants, and industrialization.* The Hague: ORAPS WP Series: 336.
Kuznets, S. (1955). Economic growth and income inequality. *The American Economic Review, 45*(1), 1–28.
Lawry, S. W. (1983). *Land tenure, land policy, and smallholder livestock development in Botswana* (No. 78). Madison: Land Tenure Center, University of Wisconsin-Madison.
Leith, J. C. (2005). *Why Botswana prospered.* Montreal and Kingston: McGill-Queen's University Press.
Lewis, W. A. (1954). Economic development with unlimited supplies of labour. *The Manchester School, 22*(2), 139–191.
Lindert, P. H. (1986). Unequal English wealth since 1670. *Journal of Political Economy, 94*(6), 1127–1162.
Lindert, P. H., & Williamson, J. G. (1983). Reinterpreting Britain's social tables, 1688–1913. *Explorations in Economic History, 20*(1), 94–109.

Lindert, P. H., & Williamson, J. G. (2016). *Unequal gains: American growth and inequality since 1700*. Princeton, NJ: Princeton University Press.
Lipton, M. (1968). The theory of the optimising peasant. *Journal of Development Studies, 4*(3), 327–351.
Lopez Jerez, M. (2014). *Deltas apart-factor endowments, colonial extraction and pathways of agricultural development in Vietnam*.
Makgala, C. J. (2006). *Elite conflict in Botswana: A history*. Pretoria: African Institute of South Africa.
Mapiye, C., Chimonyo, M., Dzama, K., Raats, J. G., & Mapekula, M. (2009). Opportunities for improving Nguni cattle production in the smallholder farming systems of South Africa. *Livestock Science, 124*(1), 196–204.
Masire, K. (2006). *Very brave or very foolish? Memoires of an African democrat*. Gaborone: Macmillan Botswana Publishing Co (Pty) Ltd.
McMillan, M., Rodrik, D., & Verduzco-Gallo, Í. (2014). Globalization, structural change, and productivity growth, with an update on Africa. *World Development, 63*, 11–32.
Milanovic, B. (2016). *Global inequality*. Cambridge, MA: Harvard University Press.
Milanovic, B., Lindert, P. H., & Williamson, J. G. (2011). Pre-industrial inequality. *The Economic Journal, 121*(551), 255–272.
Morapedi, W. G. (1999). Migrant labour and the peasantry in the Bechuanaland protectorate, 1930–1965. *Journal of Southern African Studies, 25*(2), 197–214.
Mosley, P. (1983). *The settler economies: Kenya and Southern Rhodesia 1900–1963*. Cambridge: Cambridge University Press.
Odgaard, R. (2003). Scrambling for land in Tanzania: Processes of formalization and legitimization of land rights. In T. Benjaminsen & C. Lund (Eds.), *Securing land rights in Africa*. London: Frank Cass.
Oommen, M. A., Inganji, F., & Ngcongco, L. D. (1983). Botswana's economy since independence. In *Seminar on Botswana's economy since independence (1981: Gaborone, Botswana)*. Tata McGraw-Hill.
Parsons, N. (1993). *A new history of Southern Africa* (2nd ed.). London: Macmillan Education Ltd.
Peters, P. E. (1994). *Dividing the commons: Politics, policy, and culture in Botswana*. Charlottesville: University Press of Virginia.
Platteau, J. P. (1996). The evolutionary theory of land rights as applied to sub-Saharan Africa: A critical assessment. *Development and Change, 27*(1), 29–86.
Prados de La Escosura, L. (2007). Inequality and poverty in Latin America: A long-run exploration. In T. Hatton, K. O'Rourke, & A. Taylor (Eds.), *The*

new comparative economic history. Essays in honor of Jeffrey G. Williamson (pp. 291–315). Cambridge, MA and London: MIT Press.

Quibria, M. G. (2002). *Growth and poverty: Lessons from the East Asian miracle revisited* (No. 33). ADBI Research Paper Series.

Ramsay, J., Mgadla, P. T., & Morton, B. (1996). *Building a nation: A history of Botswana from 1800 to 1910*. Botswana: Longman.

Reis, J. (2017). Deviant behaviour? Inequality in Portugal 1565–1770. *Cliometrica, 11*(3), 297–319.

Ribot, J. (2000). Decentralization, participation, and representation: Administrative apartheid in Sahelian forestry. In P. Peters (Ed.), *Development encounters: Sites of participation and knowledge*. Cambridge, MA: Harvard University Press for HIID.

Robinson, J. A., & Parsons, Q. N. (2006). State formation and governance in Botswana. *Journal of African Economies, 15*(AERC Supplement 1), 100–140.

Rodríguez Weber, J. (2015). *Income inequality in Chile since 1850*. DOL (Documentos On-line)/FCS-UM; 36.

Roe, E. (1980). *Development of livestock, agriculture and water supplies in eastern Botswana before independence: A short history and policy analysis*. Gaborone: Ministry of Agriculture.

Sala-i-Martin, X., & Pinkovskiy, M. (2010). *African poverty is falling ... much faster than you think!* (No. w15775). National Bureau of Economic Research.

Schapera, I. (1980). *A history of the BaKgatla-bagaKgafêla*. Mochudi: Phuthadikobo Museum.

Schapera, I. (1994). *A handbook of Tswana law and custom*. Münster: LIT Verlag.

Schapera, I., & Comaroff, J. L. (1991). *The Tswana* (revised ed.). London: Kegan Paul International.

Scheidel, W. (2017). *The great leveler: Violence and the history of inequality from the stone age to the twenty-first century*. Princeton, NJ: Princeton University Press.

Selolwane, O. (2013). *Poverty reduction and changing policy regimes in Botswana*. Basingstoke: Palgrave Macmillan.

Silitshena, R. M. K., & McLeod, G. (1998). *Botswana: A physical, social, and economic geography* (2nd ed.). Gaborone: Longman Botswana Ltd.

Smith, M. E. (2004). The archaeology of ancient state economies. *Annual Review of Anthropology, 33*, 73–102.

Stiglitz, J. E. (2012). *The price of inequality: How today's divided society endangers our future*. New York: WW Norton & Company.

Todaro, M. P. and Smith, S. C. (2009). Economic Development 10th Edition. Addison Wesley: Boston.

van der Ploeg, F. (2011). Natural resources: Curse or blessing? *Journal of Economic Literature, 49*(2), 366–420.
Van de Walle, N. (2001). African economies and the politics of permanent crisis, 1979-1999. Cambridge University Press.
Van Zanden, J. L. (1995). Tracing the beginning of the Kuznets curve: Western Europe during the early modern period. *The Economic History Review, 48*(4), 643–664.
Van Zanden, J. L. (2003). Rich and poor before the Industrial Revolution: A comparison between Java and the Netherlands at the beginning of the 19th century. *Explorations in Economic History, 40*(1), 1–23.
de Vries, G., Timmer, M., & de Vries, K. (2015). Structural transformation in Africa: Static gains, dynamic losses. *The Journal of Development Studies, 51*(6), 674–688.
World Bank. (2005). *World development report: Equity and development*. Washington, DC: The World Bank and Oxford University Press.
Wylie, D. (1990). *A little god: The twilight of patriarchy in a Southern African chiefdom*. Hanover, NH: Wesleyan University Press.

Internet Sources

PovCalnet. (2017). Retrieved August 2017, from http://iresearch.worldbank.org/PovcalNet/povOnDemand.aspx
UNU-WIDER. (2017). Retrieved August 2017, from https://www.wider.unu.edu/
World Bank. (2015). Botswana—Poverty Assessment. Retrieved from http://documents.worldbank.org/curated/en/351721468184754228/pdf/88473-REVISED-WP-P154659-PUBLIC-Box394819B.pdf
World Bank. (2017). World Development Indicators (2017). Retrieved May 8, 2017, from http://data.worldbank.org/country/botswana?view=chart

Archive Material

Annual Report of the Bechuanaland Protectorate. Issues 1921–1938; 1946–1965, London School of Economics Library.
Blue Books of statistics. Issues 1904–1925. UK National Archives, CO/567.
Blue Books of statistics. Issues 1926–1947. UK National Archives, DO/26.

Part IV

Part 4

7

Conclusion

7.1 Introduction

Over the past decade and a half, several African economies have experienced remarkable economic growth. In 2013, Africa was even the fastest-growing region in the world with an average increase in GDP of almost 6 per cent. The most spectacular growth was found in mineral- and fossil fuel-rich countries as they were profiting from the boom in world market prices for raw commodities driven by increasing demand from industrializing countries such as China and India. In 2015 the boom was over as commodity prices started falling due to dwindling demand and many of the growth spurts turned into busts. The period of rapid economic growth had the potential of offering a window of opportunity for many African countries to invest the increasing government revenues in alternative productive sectors thereby stimulating a diversification of the economies. However, looking at the African economies that were hailed for their economic performance just a few years ago, it is difficult to identify any systematic move away from natural resource dependency towards sectorial change and sustained long-term economic progress.

E. Hillbom, J. Bolt, *Botswana – A Modern Economic History*, Palgrave Studies in Economic History, https://doi.org/10.1007/978-3-319-73144-5_7

The commodity boom of the early twenty-first century and the subsequent slump in combination with the absence of lasting restructuring of African economies is just the latest reminder that it is not straightforward to transform resource-led growth to sustained growth and development by instigating sectoral change and structural transformation. While this challenge is a global phenomenon, its failure has been especially detrimental for the African region which is facing continuous high population growth and slow poverty reduction. In this context, Botswana is often seen as an exception to the rule. The country's independence era is perceived as an African success story wherein political stability and prudent management of the spectacular diamond wealth have resulted in an impressive long-term growth period. The country's journey from being one of the poorest and most underdeveloped territories in the world to becoming an upper middle-income country achieving significant social development has drawn much attention from both scholars and policy-makers. The question is 'what are the lessons to be learned from this case.'

In this book we have examined Botswana's success story. Its impressive long-run economic growth trajectory is undisputable, and the government's prudent management of diamond revenues is rightfully lauded. As a result of this, Botswana's experience is obviously different from that of many other countries where resource-driven growth spurts have only lasted for short periods and where poor political institutions resulted in economic collapse or even open violent conflicts. However, despite Botswana's success, we have shown that the country remains with two major challenges—to turn diamond-led economic growth into sustained economic development and to curb existing high levels of inequality in incomes and opportunities. In our aim to capture long-term developments, we have extended the analysis backwards in time to also include the precolonial Tswana cattle economy and the first growth period based on colonial cattle exports. In doing so, we have been able to add new insights into Botswana's economic history as well as trace the roots of contemporary development challenges.

This concluding chapter begins with a very brief recapitulation of Botswana's economic history as presented in the book. Next the main take-away points from the book are highlighted. The last section concludes by indicating new directions in research made possible by the present study.

7.2 A Concise Economic History of Botswana

In the 1830–1840s the period of violence and political unrest in Southern Africa known as the *Difiquane* caused a domino effect of movement of numerous population groups in the region. Some of these groups were the Tswana *merafe* that subsequently settled in the territory that is contemporary Botswana. At the time, the area was inhabited by hunting and gathering Basarwa groups that were displaced and have ever since constituted a discriminated minority group.

In the Tswana agro-pastoral system of production opportunities for successful crop farming were severely limited for climatic reasons and instead surplus production, asset accumulation, and social status were all focused around the holding of livestock generally and cattle specifically. Cattle markets were extremely limited and rather than cattle wealth being turned into cash incomes it was used to build patron–client relationships to secure access to labour and political loyalty through the cattle-lending *mafisa* system.

The low population density brought an inherent risk of a decentralized authoritarian system. However, the Twana's specific settlement patterns enabled a very hierarchical organization of society. The village was the focal point where all households had a residential compound. In addition, they held individual crop farming plots on the surrounding arable lands and could keep cattle on the communal grazing range further away. The household heads' regular return to the villages allowed for the development of a centralized governance system and gave an opportunity for the *dikgosi* and headmen to regularly reach and politically interact with their subjects, for example, at large public *kgotla* meetings.

The Bechuanaland Protectorate was established in 1885. The primary motivation for the British conquest lay neither in that the territory held documented valuable resources nor in that it had a wealthy taxable population, but in the politics of not leaving the territory to be colonized by any other European power. The initial decades of colonial rule entailed limited colonial influence and the main ambition of the administration was to set up territorial control and a taxation system. It was also a time period of increasing labour migration to the neighbouring territories, primarily to the South African mines, and Bechuanaland in many aspects developed into a de facto labour reserve. In line with the principles guiding the British Indirect Rule system, the *dikgosi* were in principle left to rule the new Native Reserves, one for each of the eight larger *merafe*.

During the second half of the colonial period starting in 1930, however, the colonial administration significantly changed its level of ambition for Bechuanaland. In the spirit of the time colonial aid started flowing into the Protectorate and the administration expanded its colonial policies with a focus on raising government revenues and creating opportunities for economic growth. Based on existing agricultural production rather than regional or global market demand, cattle exports were identified as the comparative advantage of the territory. We have argued that the impact the establishment and development of the cattle export sector had on economic, political, and social structures in both colonial Bechuanaland and later independent Botswana has commonly been underestimated. The most important colonial legacies from this time have been the establishment of natural resource-based and export-led economic growth together with the rising unequal distribution of opportunities, political influence, incomes, and assets spearheaded by the existing cattle-holding elite.

Botswana became independent in 1966 and one year later the discovery of diamond deposits was announced. In the mid-1970s diamond extractions had grown to the extent that the diamond economy definitely took over from cattle. The diamond-led growth period has been one of the most spectacular in the world, bringing Botswana from being one of the poorest countries in the world to currently being classified as an upper middle-income country with a GDP per capita of over 15,500 dollars in 2016 (2011 PPP dollars). While diamonds are in their own right an extremely valuable resource and thereby constitute a good basis for spectacular growth, it is, the prudent management of diamond incomes and the avoidance of a natural resource curse that has impressed bystanders the most. The presence of good political institutions is commonly seen as a precolonial legacy, but we have emphasized the need to problematize the 'good institutions' explanation and to recognize the limitations to the Botswana success story.

In the midst of good governance, the economy has remained natural resource dependent. There has been a lack of diversification and development of alternative productive sectors, making it difficult to see how existing growth can be maintained once diamond incomes have come to an end. With the mining sector offering limited employment opportunities the lack of linkages to other areas of the economy has resulted in high levels of unemployment as well as a dwarfed private sector unable to compete with the public sector which is fuelled by diamond revenues.

Benefits from economic growth have been transferred to the population via traditional social development in the form of education, health care, clean water, infrastructure development, poverty alleviation programmes, and so on. Impressive socioeconomic progress has primarily been explained by good political institutions and the multiparty democracy and political maturity has become a trademark for Botswana. Meanwhile, high levels of inequality in incomes and opportunities persist. While the state has been development oriented in its social policies, the absence of inclusive economic development has resulted in the creation of a dual society where poverty and underdevelopment exist in the midst of wealth and modernity. Together with the lack of diversification and sectorial change, this remains as Botswana's primary development challenge for the future.

7.3 Main Takeaway Points from the Book

Rather than repeating the various arguments presented in the book, we focus on proposing six broad clusters of takeaway points. Three of them are outcomes of the cross-cutting approaches that were suggested in Chap. 1—decompressing of history, interaction between geography/factor endowments and institutions, and the role played by the state. The following three are based on the main conclusions extracted from the three thematic chapters discussing the growth periods, challenges for economic diversification, and high levels of inequality.

7.3.1 Decompressing of History

While the identification of correlations between certain factors at various points in time can highlight potentially interesting relationships we understand this to be a point of departure for asking interesting questions, instead of providing comprehensive answers. In this study we join scholars that argue for the need to decompress history as it is only by studying all major events throughout the period under investigation that we can start to understand underlying mechanisms and drivers of change, as well as identify multicausal relationships. Only through this continuous analysis can we reach an understanding of the complexity of factors that shape a country's long-term development.

We have operationalized this decompressing of history approach in three ways. First, we have captured the whole period of the contemporary Tswana groups' presence in the area that is now Botswana, starting with their settlement in the mid-nineteenth century and ending with the country's contemporary development challenges. Second, we have paid continuous attention to all significant events found during our time period, whether they have taken place during the precolonial, colonial, or independence eras. Third, we have followed a periodization based on the identification of socioeconomic structural breaks instead of political events and used it as a key analytical tool throughout the book.

Our decompressing of Botswana's economic history has provided us with four main results. First, the understanding of precolonial legacies needs to be nuanced. While early building of state capacity has translated into an institutional competency to manage diamond incomes prudently, precolonial institutional legacy has also catered for the old cattle elite to amass political power and economic wealth. Second, we have divided up the colonial experience into two periods. For the early period 1885–1930 we agree with the notion of limited colonial influence, but for the later period of 1930 to the break with the diamond economy in 1975 we have highlighted how colonial policies, the development of the cattle export sector specifically, have had long-lasting and profound effects on the socioeconomic structures of Botswana. Third, we have argued that the current resource dependency of the economy is not new, but actually has its roots in the colonial period when the authorities established the cattle economy. For the later diamond-led growth period this natural resource dependency has meant that although export revenues have been increasing and creating financial opportunities to invest in alternative economic sectors to diversify the economy and initiate structural change and sustainable development, the Botswana government has not been able to do so. Fourth, we have shown how the currently high levels of inequality are not initially caused by the diamond economy, but have their roots in the colonial cattle-led growth period. It was the government sector and the large-scale cattle-holding elite who profited most from the opening up of export markets leading to rapid increases in income inequality. These inequalities have been institutionalized during the diamond economy, not only keeping income inequality consistently high, but also inequality in opportunity.

7.3.2 Interaction of Geography and Institutions

The last decades have seen an increasingly polarized literature with the two sides contesting the arguments of supreme explanatory power of institutions and geography. We do not see the value of such a polarization and have instead argued for the mutual interaction of institutions, on the one hand, and geography/factor endowments, on the other hand. The impact by each side is an empirical question and can only be understood and demonstrated by in-depth analysis of each empirical case at hand. Further, we have shown that in combination with the decompressing of history, such an analysis allows for the identification of changing relations over time, that is, that institutions and geography will be more or less dominant as the main driver of socioeconomic changes during different time periods under study.

We argue that the study of the economic history of Botswana provides a textbook example of the need to apply both institutional and geographical/factor endowments explanations to understand its long-term growth path. Any other approach is unable to capture all relevant mechanisms driving processes of change. Throughout, the understanding of the country's trajectories of growth and development rests on explaining the balance between access and dependence of natural resources and their management. Besides decompressing history we deliver a comprehensive analysis, from discussing the physical setup of the Tswana agro-pastoral system of production and its influence on the early creation of centralized state structures in the midst of low population density, to explaining the avoidance of a natural resource curse during the recent spectacular diamond-led growth miracle.

The approach allows us to critically discuss the common understanding that good institutions are the key explanation for Botswana's success story. With our analysis we add the following three aspects. First, we use the unique Tswana settlement pattern with its focus on village residency to explain how early development of centralized state capacity was possible despite overall low population density. Second, we discuss the interaction between the climatic preconditions for cattle rearing with water being the scarce agricultural resource, on the one hand, and the development of property rights systems governing agricultural resources and colonial export-oriented policies, on the other hand. With Bechuanaland having no valuable resources the colonial administration turned its interest towards the abundance of cattle and grazing and geared its policies towards developing a supply-driven, natural resource-dependent, and export-led cattle economy. Further, the existing customary property rights principles in combination with various borehole drilling programmes led to a concentration of water resources in the hands of the Tswana elites and resulted in a polarization of ownership not only of water points, but also of grazing land and cattle. Third, we show that the physical placement underground of diamond resources necessitates large-scale investments for extraction, and this in turn opened up opportunities for state monopoly on diamond mining, which in combination with low corruption meant that diamond incomes benefitted the large share of the population as it was invested in social development.

7.3.3 The Role of the State

Within the fields of economics and economic history there have been continuous discussions about the desired as well as the actual role of the state in development processes. What the state should actually do is, however, perhaps more a political issue than anything else. Development trajectories have been heavily influenced by state policies whether those have focused on laissez-faire or actively state-led catch-up and development. Throughout the book we have continuously discussed the rationales behind the development of specific state structures and then analysed their role in shaping Botswana's development path. We have considered multicausal relationship between geographical and financial preconditions, development of state policies, and ambitions of interest groups.

Concretely, we have traced the development of centralized state structures and early state capacity back to the precolonial settlement patterns, legitimacy of Tswana authorities, and local system of production. Further, we have categorized the colonial state as a gate-keeping state which experienced financial constrains throughout the colonial era, albeit more so in the early than in the late period. This minimalistic state focusing its resources on keeping law and order, taxing exports–imports, and investing to encourage further development of the cattle export sector had neither the means nor the inclination to diversify the economy or instigate inclusive development. The strength of precolonial political institutions in combination with the indirect rule of the colonial state meant that precolonial state structures survived within the framework of the gate-keeping state. Further, the political continuity with the Tswana cattle elite moving into government after independence meant the continued survival of the gate-keeping state. Albeit diamond incomes gave it unprecedented financial opportunities to be development oriented.

Our consistent attention to long-term interaction between economic factors and state structures has provided new insights into how the multicausal relationship between the setup of the state and its strategies for investments and taxation, on the one hand, and opportunities for economic growth and securing government revenues, on the other hand, has affected Botswana's development pathway. First, the gate-keeping state concept offers an explanation for the minimalist colonial state and the subsequent creation of a mono-product economy that is based on financial rationality. Second, the lack of a structural break, in economic, political, and social terms, between the colonial and independence eras causes us to conclude that the stability and continuity in economic and political institutions that is commonly hailed as key to Botswana's success also constitutes a development challenge. Stability has come at the cost of a lack of dynamic change while what the country needs is structural transformation.

7.3.4 The Two Growth Periods

The African region has often been equated with economic stagnation and even decline, but recent research has shown that in the long run it should instead be thought of as recurring growth. In the case of Botswana the impressive diamond-led economic growth record has overshadowed other growth periods in the country's economic history. While we analyse the diamond economy in depth we also extend our study back in time into Botswana's economic history and include an investigation of the earlier, albeit much less spectacular, cattle-led growth period.

While significantly different in their outcomes we claim that in their fundamentals, the two growth periods are both examples of natural resource-led growth and that they share many characteristics. Consequently, the roots of Botswana's current economic structures, including the challenges in terms of lack of sectorial change and high levels of inequality, can be found in the cattle-led growth period. A lesson learned is that it is not only the spectacular that deserves our attention as scholars and unless we decompress history we run a high risk of missing out on instructive periods of history. As long as the structures stay the same, a change in the sources and magnitude of growth cannot cater for change on its own.

7.3.5 Growth Versus Development

While economic growth is fundamental for increasing wage levels and government revenues and enabling consumption and investments, it is not enough for building sustainable economic systems. The main challenge for natural resource-rich economies has not been to achieve growth, but to achieve sustainable growth by instigating technological change and developing alternative productive sectors. When incomes are used for long-term investments in diversification natural resource wealth constitutes a window of opportunity and becomes a blessing also in the long run.

Despite development-enhancing political institutions and government's awareness that it will be difficult to sustain economic growth after diamonds run out unless other sectors take off, there has as of yet not been any truly successful efforts in Botswana to invest in alternative economic activity, neither to create linkages between diamonds and other sectors nor to stimulate other labour-intensive manufacturing. Rather than financing the development of alternative productive sectors, the spectacular diamond-led growth has become a trap hindering structural transformation as it has brought limited incentives for diversification.

7.3.6 Long-Term Inequality Trends

Southern Africa contains some of the highest levels of inequality found anywhere in the world and Botswana is a typical case with current estimates of income inequality with a Gini coefficient of roughly 0.6. Albeit the accuracy of official statistics can be questioned, we know much more about inequality during the independence than during the colonial era. However, if the African nations established at independence demonstrated high levels of inequality, we should infer that we need to go further back in time if we are to unearth the roots of those inequality levels. We have taken on this challenge and created social tables and computed Gini coefficients for the period 1921–1974.

To cover the whole period discussed in this book, we linked our Gini coefficients with existing numbers for the independence era.

This research has allowed us to identify the 1940s as the time when income inequality takes off in Bechuanaland and in combination with our analysis of the colonial cattle economy we explain our results by the forging ahead of the large-scale cattle holders and the government officials during the cattle-led growth period. Colonial development strategies clearly benefitted specific groups that became the long-term winners. This finding goes against the otherwise intuitive notion amongst scholars that high levels of inequality are associated with valuable natural resources, that is, diamonds in the case of Botswana.

The well-managed diamond-led growth has left the Botswana government wealthy in a regional perspective. A significant part of this wealth has been invested in broad social development. The government has not, however, launched redistributive policies to actively counter the high levels of inequality that were created during the cattle economy. As a result, Botswana is a typical case of a natural resource-rich economy characterized by high levels of inequality. While some unequal distribution of incomes does not have to be detrimental for an economy, the extreme high levels found in Botswana are a sign of underlying institutional inequality which has hindered inclusive sustainable economic development.

7.4 And Moving On …

With this comprehensive economic history study of Botswana from 1885 to today, we have tried to put Botswana's growth experience in a long-term perspective to understand the roots of current challenges. The book is one of the first in its kind, providing an in-depth qualitative and quantitative perspective to long-term development of an African country. This has generated new insights for Botswana specifically, but it also has shown the usefulness and the feasibility of such studies for other African countries. From the archives we have collected new primary data for the colonial period. Using this, we have been able to show economic development during the colonial period, in terms of incomes, employment structures, and government strategies and actions. Further, using income and population data we have been able to build social tables and measure the distribution of incomes from the early decades of the colonial period onwards. This or similar information is also available for other African countries and can be used to further our understanding of long-term development patterns in other countries and regions on the continent.

The long-term perspective and the study of all major events in the period have convinced us that the common periodization in African economic history based on political events is not always useful to understand continuity and change in the economy. We therefore did not study the precolonial, the colonial, and the independence era as separate topics. Instead, we focused on more fundamental socioeconomic breaks and divided our period under study based on those breaks. A periodization which helps to understand long-term patterns will be different for different countries. Not taking the common periodization as given has proven very insightful for our case study and might provide significant new insights for other African countries as well.

While, in all likelihood, there will be enough diamonds to drive growth in Botswana for a few more decades, the peak period for diamond-led growth has gone. Considering that diversification of the economy is a long-term process there is a need for more active efforts at instigating the development of alternative sectors immediately. If not, there is a real risk of the Botswana economy eventually experiencing the bust that it has managed to avoid for so long—a bust, not due to poor management or declining world market prices, which is commonly the case, but due to the end of diamonds. After all, it is development and not diamonds that can last forever.

It is, however, not reasonable to expect structural transformation to come about without the encouragement and active evolvement of the state. For the last few decades the Botswana government has launched numerous initiatives to encourage new sectors in the economy, alterative to diamond mining, and it has invested in social development. Despite these investments, the socioeconomic structures remain dual with a dichotomy between the rich/modern/urban and the poor/traditional/rural. At independence the Tswana cattle-holding elite took over the state from the British colonizers. While this brought political change it also cemented existing authority structures and the colonial gate-keeping state strategies. To achieve inclusive economic development more radical changes are required.

Glossary Including Tswana Terminology

Bolata A system of bonded labour, or serfdom.

Difaqane/Mfecane A period of unrest in Southern Africa during the first half of the nineteenth century.

Dikgosi Leaders of political units (plural).

Hardveld Rocky hill ranges and shallow sand, less dry than sandveld.

Kgosi Leader of a political unit (singular).

Kgotla A meeting place for village and morafe assemblies, court cases, etc.

Malata Individuals controlled within the bolata system of bonded labour.

Mafisa A system of lending out animals to subjects and relatives on a long-term basis.

Merafe Tswana term for political units (plural).

Morafe Tswana term for political unit (singular).

Sandveld Land characterized by dry, sandy soil.

E. Hillbom, J. Bolt, *Botswana – A Modern Economic History*, Palgrave Studies in Economic History, https://doi.org/10.1007/978-3-319-73144-5

Index[1]

[1] Note: Page numbers followed by 'n' refer to notes.

E. Hillbom, J. Bolt, *Botswana – A Modern Economic History*, Palgrave Studies in Economic History, https://doi.org/10.1007/978-3-319-73144-5

The manufacturer's authorised representative in the EU is Springer Nature Customer Service Centre GmbH, Europaplatz 3, 69115 Heidelberg, Germany. If you have any concerns regarding our products, please contact ProductSafety@springernature.com

Printed and bound by CPI Group (UK) Ltd, Croydon, CR0 4YY
25/09/2026
02222849-0005